9/11

The Words and Music of Jimi Hendrix

The Words and Music of Jimi Hendrix

David Moskowitz

James E. Perone, Series Editor

 PRAEGER

AN IMPRINT OF ABC-CLIO, LLC
Santa Barbara, California • Denver, Colorado • Oxford, England

Library of Congress Cataloging-in-Publication Data
Moskowitz, David.
    The words and music of Jimi Hendrix / David Moskowitz.
       p. cm. — (The Praeger singer-songwriter collection)
    Includes bibliographical references, discography, and index.
    ISBN 978-0-313-37592-7 (hard copy : alk. paper) — ISBN 978-0-313-37593-4 (ebook) 1. Hendrix, Jimi—Criticism and interpretation. 2. Rock musicians—United States—Biography. I. Title.
    ML410.H476M68   2010
    787.87166092—dc22
    [B]   2010031248

ISBN: 978-0-313-37592-7
EISBN: 978-0-313-37593-4

14 13 12 11 10   1 2 3 4 5

This book is also available on the World Wide Web as an eBook.
Visit www.abc-clio.com for details.

Praeger
An Imprint of ABC-CLIO, LLC

ABC-CLIO, LLC
130 Cremona Drive, P.O. Box 1911
Santa Barbara, California 93116-1911

This book is printed on acid-free paper ∞

Manufactured in the United States of America

Contents

Series Foreword

Although the term "singer-songwriter" might most frequently be associated with a cadre of musicians of the early 1970s such as Paul Simon, James Taylor, Carly Simon, Joni Mitchell, Cat Stevens, and Carole King, the Praeger Singer-Songwriter Collection defines singer-songwriters more broadly, both in terms of style and time period. The series includes volumes on musicians who have been active from approximately the 1960s through the present. Musicians who write and record in folk, rock, soul, hip-hop, country, and various hybrids of these styles are represented. Therefore, some of the early 1970s introspective singer-songwriters named here will be included, but not exclusively.

What do the individuals included in this series have in common? Some have never collaborated as writers, whereas others have, but all have written and recorded commercially successful and/or historically important music and lyrics at some point in their careers.

The authors who contribute to the series also exhibit diversity. Some are scholars who are trained primarily as musicians, whereas others have such areas of specialization as American studies, history, sociology, popular culture studies, literature, and rhetoric. The authors share a high level of scholarship, accessibility in their writing, and a true insight into the work of the artists they study. The authors are also focused on the output of their subjects and how it relates to their subjects' biographies and the society around them; however, biography in and of itself is not a major focus of the books in this series.

Given the diversity of the musicians who are the subject of books in this series, and given the diversity of viewpoint of the authors, volumes in the series differ from book to book. All, however, are organized chronologically around the compositions and recorded performances of their subjects. All of the books in the series should also serve as listeners' guides to the music of their subjects, making them companions to the artists' recorded output.

James E. Perone
Series Editor

Acknowledgments

Heather, Katie, and Jack, thank you, for all of your wonderful support through several book writing projects. Your unfailing patience and encouragement sustains me through lengthy projects such as this one. Lucas—this one's for you, buddy. Your constant enthusiasm for making and discovering new music is a wonder to witness. Also, the research trip to Seattle would not have been half as memorable without your company.

Thanks also to Dr. Walter Aaron Cark for his sage advice as I began my advanced studies in musicology. If not for his assistance in studying music that was not part of the canon I would not be able to pursue the type of research and writing that interests me the most. In addition I thank Daniel Harmon, the acquisitions editor, and James Perone, the series editor, for their help in completing this book. Thanks also go to Photofest for their kind permission to use the images that appear in the volume. Finally, I thank Joe Jurgensen, who provided early encouragement and assistance as this project was getting off the ground.

Introduction

James "Jimi" Marshall Hendrix (born Johnny Allen Hendrix) was a bit of an American music enigma during much of his professional life. As a young Seattle-born guitarist, Jimi caught the spirit of American roots music and rock and roll. His upbringing was difficult with a father who was absent at his birth, as he was away at war, and a mother who was barely more than a child herself when Jimi was born. Moving frequently and often in the care of those who were not his parents, Jimi began to seek refuge in music. Once reunited with his father, Al, Jimi convinced Hendrix senior to buy him his first stringed instruments. From there Jimi made many failed attempts at success in the music business. He suffered on the chitlin' circuit as a sideman and was never able to get traction for his own bands in the United States. However, once he met Bryan "Chas" Chandler (bass player for the Animals) and the pair traveled together to England, Jimi quickly conquered the musical world.

Although Jimi lived a far-too-short twenty-seven years, his level of importance during his life and his influence in death is difficult to overstate. He was one of the original guitar gods whose name was mentioned during his life in the same sentences with Eric Clapton, Jeff Beck, and Pete Townshend. His ability to synthesize musical styles was also a thing of legend. As he was reared on American blues and R&B, he was able to adapt these styles and infuse them with the more modern current of sixties psychedelia.

Jimi often chose to let his guitar playing speak for him with the vocals and the guitar line always vying for center stage—and the guitar typically winning. With that, Jimi's guitar playing became the thing of legend that guitar players since have been trying to achieve or even imitate. However,

Jimi was also an introspective and intelligent lyricist. Many of his songs were born of the family turmoil he experienced as a youth or the rarified space that he occupied as an adult. It was not by mistake that Jimi chose to surround himself with only a handful of daily companions/musical partners. He was leery of being misunderstood by strangers, often on the receiving end of barbed comments due to his appearance, and constantly searching for lost love from the female gender—either in the form of his mother or through his adult relationships.

Although he was only able to release three studio albums during his brief life, his high level of musical significance has repeatedly been attested to over the past forty years. The posthumous albums have now climbed over one hundred releases between sanctioned and unsanctioned releases both live and studio-oriented. Further, sustained interest in his music has remained unabated over the years. He was inducted into the Rock and Roll Hall of Fame as a member of the Experience in 1992 and has won several Grammy Awards. The Experience Music Project in Seattle has featured Jimi's legacy and memorabilia in a museumlike setting since its creation in 2000. Possibly more significant than the awards and accolades is the simple fact that Jimi's music continues to be released as the miles of tape that he left at his death continue to be mined for precious gems as attested to by his most recent album, *Valleys of Neptune*, released March 9, 2010. Enthusiasm for Jimi's music shows little sign of wearing thin as this new album was as eagerly anticipated as any of the early works.

SCOPE AND ORGANIZATION OF THIS BOOK

Like the companion volumes in this series, this book focuses on the life of Jimi Hendrix as told through an in-depth investigation of his music, lyrics, and major recordings. Weight and priority were given to studio albums with special attention paid to the autobiographical nature of the lyrics. Jimi purposely infused his lyrics with his favorite themes, such as science fiction, fantasy, comic book and cartoon characters, love, loss, redemption, gods, mythology, and outer space. The biography of his life is discussed as it relates to his music, and additional details are supplied as framework in which to place his musical output. As was the case with most of the musicians included in the series, the opening material is straight-ahead biography until the artist began producing documented music of some sort—in Jimi's case in bands in the Seattle, Washington, area.

An oddity in Jimi's biography is the inconsistency in details. The fact is that Jimi's life is fairly well documented through a host of existing biographies and his official Web site, which is run by his estate. That said, there are still many aspects of his life that are presented as conflicting information amongst these sources—many of these are included here with considerable effort made to reconcile the discrepancies. Most existing writing on

Jimi separates his life from his music. The aim of this volume was to avoid that separation and allow Jimi's own lyrics to tell the story of his life as much as possible.

Like its companions in the singer-songwriter series, this volume is meant to be a guide to the recordings it discusses. As a result, I have included a selected discography, which includes all of the songs mentioned in the text, specifically those written, cowritten, or recorded by Jimi regardless of who he was playing with at the time.

The Early Years: Teeth Cutting and Life as a Sideman

The guitar legend that the world knew as Jimi Hendrix was born Johnny Allen Hendrix on November 27, 1942. Jimi's seventeen-year-old mother, Lucille, gave birth to him at Seattle's King County Hospital at 10:15 A.M. Jimi's father, James "Al" Hendrix, was not a presence in his young life as he had been drafted, denied leave, and was about to be deployed overseas. Lucille was not at the point of her young life where settling down with a baby was part of the plan. Matters were made worse by her having little money and no stable place to live. Help came in the form of Lucille's mother, Clarice Jeter. Jimi's grandmother moved to Seattle to help Lucille raise her young son. Both Clarice and Lucille worked menial jobs to try to make ends meet and support Jimi. The result of this was that Jimi often went without proper care during working hours. Clarice was working as a housekeeper for a family called the Maes.[1] The Maes offered to help look after Jimi while Clarice and Lucille were at work. The unfortunate downside of this was that Lucille began leaving Jimi in the care of others while she spent evenings out dancing and spending time with other men, instead of just while she was at work.

An aspect of this association with the Mae family was that Jimi often ended up in the care of their then twelve-year-old daughter, Freddie. In addition to Freddie's watch, her mother Minnie also looked after young Jimi. In fact, at one point in Jimi's infancy, he stayed with the Maes as Lucille was missing and her mother could not both work and care for the child full time. This arrangement was in effect off-and-on for much of Jimi's young life.

Although Lucille was married to Al, Jimi's father was not in Seattle and Lucille began running around with other men. This was invariably to Jimi's detriment as Lucille would drag Jimi with her to follow around her love interests. One such man was John Williams, a rough-and-tumble character who came to Seattle from Kansas City. Lucille and this man paired up and soon she was dragging Jimi around to wherever the two would go. At times, Lucille's own mother did not know where her daughter and grandson had disappeared to for long periods of time. In the course of this turmoil, Jimi contracted pneumonia.

As it was soon completely apparent that Lucille could not care for herself, let alone a child, her mother took Jimi in even as she was working full time to care for herself. Soon after, Delores (Clarice's sister) enlisted the assistance of a friend from the Pentecostal Church, a Mrs. Champ. Mrs. Champ, one of Clarice Jeter's friends, offered to take Jimi in and provide a more stable environment for him to grow up in.[2] This change of care also caused a change in locale. Jimi moved to Berkeley, California, to stay with Mrs. Champ and she informed Al of his son's new address.

Al remained out of the country during Jimi's early years. In 1945, he was discharged from the military and able to return to Washington. Upon his return, Al went to Berkeley and collected his son and the pair returned to Seattle. Regardless of her infidelity during Al's absence, Lucille and Al were again a pair and Jimi had his first real family experiences. With Al back in the picture, Jimi's name was legally changed from Johnny Allen Hendrix to James Marshall Hendrix. The Hendrixes settled down into a period of tense domesticity. Lucille continued to pine for her freedom even as she gave birth to the family's second son, Leon Morris Hendrix.

Eventually, in December 1951, Al and Lucille divorced. Al was granted custody of both of the boys. Despite his best efforts, Al was unable to simultaneously care for the boys and work. His long hours spent trying to make subsistence pay meant that the boys were often without supervision. Leon was often left to tag along with Jimi as their father was at work. Their mother would appear now and then and tempt the boys with unconditional love, but the pair was largely inseparable and stayed with Al. When Lucille came around she lavished affection and attention on the boys making them feel like the center of her world, but those occasions were few and brief. It was at this early age that Jimi began to develop his fascination with science fiction and cartoon superheroes, which was begun by the cinema shows that Al took the boys to watch. Although it was clear that Al was doing his level best to care for the boys, times were tough and he was out of the house for long work shifts. Jimi at times found himself again in the care of others, including those at Freddie Mae's house.

Tragedy struck on February 2, 1958, when Lucille died suddenly. This left young Jimi heartbroken, and with little outlet for his emotions he turned inward. As a child, Jimi clearly pined for a closer releationship with his mother. After her passing, he often reflected on her loss and being raised without her left a mark on him that was evident his entire life. Although, Jimi was relatively aloof as an adult and rarely spoke publically about his family he repeatedly referenced his mother in the lyrics of his songs. Through this it is clear that his mother remained in his heart and was often on his mind throughout his life.

At this time, music began to be an outlet for Jimi's feelings. His father noticed that when he told Jimi to sweep up around the house he would instead find broom straws strewn about where Jimi posed with the broom as he pretended to play the guitar. Al bought Jimi a ukulele so Jimi could try his hand at music. Jimi's interest in music deepened and, eventually, Al bought Jimi a guitar "from a friend for five dollars."[3] Although the acoustic guitar that Al had purchased was strung in the traditional right-handed method, Jimi reversed the strings to play left-handed. Now that he had a musical outlet, Jimi's guitar playing took on an ever-increasing role in his life. He quickly realized that he had a strong sense of pitch and was able to tune his own guitar shortly after picking it up for the first time.

At first happy to have any guitar, Jimi soon began asking his father for an electric setup. Recognizing his son's innate ability, Al was persuaded to buy Jimi an electric guitar. Al also bought a saxophone so that he and his son could connect on a musical level.[4] Soon enough Jimi ended up in his first band when he joined the Velvetones.[5] His band allowed him access to an amplifier and another guitarist to learn from. Jimi joined the group in the summer of 1958. After several months, in late 1958, the Velvetones went through a lineup change that also caused a name change to the Rocking Teens. In the summer of 1959, part of the Rocking Teens membership broke away and formed the Rocking Kings. The Rocking Kings included Lester Exkano on drums, Walter Harris on saxophone, Ulysses Health on guitar, Web Lofton on saxophone, James Thomas on guitar, and James Woodbury on piano and vocals. Jimi also played guitar but he was covering the bass parts as there were already lead and rhythm players in the band.

At this point Jimi was playing the solid body electric guitar that Al had bought him, a Supro Ozark 1560S. Although playing bass parts, Jimi was learning from being around two other guitar players. The Rocking Kings played together for about a year and had relatively regular gigs in local Seattle venues. They even won an *All-State Band of the Year* competition in 1959. After one Rocking Kings show, Jimi's guitar was stolen. Although Jimi was heartbroken, Al did not have the means to buy him a new one. Help came from Jimi's aunt, Mary Hendrix, who took pity and bought Jimi a Danelectro electric guitar.[6] After the Rocking Kings broke up at the end of 1959, Jimi went on to play with Thomas and the Tom Cats, which was formed by James Thomas who had managed the Rocking Kings. In Thomas and the Tom Cats, Jimi had the opportunity to play guitar parts and he began to develop his own guitar style.

As music was gradually taking over Jimi's life, his work at school began falling by the wayside. In October 1960, Jimi left Seattle's Garfield High

School without graduating. With little direction outside of music, Jimi began working with his father as a landscaper. His heart was not in this work and the two soon ended their work relationship. This left Jimi with little means for making money and soon he ran afoul of the law. At age nineteen, in the summer of 1961, Jimi was arrested for an incident involving a stolen car. He spent a week in jail and received a two-year suspended sentence because he agreed to join the military. At this point, Jimi left for basic training and his aspirations in music came to an abrupt standstill.

In the military, Jimi opted into paratrooper training, becoming a member of the Screaming Eagles 101st Airborne Paratrooper squad. He was stationed at Fort Campbell, which is located between Hopkinsville, Kentucky, and Clarksville, Tennessee. Adjusting to the life of a soldier was difficult for Jimi as he was not used to the uniform dress and rigid schedule. This was made worse by his decision to leave his guitar in Seattle with Al. While serving, Jimi met several people who would have a great deal of impact on his later life; probably the most important was Billy Cox. After getting used to life on base, Jimi asked Al to send him his guitar so that he could again have his own instrument to practice on. During his time at Fort Campbell, Jimi gradually returned to music and this is where he and Cox connected as Cox was a bass player. With Cox, Jimi formed a band called the King Kasuals along with drummer Gary Ferguson. The group experienced a degree of success playing in the rhythm and blues style in venues on and around the base.

Less than a year into Jimi's army service he broke his ankle during a jump and was subsequently discharged. With his service to the country complete, Jimi and Cox moved to Nashville and reformed the King Kasuals. They managed to land a regular playing job at the Club Del Morocco in Nashville.[7] During his stint with the King Kasuals, Jimi hooked up with guitarist Larry Lee. Jimi and Lee struck up a friendship and in late 1962, Jimi, Cox, and Lee joined Bob Fisher and the Barnevilles for a monthlong tour supporting the Marvelettes and Curtis Mayfield and the Impressions. In late 1963, Jimi joined Bobby Taylor and the Vancouvers, a band that had a regular gig at Dante's Inferno nightclub. This pairing was brief and in a few months Jimi joined "Gorgeous" George Odell. With Odell, Jimi ground out a living playing southern rhythm and blues on the chitlin' circuit.[8] Back in Nashville, Jimi again hooked up with Lee who introduced him to a promoter who encouraged Jimi to go to New York to make more money. The Nashville area was filled with talented guitar players and it was difficult to catch a break with so much competition.

By 1964, Jimi relocated to New York. Along the way he made a fortuitous stop in Philadelphia where he sat in on a recording session with saxophonist Lonnie Youngblood.[9] Jimi provided guitar parts for Youngblood's songs "Go Go Shoes" and the B-side "Go Go Place." The single was released in late 1963 on the Fairmount Records label. Jimi also recorded the songs "Soul Food (That's A What I Like)" and the B-side "Goodbye, Bessie Mae" with Youngblood. These two songs were released on Fairmount in early 1964. Jimi's experience with Youngblood was his first foray into the world of the professional recording artist.

Jimi's arrival in New York was not as grand as he had anticipated. Riding the high from the Youngblood sessions, Jimi soon learned that the performing opportunities in New York were not what he had expected. With little work and less money, Jimi turned to nightclub jam sessions to keep his guitar playing fresh. While working at the Palm Café Jimi met Fay Pridgeon, "an ex-girlfriend of Sam Cooke."[10] Fay—whose full name was Fayne—took Jimi in and together they lived in Harlem while Jimi continued to look for playing jobs. Back at the Palm Café, Jimi met an associate of the Isley Brothers and through this connection he got picked up as the group's new guitarist.[11] In 1964, Jimi was part of the Isley Brothers backing band when the group went into the studio and recorded "Testify" with B-side "Testify II." The group then went on a tour of the United States and Canada that took Jimi back to the West Coast.

Back in Seattle, Jimi managed to miss the tour bus as it left for the next show and again had his guitar stolen. Fortunately for Jimi, the Isleys prized his playing enough to allow him to return to the tour, even giving him his first Fender electric guitar, a Duosonic. With the Isley Brothers, Jimi recorded several other songs including "The Last Girl" with B-side "Looking for a Love," which was released in November 1964, and "Move Over and Let Me Dance" with B-side "Have You Ever Been Disappointed?" released in 1965. Although Jimi was working for a professional touring and recording band, he aspired to have greater creative control of the music that he played. To that end, Jimi left the Isley Brothers when the tour stopped in Nashville.

Although his intentions were to strike out on his own, the realities of needing a steady income soon took over and Jimi went back to work with "Gorgeous" George Odell. In late 1964, he also landed a spot with Little Richard's backing band. Jimi played with Little Richard for the rest of 1964 and into 1965. During that period he toured and recorded as Little Richard's full-time guitarist. In this capacity, Jimi appeared on at least one single titled "I Don't Know What You've Got but It's Got Me (Part I)" with B-side "I Don't Know What You've Got but It's Got Me (Part II)." Also during this period, Jimi met the leader of the band Love, Arthur Lee. Lee recruited Jimi to play guitar for a single being recorded by singer Rosa Lee Brooks.[12] The song was called "My Diary" with B-side "Utee" and was released on the Revis Records imprint in mid-1965. "My Diary" was written by Lee and "Utee" is credited to Brooks. Although Jimi was working, he was not happy with continuing to be a sideman, and playing with Little Richard's backing band, the Upsetters, was not panning out. Jimi quit the Upsetters in the summer of 1965 and returned to Fay Pridgeon and New York.

In late 1965, Jimi caught the free spirit coming out of New York City's Greenwich Village and, without Fay, moved to the Village. At this same time, Jimi met Curtis Knight and soon joined his band the Squires.[13] Through Knight, Jimi met Ed Chalpin, who was working as a producer. Chalpin recognized Jimi's talent and signed him to an exclusive production deal with PPX Enterprises that lasted for the next three years. While Jimi assumed that this was a positive step forward for his career, the reality of the deal was that it only cut the young guitarist in for 1% of the royalties and that was after all other expenses were paid.

With Knight and the Squires, Jimi recorded several singles including "How Would You Feel?" with B-side "Welcome Home," "Hornet's Nest" with B-side "Knock Yourself Out," "How Would You Feel?" with B-side "You Don't Want Me," "How Now" with B-side "Flashing," "The Ballad of Jimi" with B-side "Gloomy Monday," and "No Such Animal (Part I)" with B-side "No Such Animal (Part II)." Knight singles that included Jimi were released from late 1965 to early 1971. Although Jimi was again a working professional musician, he remained unhappy in the sideman role. As a result, he decided to start his own band. Calling the group Jimmy James and the Blue Flames, Jimi recruited a small backing group and for the first time took the lead guitar and singer role.

The Blue Flames played at the Café Wha? in Greenwich Village where they were exposed to a variety of New York bohemians in the middle of the 1960s. Jimi was not working on original material at the time; instead the Blue Flames did cover versions of hits such as "Wild Thing," "Hey Joe," and [Bob] Dylan's "Like a Rolling Stone."[14] As Jimi and the Flames ground out an existence through early 1966, Jimi's guitar playing (and gimmicks such as playing with his teeth) began to catch the attention of a wider audience. Linda Keith saw Jimi play and was taken with his potential.[15] She convinced Bryan "Chas" Chandler, who was the bass player for the original Animals, to see Jimi perform.[16] Chandler was setting up a management company and Jimi fit nicely into the roster of hot, young performers that Chas wanted to cultivate. The catch was that Chandler's connections were mostly in Europe so he recommended that Jimi relocate to London. With few other options to get ahead in the music business, Jimi packed his meager belongings and left New York with Chandler in late September 1966.

In London, Chandler set about the business of holding up his promises to Jimi. He soon introduced the young guitar player to Eric Clapton, who had recently exited John Mayall's Bluesbreakers and formed Cream with Jack Bruce and Ginger Baker. Chandler even got Jimi on stage with Clapton for a jam on Howlin' Wolf's song "Killing Floor." With this, Jimi instantly established himself as a force to be reckoned with on the London music scene. Unable to work as a soloist, Jimi needed to assemble a backing band. Because of his long tenure as a sideman, Jimi was well able to cover both lead and rhythm guitar parts, so he needed a bass player and a drummer—the rock and roll power trio. Noel Redding learned that Chandler was trying to assemble a group around Jimi and auditioned on bass, although his first instrument was guitar. The two clicked and Noel joined Jimi's fledgling outfit. That left the role of drummer yet to fill. John "Mitch" Mitchell played with Jimi and soon enough rounded out the trio that was given the catchy name the Jimi Hendrix Experience.

Overnight Success (1966–1967)

Now that Jimi had a formal band, he and Chandler needed experienced management in the music business. Chandler recruited Michael Jeffery to handle the business matters of the Experience.[1] Chandler and Jeffery signed Jimi to a management and production contract, not realizing that he was still under contract to Chalpin and PPX, and Noel and Mitch were signed to a production contract as support for Jimi. With signed contracts the Experience went into rehearsal preparing for a brief French tour in support of Johnny Hallyday.[2] The four-day tour took the Experience to France in early October 1966 where they performed at L'Olympia in Paris. Their time on stage was limited as a warm-up act and they had no original songs. As a result, their "set [list] included cover versions of 'Killing Floor,' 'Hey Joe,' and 'Wild Thing.'"[3] Although the tour got the Experience in front of their first live audience, it did not provide them much in the way of monetary payment.

The most expedient route to money was for the Experience to record and release a single that they could sell. Chandler convinced Jimi to use his cover of "Hey Joe" for the Experience's first single—Jimi had wanted to use "Killing Floor." The B-side to the first single was also a contentious point. Jimi wanted to use another cover version and Chandler was prodding him to write a song of his own. Chandler prevailed and Jimi set about the task of writing his first original song, "Stone Free." On December 16, 1966, the Jimi Hendrix Experience released their first single on the United Kingdom imprint Polydor.

Also in December 1966, Jimi and the Experience played a series of club dates at the Ram Jam Club, Guild Hall, the Upper Cut, and Blaises

Club. Chris Welch offered the following description of the December 21 show:

> Jimi Hendrix, a fantastic American guitarist, blew the minds of the star-packed crowd who went to see him at Blaises Club, London, on Wednesday. Among those in the audience were Pete Townshend, Roger Daltrey, John Entwistle, Chas Chandler, and Jeff Beck. They heard Jimi's trio blast through some beautiful sounds like "Rock Me Baby," "Third Stone From the Sun," "Like a Rolling Stone," "Hey Joe," and even an unusual version of the Trogg's "Wild Thing." Jimi has great stage presence and an exceptional guitar technique which involved playing with his teeth on occasions and no hands at all on others! Jimi looks like he is becoming one of the big club names of '67.[4]

With this appearance before two-thirds of the Who, as well as other music notables, Jimi and the Experience were on their way to making a mark on the world.

"Hey Joe" was a song that Jimi had long been conversant with as it exists in a wide variety of versions. The song was originally written by California folk singer Billy Roberts who sold it to Dino Valenti who licensed it under the name Chet Powers. Fast versions of the song exist, but Jimi was most influenced by folk singer Tim Rose's slow, bluesy version. The earliest known recording of the song comes from a band called the Leaves and was released in late 1965. The Experience recorded their version in October 1966 with Chandler handling the production at Pye Studios in London.[5]

The song tells the story of a man "Joe" who shot his wife as the result of catching her cheating on him. He owns up to the action but then has to escape to Mexico to avoid the consequences. Though not truly a "traditional" song, it did possess the ". . . archetypal nature of its tale of infidelity and bloody revenge that it sounded like a murder ballad which had been handed down through the generations."[6] Musically, the song opened in the standard blues fashion with a distinctive guitar lick that led into Jimi singing the open lyric twice. Each instrument and the vocals were all equally present and Jimi worked a direct call and response between his singing and guitar playing. The song unfolded slowly as Jimi told the story before fading out at the end. Female vocal backing was added by the Breakaways, which was composed of Vicki Haseman, Margo Quantrell, and Betty Prescott. As Richie Unterberger noted, Jimi's version of "Hey Joe" (along with how he would handle several songs by Bob Dylan) was a testament to his ability to interpret a well-known song and remake it in his own style.

The first song that Jimi wrote, "Stone Free," was an anthem to the freedom of the late 1960s—as well as his own belief in personal freedom. Jimi sang and played in an uninhibited manner and the song was much more in the rock style than "Hey Joe." With this song Jimi asserted his artistic independence and also began discussing his life in the lyrics of his songs. The opening verse began by Jimi discussing his long-standing traveling ways referencing being in a different city every week. The verse ended with mention of being singled out because of his clothes and then drove into the chorus where Jimi puts everything behind him by moving on. The second verse was about the many women that entered and exited Jimi's life and his desire to keep moving before getting pinned down. It was ". . . a declaration of intent to be footloose and fancy free, not tied to any one place or existence— certainly not by those who put down the clothes he wears, who 'don't realize they're the ones who's square.'"[7] The song then wound around through several repetitions of the chorus before chugging to a halt. With this song, Jimi asserted his songwriting skills, his independence, and his feeling about living a free life.

The first single came out on Polydor, but Chandler and Jeffery had actually brokered a deal with Chris Stamp and Kit Lambert, the Who's management team, who were launching their own Track Records imprint. The new label was not ready for use when the first single was ready to go so Polydor was used as a substitute. Jimi's management was convinced to sign to the fledgling label because Stamp and Lambert also promised to get the Experience an appearance on the British music show *Ready Steady Go*.[8] Not only did the Experience play *Ready Steady Go*; they also had an appearance on *Top of the Pops*.[9] With a single out and two television appearances in rapid succession, the Experience jumped straight to public popularity. In the wake of their newfound fame in the United Kingdom, Jeffery delivered a lucrative deal for the band from the Warner Brothers imprint in the United States.

In early November 1966, the Experience had a four-day stand at the German club called the Big Apple, in Munich. From November 8 to November 11, the band worked to increase their fan base in Germany. Additionally, it was during one of these shows that Jimi smashed his first guitar on stage. What began as an accident turned into one of Jimi's signature moves on stage. According to Glebbeek and Noble, Jimi had been pulled into the audience by an overzealous fan and in trying to return to the stage he damaged his guitar. As it was already unplayable, he set about smashing it completely to the amazement and pleasure of the crowd.[10]

On the heels of their German appearance, the Experience went back in the studio to parlay their early success into more material on record. The group's next single was released on Stamp and Lambert's Track Records imprint with "Purple Haze" on the A-side and "51st Anniversary" on the B-side. Both songs were originals written by Jimi and had distinct and vaguely autobiographical stories behind their lyrics.

Released on March 3, 1967, "Purple Haze" has been considered by many as Jimi describing a drug-induced haze. The reality of this song was that it was influenced by Jimi's interest in reading science fiction books. The lyrics were based, at least in part, on the Philip José Farmer book *Night of Light*.[11] Early drafts of the lyrics for "Purple Haze" were as many as ten pages long.[12]

The Jimi Hendrix Experience 1968, shown: Mitch Mitchell, Jimi Hendrix, Noel Redding (Courtesy of Photofest)

Part of Chandler's role in Jimi's early songwriting was to work with him to trim such things down into manageable, and marketable, length. In an interview published in the music magazine *New Musical Express* in 1967, Jimi went on record describing his concept for "Purple Haze": "I dream a lot and I put a lot of dreams down as songs. I wrote one . . . called 'Purple Haze,' which was all about a dream I had that I was walking under the sea."[13]

The song was written in December 1966 and was recorded first at DeLane Lea Studios in London. With the success of "Hey Joe," Chandler moved the recording session to Olympic Studios and there "Purple Haze" took form. With Dave Siddle at the controls, as session engineer, the Experience ripped into "Purple Haze" by beginning the song with the sinister sounding tritone interval creating an opening dissonance, long described as the "Devil in Music." Unique features of Jimi's playing on the song also included the use of the dominant 7 sharp 9 chord that became known as the "Hendrix chord." The sonic landscape of the song was further enhanced by the use of the effect pedal called the Octavia that had been developed by Roger Mayer, as well as the Fuzz Face distortion effect.[14]

The song ended with aggressive use of the vibrato or whammy bar. All of these electronic and performance-based alterations to their sound quickly gave the Experience a unique quality to their music that was unmatched at the time. "Purple Haze" was a major success for the Experience as it entered the United Kingdom charts at number thirty-nine and peaked at number three, selling more than one hundred thousand copies.[15] Released in the United States in June 1967 on the Reprise imprint, the song went to number sixty-five and helped to increase the popularity of the Experience in America.

Released as the first B-side of the "Purple Haze" single, "51st Anniversary" was another original song that made a poignant statement about relationships and loss. Jimi presented the lyrics counting backwards through a couple's married life, starting with fifty years, then thirty, twenty, ten, and three. The opening optimism of the couple looking forward to their "51st Anniversary" disappeared quickly as the stress of the early part of the pairing comes to bear. There are certainly autobiographical elements to the lyrics in the latter half of the song. Jimi referenced his mother Lucille's young age of seventeen when she married his father. He also directly noted that she was not ready to put away her partying ways (or interests in other men). Jimi himself said that the first half of the song was meant to describe marriages in general and the second half was about his own life. The main point that Jimi was making throughout the song was that he would not be tied down in the manner that others referenced in the song were.

The music of "51st Anniversary" was similar to that of "Purple Haze," but without the heavy dissonance and a little less of a psychedelic quality. Here Jimi mixed elements of the blues, and mid-1960s psychedelia, along with a healthy dose of straightforward storytelling. Several standard blues devices were present in the lyrics. Jimi repeated many lines twice in addition to moving back and forth between singing and speaking in the country blues fashion. Mitch and Noel left the focus on Jimi's singing and guitar playing, with relatively light beat keeping on the drums and the bass often doubling the guitar. The song ended with a repeated note figure that simply faded out.

During the production of the early singles, the Experience was an increasingly active live band. In November and December 1966, the group played shows in and around London including Hounslow, Brixton, Bromley, Southampton, and Folkestone. As 1967 dawned for the Experience, live appearances and touring took an even greater role. The group played numerous English dates through January and February. In March, in addition to dates in England, they returned to Germany for a three-day run at the Star Club in Hamburg. The final day of March found the Experience booked onto a package tour with a host of unlikely other bands on the lineup. For the entire month of April, the Jimi Hendrix Experience toured England on a concert bill that included Cat Stevens,[16] Engelbert Humperdinck,[17] the Walker Brothers (on their farewell outing),[18] the Californians, and the Quotations. The shows were all booked into large cinemas and the Experience had little time to do more than play a five-song set.

As a means of setting the band apart from the other acts on the bill, the idea was hatched to light Jimi's guitar on fire on stage during the opening show on March 31, 1967, at the Astoria in London. Journalist Keith Altham, along with Chandler and the Experience, hit on the idea of pouring lighter fluid on Jimi's solid body guitar to get it to catch fire—since a solid bodied guitar simply would not burst into flames. Roadie Gerry Stickells was dispatched to get the lighter fluid and the Experience went on stage after the Californians. The "short set comprised 'Foxey Lady' and 'Can You See Me?' plus 'Hey Joe' and 'Purple Haze.' The final song 'Fire' was also new and, at the climax of the song, Jimi touched the lighter to the petrol-soaked guitar."[19] The on-stage spectacle gained Jimi huge media attention. Reports vary about the response of the promoter and house security.[20] Regardless, the deed was done and with it Jimi's stage performance style was vaulted into infamy.

The package tour ground on. Although it was a strange collection of groups, on-tour reports indicated that all of the various band members got along, even including practical jokes of each other on stage. The only standout was Cat Stevens who generally kept away from the antics of the other musicians. For thirty-one days, the tour moved around England from London to Leeds, from Cumberland to Lancashire, and from Manchester back to London. In the end, although a strange choice, the Experience gained enormous exposure from the tour. In accord with the maxim that there is no such thing as negative publicity, the group was receiving unprecedented media attention and the buzz was building for their next single.

Back in the studio, the Experience recorded two more Jimi originals. The A-side of the release was "The Wind Cries Mary" and the B-side was "Highway Chile." This third single was released May 5, 1967, and marked the first Experience single that was anticipated by the waiting public. Well adjusted to playing with each other after the April package tour, the Experience recorded "The Wind Cries Mary" in only twenty minutes.[21] This new song was unlike anything Jimi had played or written in the past. The lyrics were a touching love song to Jimi's then girlfriend Kathy Etchingham (her middle name is Mary). Jimi had met Etchingham on his first day in England when Chandler asked her to walk him to his hotel. They struck up an immediate friendship and subsequent relationship that was at times tumultuous. Although the pair eventually broke up, they remained friends for the rest of Jimi's life.

The song was the first that Jimi wrote that cast his voice as the main feature, with his guitar serving a support role. The four verses of the song were divided in half by a guitar solo in between verses two and three. Although a solo, it lacked any of the pyrotechnic elements of much of Jimi's later playing. Describing the song as close to folk-rock as Jimi ever came, Richie Unterberger described it as ". . . Curtis Mayfield-esque guitar riffs, smooth and note-jammed, but lilting and restrained, avoiding overplaying or the kind of volume and distortion Hendrix was habitually employing to make his more aggressive points by early 1967."[22] The content of the lyrics describes a couple who were not getting along and casts them as being separated and lonely with their relationship in pieces. Kathy admitted that her relationship with Jimi was often quite rocky and that the song was likely inspired by one particular fight during which Jimi accused her of cooking with dirty pans.

"A heated argument ensued, culminating in Etchingham hurling plates and pans about the kitchen of their flat before storming out to spend the night at the house of the Animals vocalist Eric Burdon."[23]

"Highway Chile" was the B-side to "The Wind Cries Mary." The basic tracks for the song were laid down at Olympic Studios on April 3, 1967. Stylistically, the song was a rollicking mixture of rock and electric blues. Here Jimi used a signature guitar hook that opened the song and was repeated in each chorus section. Structurally, Jimi paired two verses before moving to the chorus and the song progressed through this pattern twice with a short guitar solo inserted after the second chorus. The content of the lyrics described a wandering guitar player with a guitar slung across his back who was wronged by a woman and will never settle down. Vaguely autobiographical, the lyrics of "Highway Chile" seemed to describe Jimi's early life without making direct reference to any specific circumstances. "Things might not have been quite so bad for some of the time when Hendrix was struggling on the chitlin' circuit and in Harlem, but they were similar enough to the circumstances he outlines here to suspect that this is a bit of a self-portrait."[24]

During May 1967, the Experience toured around England, went back to Germany, and expanded their traveling. On May 19, the group made its first appearance in Sweden with three shows in various locations. They then played in Helsinki, Finland, before returning to Sweden for two more shows. The concert in Helsinki was a disaster and the Experience and its road crew were harassed for their appearance. The group never played in Finland again. The month ended with a multiact show in Lincolnshire called *Barbeque '67*. This concert also featured Cream,[25] Pink Floyd,[26] Zoot Money,[27] and the Move.[28] The Jimi Hendrix Experience was the headliner and performed for a packed house.

With three successful singles on the market and an aggressive touring schedule, the members of the Experience should have been enjoying their first real taste of financial success. However, that was not the case as the money coming in from their musical exploits was not filtering down to the three actually making the music. Jimi, Noel, and Mitch confronted Chandler and Jeffery about the disparity. The three were sent away with enough money to ease the situation for the moment, but this was a direct harbinger of things to come. At that time, "there was an oral agreement between Jimi, Noel, and Mitch that all income would be divided on a 50-25-25 basis with Jimi taking the biggest share, rather than Noel and Mitch being on a wage."[29] This not only gave Noel and Mitch more of a fair share; it also indicated that Jimi valued their contributions to the Experience's music.

Are You Experienced?

The summer of 1967 was extremely eventful for the Jimi Hendrix Experience. In May the group released its first full-length album, *Are You Experienced?*

The record was issued on the Track imprint in the United Kingdom on May 17, only twelve days after the release of "The Wind Cries Mary" single. In June, the Experience made their United States debut by appearing on the *Monterey International Pop Festival* in Monterey, California. *Are You Experienced?* was released in the United States in August on the Reprise label and the group toured the United States throughout June, July, and August. The original Track label imprint for the United Kingdom album front was a picture of the band taken by Bruce Fleming. The Reprise imprint release in the United States was fronted by a circular picture of the group with a pale green background, with a list of tracks and another band picture on the back.

Are You Experienced? was recorded in London over the course of several months, October 1966 to April 1967. Chandler was the producer on the record and Dave Siddle was the engineer at De Lane Lea Studios. The record was mastered at Olympic Studios by Eddie Kramer and was released on May 17, in the United Kingdom. *Are You Experienced?* was a smash hit and spent thirty-three weeks on the charts peaking at number two, behind the Beatles' *Sgt. Pepper's Lonely Hearts Club Band*. The record was then released in the United States on the Reprise imprint on August 8, strangely, with a slightly different song list.

The Track release in the United Kingdom contained the following songs: "Foxey Lady," "Manic Depression," "Red House," "Can You See Me?" "Love or Confusion," "I Don't Live Today," "May This Be Love," "Fire," "Third Stone From the Sun," "Remember," and "Are You Experienced?" The United States release on the Reprise imprint contained "Purple Haze," "Manic Depression," "Hey Joe," "Love or Confusion," "May This Be Love," "I Don't Live Today," "The Wind Cries Mary," "Fire," "Third Stone From the Sun," "Foxey Lady," and "Are You Experienced?" The difference in tracks appearing on the album may have been done to expose the American audience to the singles that had previously been released only in the United Kingdom.

The album began with "Foxey Lady" and a wash of feedback. Here Jimi was, on the prowl chasing after a woman he desired (some say Heather Taylor,[30] who would later marry Roger Daltrey, the singer for the Who).[31] Lyrically, the song was loaded with sexual innuendo as Jimi called her out and tried to entice her to come home with him. The song itself did not have a great deal of different lyrics; Jimi simply staked his claim on this woman and would not be denied. Musically, the Experience grooved together with the guitar forward in the mix. Noel and Mitch were relegated to relatively light beat keeping throughout most of the song. Richie Unterberger described the song's opening as "[a] parade of arresting opening riffs that Jimi was seemingly summoning up at will by early 1967 continued at the beginning of this track, which kicks off with a slow fade-in of wiry, fluttering notes, like an insect buzz slowly making its way through your speakers."[32] At about two-thirds of the way through, the musical tension increased and led into the solo where Jimi displayed his virtuoso guitar chops. After the solo Jimi repeated the second verse after which the song wound down to end with Jimi raking the edge of his guitar pick against one of the strings.

The second song on the United Kingdom release was "Manic Depression" which was described by Peter Doggett as "an epic of confusion and slightly amused despair."[33] Recorded in February and March 1967, the lyrics of this song were a direct statement about Jimi's impressions of the world. In straightforward language he asserted that while most things around him were a "frustrated mess," his solace was always found in music. The genesis for the song was a comment that Chandler made to Jimi about him acting like a manic depressive. From this, Jimi carved out the lyrics for the song which ended up being a foreshadowing of some of the fears and doubts that he had later in his life.

Musically, the song was an oddity in Jimi's catalogue and in rock and roll music in general, in that it was written in triple meter while most songs in this style are in a four-four time (certainly there are rock songs in three, but not very many). The song began in a mellow manner with all three instruments evenly matched. As the lyrics unfolded, tension built and drove to the guitar solo which was so frantic that it almost stopped working with the lines being laid down by the rhythm section. For all of the accolades eventually heaped on Jimi's guitar playing, Mitch and Noel could hold their own and their performance on this song was described as "Redding plots a moody, aggressive line; he sounds real mean . . . [and] Mitchell's dominant, octopus-on-speed provides the 'manic' element."[34]

Jimi got back on track for the third verse and the song drew to a close with him speaking the word "depression." The lyrics here were quite telling of Jimi's temperament. Generally, he was categorized as being shy and withdrawn but he did have a notorious temper and a tendency for moodiness. Jimi said of the song, in a live performance in 1968, that it was "a story about a cat wishing he could make love to music, instead of the same old everyday woman."[35]

"Red House" was Jimi's grounding in the blues on display. A slow deliberate presentation in the standard mode of the 12-bar blues style, here Jimi put his outstanding guitar playing on display. As is the case with many blues numbers, the lyrics of this song were about the pain of love lost. Typical of the presentation of the lyrics in the blues, Jimi sings the opening lyric twice and the entire song was a call and response between Jimi singing and Jimi playing guitar. In the second verse Jimi discovered that his key no longer unlocked the door and he has been put out. In an unusual twist, the loss of his love interest did not have the effect that was normal for the style. Instead of ending with a lament about lost love, Jimi's spirits were lifted because he still had his guitar. The song ended with him taking this one step further with the sentiment that since this woman did not love him anymore, "maybe her sister will."

Recorded in November 1966, "Can You See Me?" was divided into four verses with a guitar solo in the middle of the song. Although the cut was recorded early enough that it could have been released as a single, it was not available until this album version. Lyrically, Jimi sang in a plaintive manner about another love interest who cast him aside. The first verse had him begging for her affection and the second verse had him crying about losing her. After the lively solo, Jimi asked if the object of his attention could hear him singing to her and in the final verse Jimi resigned himself that his song was falling on deaf ears. The lyrics showed Jimi's heart laid bare; however, the music of the song was up-tempo and driving. The vocals were double tracked and the guitar panned from side-to-side for an enhanced stereo effect. Additionally, "Hendrix's use of fuzztone [guitar effect] is clearly getting more advanced than it had been when the Experience first entered the studio, at times approximating a violinlike tone in its thick sustain."[36]

"Love or Confusion" was also recorded in November 1966 and again illustrated Jimi's feelings of uncertainty regarding love and his place in the world. Constructed much in the same way as "Manic Depression," here Jimi linked together lyrics that asked a series of questions about time, space, and love. Jimi's anxiety level increased through the course of the song unfolding which he referenced through his pounding head and burning heart. The song again cast Jimi as the seeker of comfort and affection that was not forthcoming with Jimi left alone and unsettled. Musically, "Love or Confusion" had a variety of alterations made to the basic tracks which gave the song a psychedelic or otherworldly quality. The opening guitar sound had the quality of a sitar causing an Indian feel. Jimi's vocals were passed through an echo effect making them sound distant and "spacey." The guitar playing on the track was solid as usual and the song ended with Jimi stating the word "confusion" and working the whammy bar as the sustained tone of his guitar faded out.

In concert, Jimi frequently dedicated "I Don't Live Today" to the American Indians and the sentiment of the lyrics applied equally well to the circumstances of the native American people as well as to Jimi's own life. In fact, Jimi was one-sixteenth Cherokee Indian. The song was recorded in February 1967 and Peter Doggett called it "a magnificently malevolent psychic voyage"[37] Lyrically, Jimi painted a bleak picture of a miserable life that lacked even sunlight. Here Jimi's sympathies were with the displaced Native American population who felt they were marginalized and forced from a once-proud existence to the edge of American society. The only possibility for peace was that "maybe tomorrow" things would improve.

Musically, "I Don't Live Today" was a whirling adventure in studio techniques and sound manipulation. The song opened with Jimi playing a rhythm guitar part, but with another guitar part overdubbed that was composed of long sustained notes that float above the texture of the band. This additional guitar part was further manipulated through the use of the whammy bar bending the sound up and down. "... 'I Don't Live Today' is as strong as all but the very best tracks on *Are You Experienced?*, the vocals complemented at every turn by pounding riffs before transitioning into a proud, glowering chorus which in turn makes an unpredictable switch into double time."[38] The solo, which hits about two-thirds of the way through the song, was noted as Jimi's first use of the wah-wah effect.[39] The wah-wah effect made the guitar sound like a human voice and also allowed Jimi to alter the pitch he was creating through the use of a foot pedal that swept the pitch up and down creating a glissando (or stream of pitches moving high to low and back).[40] After the solo, Jimi sang another verse and the song began dissolving into an uncontrolled frenzy. At one point the sound stopped altogether only to begin again. The sound of all of the instruments dropped out several times as Jimi spoke the final lyrics about getting experienced accompanying himself with several hand claps.

Recorded in April 1967, "May This Be Love" contained a much different sentiment than "Manic Depression" or "Can You See Me?" The song was also known as "Waterfall" because Jimi used the metaphor of a waterfall to describe a love interest who made him feel safe and comfortable. In the lyrics, Jimi's waterfall took away his worries and protected him from damaging comments that others made—it was a tender love song. However, the lyrical content of this song was fairly short with two chorus statements and one verse. Gone was the storytelling and extended discussions that Jimi had in other songs on the album. The material that the members of the band presented here focused almost exclusively on Jimi's guitar playing. After he stated the lyrics, the song continued for an extended period with the guitar work taking prominence. This divided the song in half with the first half containing the lyrics and the second reserved for the guitar playing.

Often mistakenly called "Let Me Stand Next to Your Fire," the lyrics for "Fire" came at least in part from an exchange at the New Year's Eve party at Noel Redding's mother's house in 1966. Jimi reportedly asked if it would be all right for him to stand next to the fireplace. The lyrics of the song again dealt with relationship issues, this time cast in a fairly straightforward verse and chorus exchange. Jimi related being with a love interest to standing next to her fire and made his case for the two pairing up. " 'Fire' is not only as catchy as any single by the Experience or any other major act of 1967, it teems with as much energy as anything the group cut, and if it's not quite as carnal as 'Foxey Lady', it certainly has more than enough hormonal heat to go around."[41] Musically, the song was one of the faster paced on the album. It opened with Noel's bass part doubling Jimi's guitar. The Octavia effect pedal was used on Jimi's line to double the notes that he was playing an octave higher, which gave the guitar sound more body and presence.

"Third Stone From the Sun" was the first of many efforts by Jimi to create in his music an "otherworldliness." He achieved this here by beginning the lyrics of the song with an exchange between the Star Fleet and the Scout Ship. The exchange was:

> Star Fleet to Scout Ship. Please give your position. Over.
> I'm in orbit around the third planet from the star called the Sun. Over.
> You mean it's the Earth? Over.
> Positive. It is known to have some form of intelligent species. Over.
> I think we should take a look.[42]

Interesting enough on its own, Jimi complicated matters further by having the exchange recorded such that it is unintelligible unless played back at 66 $2/3$ rpm, twice the normal playback speed for an LP. Jimi himself provided the voice for the Star Fleet.

The lyrics of "Third Stone From the Sun" were the impressions of the Scout Ship upon investigating planet Earth. Jimi noted the planet's beauty and majesty, but admitted that he did not understand the people and therefore wanted to leave (maybe a sentiment that he truly held). The song was an interesting experiment and laid the groundwork for Jimi to further explore other types of tape manipulation and effects on the human voice in later recordings. The lyrics themselves were all spoken and seemed to have been inspired by Jimi's interest in science fiction, as discussed regarding "Purple Haze." The music of the song was unlike anything else that the Experience had put out to that time. Stylistically, it was reminiscent of the surf rock style that was mentioned at the end of the lyrics. Unterberger noted, ". . . much of what Jimi did with the guitar translated the R&B-blues-soul sensibility to the psychedelic age, here he does the same for the kinds of riffs associated with surf music, or perhaps the Northwest combos like The Ventures that had been a key part of his adolescent musical education."[43] Although it had very few words, the largely instrumental song was the longest on the album.

The spaced out journey that was "Third Stone From the Sun" was immediately contrasted by the straight-ahead rhythm and blues of "Remember." Here Jimi returned to his stylistic roots from his days on the chitlin' circuit. As Doggett stated, ". . . [this] song, recorded on February 8, 1967, was proof that Jimi had spent a couple of years on the American R&B circuit."[44] That meant that the dynamics of the instruments were kept even and the vocals were forward in the mix and the overall impression of the song was similar to that of the Stax label stylings of Otis Redding. Structurally, the song contained six verses without any true chorus sections. After the third verse, Jimi took a short solo and then continued his story of loss. Moving into the fifth verse the music modulated up a step in accord with the rhythm and blues style. Lyrically, Jimi was again lamenting the loss of a love which silenced the sweet singing of the birds and the bees. The lyrics of the first half of the song discuss how the loss affected things around Jimi and the second half discussed how it affected Jimi himself. The song faded out with Jimi calling the woman back home by telling her to "stop jiving around."

"Are You Experienced?" the title track of the album, appeared as the last song on side two for both the United Kingdom and the United States releases—not a common position for such a prominent song. This song became one of the most popular on the album with the double meaning of the lyrics referencing the name of the band along with "experiencing" Jimi himself. Of the ". . . experience that Jimi makes so much of here, it could be sex or it could be drugs, particularly of the psychedelic sort . . . [or] both, given his predilection for missing the two and the counterculture's appetite to hear both subjects addressed more openly in songs than had seemed possible even a year or two previously."[45] The lyrics and music of the song unfolded in a straightforward verse and chorus alternation with a guitar solo after two verse/chorus pairings. The content of the lyrics found Jimi encouraging the listener to join him for a host of new experiences both real and imagined. Musically, this was the only song on the album that included the use of the piano. Jimi played the piano part and it created a chiming effect in the overall texture of the group. Another interesting addition to this song was the use of guitar, bass, and drum overdubs that were played backward. The overall sound was at times cacophonous, but it still worked and all of the various parts hung together to create an interesting product. The group texture of the song ended; then there was a single guitar blast that hit abruptly creating the actual end.

A month after *Are You Experienced?* was released in the United Kingdom the single "Purple Haze" with B-side "The Wind Cries Mary" was released in the United States. Now that the Experience had conquered the United Kingdom, it was time for them to invade the United States. The band's takeover began with an appearance at the *Monterey International Pop Festival* on June 18. Earlier in the day, the Who had played a blistering set that Jimi feared would upstage his own band. After the Who, the Grateful Dead played and then the Jimi Hendrix Experience took the stage. Jimi pulled out all the stops and used every one of his tricks accumulated over the course of trying to get noticed early in his career. He played with his teeth and behind his back; in addition he created great waves of feedback sliding the neck of his guitar over his mic stand and on the edge of his amplifier cabinets. Noel and Mitch matched Jimi's energy and the Experience put on a set that remains remarkable forty years later.

With his freak flag flying, Jimi took the stage wearing a pink feather boa and promptly put down a scorching version of "Killing Floor."[46] The Experience followed this with "Foxey Lady" and "Like a Rolling Stone"—covering Bob Dylan in a manner that really got the crowd's attention. Next came "Rock Me, Baby," "Hey Joe," "Can You See Me?" "The Wind Cries Mary," and "Purple Haze." The final song of the set was a cover of the Troggs' song "Wild Thing."

Just before the song, Jimi talked to the audience from the stage. He was setting them up for what was about to happen in his typical understated manner.

Monterey Pop (Documentary, 1968), Directed by D. A. Pennebaker, shown: Jimi Hendrix (Courtesy of Photofest)

He said, "I could sit up here all night and say thank you, thank you . . . I just can't do that . . . so what I want to do, I'm going to sacrifice something right here that I really love . . . don't think I'm silly . . . so I'm not losing my mind. This is just for everybody here, this is the only way I can do it . . . Don't get mad, no."[47] After this, Jimi blasted into the song and gave the audience the concert climax they were looking for to end the set.

During the song, Jimi played with one hand, played behind his back, and created great walls of distortion. As the song reached its climax and the amplifiers howled, Jimi put his guitar on the stage and knelt over it, pulling on the whammy bar. As new levels of distortion and feedback were reached Jimi began squirting lighter fluid on the face of the guitar and then struck a match. The image of Jimi kneeling over his burning guitar at Monterey became one of the most iconic pictures of the era. At that point the audience was hearing the sound of Jimi's guitar burning through Marshall amplifier stacks all turned up to ten. Next, Jimi leapt to his feet, swung his guitar over his head, and brought it down against the stage—still feeding back through the amps. The neck broke and soon enough Jimi's guitar was completely destroyed. He then picked up a few pieces and tossed them out to the audience. The Experience's set ended and some members of the crowd went crazy while others sat in stunned silence.

After making a huge impression at Monterey, the Jimi Hendrix Experience spent the summer of 1967 touring the United States. From June 20 to June 24, the Experience took up residence at the Fillmore West in San Francisco, California.[48] They followed this with other California shows playing in Santa Barbara and then moving on to Los Angeles for a night at the storied Whisky a Go Go.[49] While on the West Coast, Jimi became friendly with several members of the band the Monkees. Peter Tork, a member of the Monkees both during the television show and for the touring band, introduced Jimi to "Joni Mitchell, Judy Collins, David Crosby, and Mike Bloomfield."[50] Although they were friends of the Monkees, Chandler and the Experience were quite dismayed to hear that Jeffery had booked the band to open for the Monkees on a nationwide tour. Regardless of their initial response, the Experience went to the East Coast for the tour. They played several nights at New York's Scene Club in addition to playing the Rheingold Festival in Central Park on July 5 where the four-song set list was "Purple Haze," "Hey Joe," "Like a Rolling Stone," and "Wild Thing."

Next they spent a week in the South playing two shows in Florida followed by two in North Carolina. Things were not working out with providing tour support for the Monkees, who had a very clean and prepackaged image from their television show. The Experience went on directly before the Monkees and this meant that the crowd spent the Experience's set clamoring for the headliners. The tour pressed on to New York for a three-night stand at the Forest Hills Stadium. During these shows things reached a breaking point. Jimi would blaze through the Experience set at breakneck speed just to get off stage, and the level of playing was not high.

Recognizing that this could not go on, Chandler arranged an out with the tour promoter, Dick Clark.[51] Chandler and Clark cooked up a story that the Daughters of the American Revolution were protesting the Experience being on a tour that clearly pandered to a young audience. The ruse worked and the Experience was able to bow out of the rest of the tour having played only seven shows. In an interview with the magazine *New Musical Express* on July 29, 1967, Jimi teased that he thought the Experience would be replaced on the tour by "Mickey Mouse." Jimi went on to quash rumors that there had been racial segregation on the tour. He stated that he, Peter, and Mickey (all four members of the Monkees are white) were friends and spent time together throughout the opening of the tour.

After leaving the Monkees' tour, Jimi returned to New York where he rekindled his relationship with Fay Pridgeon. Fay marveled at how much

Jimi's career had progressed in the relatively short period that he had been away. He also hooked back up with some of his old musician friends like John Hammond, Jr. for jam sessions.[52] Also at this time, Jimi and the band continued to play live. They played a series of shows in New York City alternating between the Salvation Club[53] and the Café Au Go Go.[54] The Experience then picked up a series of four shows at the Ambassador Theater, in Washington, DC, with the band Natty Bumpo opening.[55]

Mid-August 1967 found the Experience continuing to play live as much as possible. On August 13 they performed as part of the *Keep the Faith for Washington Youth Fund* concert in Washington, DC. This was followed by a run out to Michigan to play at the Fifth Dimension Club. The middle of the month culminated in a show at the Hollywood Bowl with the Mamas and the Papas, on August 18.[56] The Experience then played the next day at the Earl Warren Showgrounds in Santa Barbara with Moby Grape,[57] Tim Buckley,[58] and others. After these West Coast shows, the Experience returned to England having generated a strong and ever-growing American audience. Also in the middle of the month, the group released another single, "Burning of the Midnight Lamp" with B-side "The Stars That Play With Laughing Sam's Dice." This single came out on the Track imprint in the United Kingdom and was not released in the United States at the time.

Before leaving for England, Jimi had dinner with Chalpin hoping that his deal with PPX had passed into distant memory. Sadly, this was not the case and although Chalpin was polite at first, he soon informed Jimi that PPX was pursuing legal action against Track and Polydor. Additionally, Jimi was reminded that, legally, he worked exclusively for Chalpin and PPX until October 1968. Even with this tense situation brewing, Jimi agreed to go into the studio to record with Curtis Knight, with Chalpin producing. The agreement was that Jimi's name would not be used (an agreement that was not honored). Further, in later interviews, Jimi claimed that he was just jamming and did not realize that the session work could be subsequently issued. In addition to pursuing litigation against the United Kingdom labels that Jimi had recorded for, Chalpin also released a series of Curtis Knight records highlighting the fact that Jimi had played on them—thus making him (Chalpin) a handsome sum, which Jimi saw nothing of.

The new single, "Burning of the Midnight Lamp," did not appear on an album until *Electric Ladyland* in 1968, but as a single showcased Jimi's ever-expanding skills. The song featured Jimi using the wah-wah pedal in addition to adding an electric harpsichord opening melody. Jimi's vocals were multi-tracked and for the backing vocals Jimi's voice was passed through a mellotron effect.[59] Another alteration to the sound on this song was the inclusion of the tambourine. Jimi reportedly penned the song on a cross-country flight from Los Angeles to New York.

The song began with a wah-wah altered guitar part that led into the first verse in which Jimi described being in a lonely state that lasted through night and day and left him in a state of desperation. The verse ended with the return of the wah-wah guitar line from the opening with Jimi singing the sole line of the title of the song with a single word added, "alone." The second verse continued that same sad and lost sentiment—that a cross-country flight and constant touring could create. After the second verse, Jimi launched into a guitar solo that again made use of the wah-wah effect and carried the song back into the third and final verse. The song's structure exhibited long verse statements that were narrative and emotion filled that end in a single line refrain/chorus statement—this was a popular compositional method for Jimi. Although "Burning of the Midnight Lamp" was not the standout hit that the earlier singles had been, Jimi commented at the time that it was "the best one we ever made."[60]

The B-side of the single contained the song "The Stars That Play With Laughing Sam's Dice." The title was a not-so-veiled reference to "STP with LSD," both of which were popular hallucinogenics in the 1960s. The makeup of the sound on this song was different than most by the Experience. Here Jimi cast himself as the "friendly neighborhood experience maker" and there was an added ensemble of singers who were dubbed the Milky Way Express. Structurally, the song lacked any resemblance to a standard verse/chorus rock and roll piece. Jimi began with a four-line opening lyric that stated the title of the song followed by what could be described as the effects of taking hallucinogens—a cosmic journey through the universe. The Experience then launched into an extended jam during which Jimi's voice was mostly lost in the din of the instruments. The guitar wailed while Noel and Mitch held down the groove. During the body of the song, Jimi proclaimed himself the tour guide for the group. The Milky Way Express came on board and off they all went to the sounds of howling and whistling. Jimi referenced passing Saturn and Mars as he asked the travelers not to throw cigarette butts out the window. There was also a subtle hint of drug-induced paranoia when Jimi shouted "Don't open the door!" Doggett described the song as ". . . joyous cacophony of psychedelia and studio madness."[61]

In mid-1967, the Experience was immersed in the psychedelic drug culture with this song serving as a prime example. Additionally, Jimi was a notorious fan of the Beatles, and their album *Sgt. Pepper's Lonely Hearts Club Band* was issued in June 1967. On it was the song "Lucy in the Sky with Diamonds." Written by John Lennon and Paul McCartney, the song made direct reference to LSD in its title and through the psychedelic images its lyrics evoke. Although Lennon denied to his death that the song was about hallucinations caused by LSD—he claimed it was about a picture that his son Julian drew—McCartney later went on record saying that the drug references were pretty obvious.

Taking Control
(Fall 1967–1969)

AXIS: BOLD AS LOVE

Riding the wave of success from the early singles and successful United Kingdom and United States tours, the Jimi Hendrix Experience returned to London in the fall of 1967 for the purpose of going into the studio to cut their sophomore album. Enshrined in London's Olympic Studios, the trio set about the work of recording new songs. In the studio for this record were Jimi, Noel, and Mitch, along with Chandler handling production and "song shortening" duties. Eddie Kramer was the engineer of record for all the sessions and George Chkiantz was tape operator. The product of the work done by all over the next several months was *Axis: Bold as Love*, the second official Jimi Hendrix Experience album, which was released in the United Kingdom on Track in December 1967 and on Reprise in the United States in January 1968. The record went to number five in the United Kingdom where it sat on the charts for sixteen weeks and to number three in the United States where it charted for fifty-three weeks.[1] The album was released in a gatefold sleeve that allowed the full album art to be viewed when the jacket was unfolded. The image was of the Hindu devotional painting called "Viraat Purushan-Vishnuroopam," which illustrated the various forms of Vishnu with Jimi, Noel, and Mitch's faces superimposed. The inside of the gatefold sleeve was a large black and white image of the group painted by Roger Law. The United States issue on the Reprise label included lyrics for each song inside surrounding the painting.

In fact, the initial tracking for several of the songs on the new album began as early as May 5, 1967, at Olympic. Early tracking for "EXP" and "If 6 Was 9" began at this time. All the while, the band continued to perform live at venues such as the Imperial Ballroom in Lancashire and the Saville Theater. There followed the long string of dates in Germany, Sweden, Denmark, and Finland as noted above. On October 1, 1967, Jimi and the Experience were back in London recording more tracks for their second album. They laid down "Little Miss Lover," "Got Me Floatin'," and "One Rainy Wish" followed by more work on "Little Miss Lover" and "There Ain't Nothing Wrong," on October 5. The recording sessions for the new album were interrupted by more live shows around London and in Paris. On October 25, the group recorded "Little Wing," "Electric Ladyland," and "South Saturn Delta." The following day they recorded "Wait Until Tomorrow" and "Ain't No Telling," with "Spanish Castle Magic" tracked on October 27. "Castles Made of Sand" and "Bold as Love" were recorded next with "Up From the Skies" and some reworking of earlier tracks on the 29th. The month ended with the recording of "She's So Fine" and the mixing of the album.[2] Not surprisingly, many of the songs on the album focus on Jimi's longing for female company in one form or another. Those not focused on love or affection were statements about Jimi's personal impressions of relationships and the counterculture of the late 1960s.

The album kicked off with another testament to Jimi's interest in science fiction and space. "EXP" (working title "Symphony of Experience") was not a traditional song by any stretch; it was an interview between "Mr. Paul Caruso" (Jimi) and a Radio Station EXP Announcer (Mitch).[3] The topic of the interview was the question of whether or not spaceships exist. Mitch's and Jimi's voices were rendered unrecognizable through the use of tape speed manipulation and newly available effects pedal technology. The interview concluded with Jimi (the spaceman) departing in his spaceship. The instrumental sounds heard after the "interview" ended were created by the destruction of several electric guitars while plugged in and turned up to ten. There were no conventional bass or drum parts.

"Up From the Skies" was a psychedelic talking blues in which Jimi discussed his impressions of the world. Through the course of four verses, Jimi discussed family, his impressions of the "love the world" 1960s, and the universe. The chorus statement was just a single line beginning with the question, "is this true?" The three instruments laid down a steady and propulsive groove featuring Jimi's guitar run through the wah-wah effect. Mitch's drumming was given an air of subtlety with the use of brushes instead of sticks. The overall effect was enchanting with all of the words clearly audible and a delicate closing fade. With "Up From the Skies," Jimi introduced the first of many abrupt shifts of mood that mark the album as a whole—from the spaced out interview of "EXP" to the gentle restraint of this song. Musically quite different, the lyrics of "EXP" maintain Jimi's fascination with science-fiction-oriented themes. Here he ". . . takes the guise of a curious, well-mannered alien descending to Earth to find out more about its peculiar residents . . . [claiming] to have lived here before the Ice Age indicates that he's revisiting the planet he once called home, though—typically for Jimi— what he finds doesn't quite live up to what he might have hoped for."[4]

The third track on the album was "Spanish Castle Magic." Here Jimi played guitar and sang along while adding a piano line. Noel's bass part was played on a Hagstrom 8-string bass, which in turn led to the popularity of this particular instrument (in fact it is still a featured instrument in the Hagstrom line of basses). The Spanish Castle about which this tune was written was a reference point from Jimi's earlier life. The Spanish Castle Club was located about twenty miles south of Seattle. The unique feature of the club was that the exterior was built to resemble an authentic Spanish castle.[5] The club must have occupied some type of special place in Jimi's heart since he wrote a song about it many years after leaving the Seattle area. The song was built of two verse/chorus alternations with the chorus repeated twice at the end before fading out with a guitar solo. This type of arrangement was quite popular at the time and resulted in a song form that was chorus heavy and endweighted. The song opened with Jimi in a cosmic mood saying that he could get to the club by flying on a dragonfly. He went on to describe that the club was not in Spain, but that it was a groovy place with its own "magic." The song was not solely about the club itself, ". . . its images of clouds of cotton candy and travelling by dragonfly, it might well have owed at least as much to his science-fiction reading and drug ingestion . . . it's a reflection not just of his roots, but also of how very far he had travelled from them by late 1967."[6]

"Wait Until Tomorrow" began with a subdued sounding Experience with Mitch using the side-sticking technique for the opening—that is, having the left stick turned on its side and using it to hit the rim instead of the head of the drum. The song itself was in the traditional verse/chorus form with the chorus containing high harmony singing performed by Mitch and Noel. The topic of the lyrics of this song was about Jimi paying a visit to Dolly Mae with the purpose of the pair running away. Interestingly, Jimi got in a bit of a jam as his love interest had invited him over to take her away and when he arrived she tried to make him "wait until tomorrow" before she would go. Jimi used the second verse to try to convince Dolly Mae to come down the ladder to him; unfortunately, in the third verse Dolly's dad spotted Jimi and shot him, after which Jimi expired. The chorus words were the same for the first two repetitions, during which Dolly was putting Jimi off. For the third and final chorus, Jimi changed the words to illustrate that he had been shot, saying that it was good night forever but at least he did not have to wait for her anymore. The persona that Jimi took on in the song resulted in a ". . . cool, laidback but still concerned piece of romantic role-playing, wrapped around a sinuous guitar-line, and supported by some white-boy soul vocals."[7]

In fact, the high harmonies that Mitch and Noel added significantly enhanced the fairytale gist of the song.

Track five was "Ain't No Telling," another song on which Jimi employed the Octavia foot pedal. With this, the guitar sound was bigger and rounder than usual as it occupied many layers of the musical texture. The opening guitar lick was actually quite reminiscent of the opening of "Little Wing," but only for a fleeting second. There were also moments in the middle of the song where the guitar line smacked of "Stone Free." The structure of "Ain't No Telling" was a hybrid with an opening and closing chorus statement with a longer verse statement in the middle. Here Jimi was talking about leaving a woman in the morning with the hope of seeing her again soon, but there were no guarantees of this. In the verse, Jimi called the love interest Cleopatra with all of the associated head games that the Egyptian leader was famous for. Jimi led out of the extended verse with a short guitar solo before moving into the final chorus. The song was another fine example of Jimi making use of the call and response technique creating a conversation with the musical texture. There was another brief guitar solo at the end of the song which was used as a coda, instead of simply fading out.

"Little Wing" had a very unique sound that set it apart from all of the other songs on *Axis: Bold as Love*. The trio of the standard Experience instruments was enhanced by the addition of Jimi on glockenspiel, which gave the song a wonderful bell-like quality. Additionally, Jimi's guitar part was played through a Leslie speaker[8] and some of his vocals were enhanced by being passed through a Pultec filter.[9] Jimi said the song, " 'Little Wing' is, like, one of these beautiful girls that come around sometimes . . . a very sweet girl that came around and gave me her whole life and more if I wanted it. It is based on a very, very simple Indian style. I got the idea, like, when we were in Monterey."[10] Musically, the Experience was in very tight form for this song. The various lines created a perfect complement to Jimi's voice and guitar playing. Although Jimi wrote many songs about love and relationships, this was one of the few that could be classified as a ballad. Lyrically, Jimi wrote two free-form verses with no traditional chorus statements. Images of animals, moonbeams, and fairytales were tossed about in the first verse. The second verse referenced how this person was able to brighten Jimi's mood in times of sadness. Jimi created a "painting [of] one of his most romantic (and some would say idealized) portraits of a woman . . . who might be true, or at least one so unselfish as to be unlikely to be found in Jimi's real life."[11] The song climaxed at the end of the second verse with the title words being sung. There followed an extended guitar solo that faded out to create an end.

The A-side of the album closed with "If 6 Was 9," a bold and direct assertion of Jimi's individuality. Here again, Jimi cast the song in a series of three verse statements with a chorus after the first two. There followed an instrumental break that led into the third verse which was periodically interrupted by guitar flourishes.[12] The music of the song gradually took over the lyrics as it progressed into a jam-sounding ending. Lyrically, Jimi did include a spoken word fourth verse that again affirmed his individuality. Overall, the sentiment of the words of this song was Jimi proclaiming his countercultural status. He laid claim to his position as an outsider and through the course of the song made it clear that that was how he felt the most comfortable. The button-down business world could say what they wanted; he was "gonna wave his freak flag high."[13] The difficult to discern spoken-word fourth verse was his most direct statement of freedom. He stated that since he was the one who had to be accountable for his actions and appearance when the final day of reckoning came, then he should be able to live his life the way he wanted to.

Adding to the mystique of this track was an interpretation of the title itself, "at a time when even the merest allusion to a certain sexual position was taboo, the title of 'If 6 Was 9' couldn't help but bring a knowing wink to the eyes of those looking to find hidden (or not so hidden) meaning in the works of their psychedelic heroes."[14] An interesting aside to this song was that it became a late 1960s countercultural mainstay with its use on the soundtrack to the 1969 film *Easy Rider*.[15] Musically, the song contained several atypical additions for the Experience. Jimi added a wooden flute part at the end of the track and Gary Leeds, Graham Nash, and Michael Jeffery all added the sound of foot stomping.[16]

"You Got Me Floatin'" was the first song on the B-side of the album. Here Noel was again playing his part on the Hagstrom 8-string bass and there were added vocal harmony parts by Trevor Bolder and Ace Kefford and Roy Wood.[17] Additionally, Jimi overdubbed a backward guitar track which was layered on top of the standard band sound. Musically, the song was a rollicking ride through a series of verse and chorus exchanges about how a woman had enchanted Jimi. "You Got Me Floatin'" was "formulaic R&B, in the tradition of 'Ain't No Telling,' with only the cross-speaker fades to pull it into the psychedelic age."[18] The song began with the chorus which set the mood and the tempo, along with identifying how strongly Jimi felt about this particular love interest. There followed two verse and chorus alternations that emphasized this sentiment. The middle of the song contained an extended instrumental break featuring Jimi's guitar playing with Mitch and Noel holding down a steady groove. In the second half of the song, Jimi described how the woman's parents were aware of his amorous desires, but they were cool because they knew he was in love. The song ended with a jam on the final chorus statement filled with wailing guitar and vocal harmonies that eventually fade out.

The second song on the B-side of the album was "Castles Made of Sand." Musically, the song was in the mold of Jimi's talking blues style pieces. The trio played a straightforward groove with little embellishment beyond an overdubbed backward guitar line played by Jimi. The opening, and closing, guitar lick sounded vaguely Indian. Structurally, the song contained three wordy verses with three short chorus statements built of a lyrical couplet.

The meaning behind the first verse was likening a failed relationship to the fleeting nature of a sand castle built on the shore only to be reclaimed by the ocean waves. It was likely that the topic of the lyrics was referencing the rocky relationship of Jimi's own parents. In the first verse they were cast as a fighting young couple. The second verse extended that metaphor to include references to an Indian warrior who preparing for battle was instead killed in his sleep, potentially describing the lost ambition of Jimi's father. The third verse described a young woman who was handicapped by circumstances that led to her taking her own life. If verse two described Jimi's father, then verse three must be about the lifelong struggles and untimely death of Jimi's mother. Similar to "51st Anniversary," here Jimi ". . . never sounded more vulnerable, or more involved in the spirit of the song."[19]

"She's So Fine" was an anomaly on an Experience album so far as it was not written by Jimi but rather by Noel. Jimi likely allowed it because he knew that Noel wanted more control over the band's direction and the greater the input from the other members of the Experience the more ownership they took over the band's ultimate success. Not surprisingly, the song had a greater bass guitar presence than most others on the album. Structurally, the song was a verse and chorus alternation with three verses likening a woman's features to various birds and images from nature. The song contained a great deal of high harmony vocal parts throughout the verse statements and the entirety of the choruses. Two-thirds of the way through, the song broke down into a guitar solo where Jimi briefly took the forefront. Noel said of the song, ". . . [it] was about hippies. I had seen some bloke walking about with an alarm clock around his neck, attached by a bit of string."[20] This image found its way into the opening line of the first verse.

The album then concluded with three songs all penned by Jimi. "One Rainy Wish" again cast the Experience in their traditional roles. Here Jimi's guitar was enhanced through the use of the Octavia pedal and some of his vocals were modified through the use of automatic double tracking (ADT).[21] The guitar part that Jimi used through much of the song was a descending cascade of notes that created a musical image of the rain described in the song's title. The lyrical content likened one of Jimi's love interests to a flower preserved in time. He created an ideal landscape into which he and this woman were immersed, with stars, mountains, and eleven moons. Overall, the sentiment of the song came across as the perfect euphoria of love—or imagined love, as he described the whole scenario in the final verse as a dream. The Experience's instrumental lines float along and spin around until the song fades to end.

"Little Miss Lover" again had Jimi using the Octavia effect on his guitar as well as the Pultec filter on his voice—for the purpose of giving both parts greater presence in the mix. Noel flexed his bass chops on the Hagstrom 8-string and both he and Mitch provided background vocals. There was also an added tambourine line played intermittently throughout the song. Structurally,

Jimi returned to his verse heavy/no chorus setup. This narrative approach to lyric writing was not the norm in popular music. The standard verse and chorus alternations were a time-honored song form and the bread and butter of much of rock and roll. However, Jimi used the narrative plan to outstanding results. The issue with avoiding a standard chorus was that the chorus typically contained the hook, or most memorable lyric and melody of the song. Regardless of writing songs without standard chorus statements, Jimi was still able to craft extremely catchy and memorable songs. Of the track, Doggett said "from dream to sexual desire, as Jimi revived the lusty spirit of Don Covay or Wilson Pickett's R&B with a guitar riff that would have delighted James Brown."[22] The three verses in "Little Miss Lover" were a direct and open invitation for a woman to hook up with Jimi. From the words of the song's title to the content of the first two verses, Jimi was on the prowl. After the second verse, the song moved into a guitar solo with a few sparse lyrics. The final verse continued Jimi's plea which ended in a gradual fade-out. Musically, the majority of the song had a funky-sounding groove that carried the sexual tension and edge.[23]

The final song on *Axis: Bold as Love* was the title track "Bold as Love." Much has been made of the use of the word "Axis" in the album title and in the central lyric of the song. Some speculate that it referred to the Axis versus the Allied powers in World War II; others speculate that it referenced the axis on which the earth spins. Regardless, other lyrics in the song were more straightforward and easier to decode. The song was constructed with two verse statements and two chorus statements. The first verse described a series of emotions by giving them each a persona. Jimi used the second verse to compare his emotions to colors and associated each of them with certain deeds or achievements. "After two verses, he decided he could speak more eloquently with his guitar, setting out on a liberating one-minute solo that faded away then (in what Jimi called elsewhere a 'slight return') regrouped with renewed energy to restate the melodic theme of the song."[24] Both choruses were the same and served as the focal points of the texted portion of the song.

Musically, the song contained several additions to the typical Experience power trio. Jimi added a harpsichord line to broaden the sound of the usual three pieces. Mitch's drums are phased, meaning that the recorded drum sound was split into two signals and altered to allow for the effect that the sound was sweeping back and forth from one speaker to the other. The session engineers Eddie Kramer and George Chkiantz created this effect for the song. About phasing, Jimi reportedly said "that's the sound I've been hearing in my dreams!"[25] A unique feature of the song was that after the section containing lyrics was complete, the group ripped into an equally long instrumental section with soaring guitar lines and pounding rhythm section accompaniment. The song actually seemed to come to a close before reaching new heights in this second section. The song faded out at over four minutes, drawing the second Jimi Hendrix album to a close. In April 1968, Jim Miller reviewed this album for *Rolling Stone* magazine and amid an uneven and at times unflattering review called Jimi "the Charlie Mingus of Rock." Miller said that "*Axis* demonstrates conclusively that he is one of rock's greatest guitar players in his mastery and exploration of every conceivable gimmick."[26]

After *Axis: Bold as Love* sessions were complete, the Experience resumed their aggressive live show schedule in earnest. In early November, the Experience played at Manchester University and then hopped a plane to Rotterdam to film the TV show *Hoepla* in the afternoon followed by an evening show as part of the *Hippy Happy Event*. Jimi opened the recording of the television show by saying "I don't know what you're used to over here, but take care of your ears."[27] The group then returned to London for a show at Sussex University in Brighton with the band Ten Years After.[28]

Next the Experience kicked off a fifteen-day tour of the United Kingdom with Pink Floyd, the Move, Amen Corner,[29] the Nice,[30] the Outer Limit, and Eire Apparent.[31] With the package tour in place, the six bands played a series of venues including Royal Albert Hall, Winter Gardens, City Hall in Sheffield, the Empire Theater in Liverpool, the Coventry Theater, Guild Hall in Portsmouth, Sophia Gardens Pavilion in Cardiff, Colston Hall in Bristol, the Blackpool Opera House, Manchester's Palace Theater, the *Festival of the Arts* in Belfast, Kent's Town Hall, the Dome in Brighton, the Theater Royal in Nottingham, Newcastle-upon-Tyne's City Hall, and Green's Playhouse in Glasgow. The tour was a grind with only five days off in a month. The Experience spent the rest of December in London with Jimi playing jam sessions at the Speakeasy Club. On December 22, the group played a holiday concert called *Christmas on Earth* in London with Eric Burdon and the Animals, the Who, Pink Floyd, the Move, Soft Machine,[32] and Tomorrow. At the dawning of 1968, Jimi was still in London playing in jam sessions at the Speakeasy and Klook's Kleek.

On January 5, the Experience embarked on an outing to Sweden and Denmark warming up for their next American tour. Next, the group began a series of West Coast shows with a concert at the Fillmore West on February 1 with Albert King,[33] John Mayall's Bluesbreakers,[34] and Soft Machine. Mick Taylor, who was playing with the Bluesbreakers, said "after the show . . . we went and played somewhere until five in the morning. It was like The Grateful Dead meets the blues."[35] They next played a three-night stand at Winterland in San Francisco followed by shows in Arizona before moving up the West Coast through California into Washington. On February 12, 1968, Jimi was back in his hometown of Seattle, Washington, to play at the Seattle Center Arena. The February shows then carried the Experience to Colorado, Texas, New York, Pennsylvania, Michigan, Toronto, and Wisconsin before returning to New York. On March 2, the Experience played Hunter College in New York with the Troggs, whose song "Wild Thing" Jimi had been covering (quite famously at Monterey) for quite some time.[36]

March began with Mitch and Noel taking a short break in the Bahamas while Jimi stayed in New York jamming nightly at the Scene Club with artists such as Eric Clapton, the Hollies, and the Doors. On March 5, recording sessions began for "1983 . . . (A Merman I Should Turn to Be)," "Moon, Turn the Tides," and "Somewhere"—these songs would begin to form the backbone of the third Experience album *Electric Ladyland*. With Mitch and Noel's return, the Experience again began gigging on the East Coast. The band played a pair of university shows in New York followed by a concert at the International Ballroom in the Washington Hilton, Washington, DC. Recording sessions continued with "My Friend" and "Little Miss Strange" at Sound Center in New York on March 13. The second half of March was filled with concerts, jam sessions, and recording sessions in New York, Massachusetts, Maine, Ontario, Connecticut, Michigan, Indiana, and Ohio.

By mid-March, Jimi realized that his management (specifically Michael Jeffery) was not making a fair accounting of the money being earned by the Experience. Jimi was the one who continually tried to get Jeffery to be open about how much the band was making for each live show and through merchandising. He took to calling Bob Levine, a member of his management staff, for updates on how profits were building. Levine noted, "Hendrix continually called . . . and ask[ed] about the poster money and what his share was."[37] Jimi often struggled to get Jeffery to be accountable for Experience earnings and instead took to talking him out of material goods such as cars, instruments, and audio gear. The majority of Jimi's money was housed in bank accounts controlled by Yameta management, a company that Jeffery had set up.

The first half of April continued the Experience's strenuous gigging and recording schedule. They played in Pennsylvania, Montreal, Virginia, and New Jersey. On April 5, the Experience played Symphony Hall in Newark, New Jersey. The evening proved to be highly emotionally charged as Jimi had just learned of the assassination of American civil rights leader Martin Luther King, Jr. King had been shot down by James Earl Ray in Memphis, Tennessee, on April 4, 1968, and Jimi used a portion of the Symphony Hall show to present a wordless, musical eulogy. He walked onstage and simply said, "This number is for a friend of mine" and tore into an improvisation "which was hauntingly beautiful . . . everyone knew what this was about—a lament for Martin Luther King," remembered Mark Boyle, Soft Machine's lighting engineer.[38]

On April 7, the Experience performed at the Generation Club in New York. It was a monumental night as Jeffery had just opened the club and the list of luminaries for the evening included B. B. King, Janis Joplin, Joni Mitchell, the Paul Butterfield Band, Richie Havens, and Buddy Guy.[39] Jimi also jammed at the Generation Club on the 9th and the 15th with a revolving cast of American blues greats.

SMASH HITS

On April 12, the album *Smash Hits* was released in the United Kingdom. The record was issued by Track Records as a means to fill the gap in between new Experience albums, as *Axis: Bold as Love* had been released in December 1967. *Smash Hits* contained little new material and was not sanctioned by the group. The *Smash Hits* release was technically the Jimi Hendrix Experience's third album, but because it was a greatest hits–type of release it was not a true third release. Track was looking to cash in on the international success of the band, but the Experience was still working on the songs that would become their third album of new material, *Electric Ladyland*. The album jacket artwork was credited to Ed Thrasher and consisted of three multicolored images of Jimi on the front and a series of four pictures of the band on the back. The pictures on the back of the album cast the Experience as Wild West gunslingers with pistols, cowboy hats, and horses. *Smash Hits* went to number four on the United Kingdom charts within two months of being released.

The songs on *Smash Hits* had almost all been previously released either as singles, on one of the two previously released albums, or both. The reissued songs were "Purple Haze," "Fire," "The Wind Cries Mary," "Can You See Me?" "Hey Joe," "Stone Free," "Manic Depression," "Foxey Lady," "Red House," and "Remember." Newer material that made the album were the songs "Crosstown Traffic" and "All Along the Watchtower"—both of which would also be on the next album, *Electric Ladyland*.

"Crosstown Traffic" was another classic example of Jimi using everyday events as metaphors for his struggles with love, relationships, and freedom. Here Jimi used the notoriously slow crosstown traffic between Manhattan's east and west sides. As Jimi considered New York his home away from home in the United States he was certainly well aware of the constant slowdowns caused by vehicles trying to navigate the congestion to get past Central Park. The lyrics ". . . aren't among Hendrix's most profound and once again express the 'don't cramp my style' attitude which might be among Jimi's less endearing attributes (at least insofar as it informed his relationships with women)."[40] In the lyrics of the song, Jimi alternated two verse statements with two chorus statements, with the song ending on a short jam of small snippets of the chorus words and music before fading out. The first verse described Jimi's desires as a speeding car that the love interest in the song was trying to get in the way of. The second verse added weight to this notion with him comparing both of their love lives as occasions of "hit and run." By the end of the second verse Jimi made clear that this woman was standing in his way and preventing him from living/driving the way he was accustomed to. The two chorus statements directly compare the woman to crosstown traffic slowing Jimi down. Each ended with Jimi saying that he was just trying to get to something better on the other side of town.

Musically, "Crosstown Traffic" fit into the mold of Jimi's talking blues-style songs. He even added a recurring kazoo part along with a piano line. Mitch and Noel maintained a steady mid-tempo groove that allowed Jimi to half speak and half sing the lyrics. Another musical addition was the high harmony vocal harmony lines in the chorus. Mitch, Noel, and Dave Mason (ironically enough of the band Traffic) were credited with singing these lines in tight harmony.[41] In addition to added instruments and vocal lines, Jimi's voice was enhanced by being run through a Pultec filter.

The other new song on *Smash Hits* was Jimi's cover of Bob Dylan's song "All Along the Watchtower." Reports on how Jimi came to hear the song for the first time differ but what is known is that as soon as he heard it he set about making his own version. Bob Dylan wrote "All Along the Watchtower" during the summer of 1966 while he was convalescing at home after a motorcycle accident. The song appeared on Dylan's album *John Wesley Harding*, which was released in late 1967—making Jimi's early tracking of his version in January 1968 even more remarkable. Dylan's original version of the song was dark and sparse in texture and conveyed his newly discovered interest in the Bible. The central lyrics of the song contained lyrics that directly reference the book of Isaiah, chapter 21, verses 5–9. Key words that Dylan kept from the Bible passage were watchtower, princes, and horsemen (riders). Although Jimi changed the musical context of the song dramatically, he maintained Dylan's lyrics. Jimi's version "connects the song's almost biblical sense of impending catastrophe to the contemporary social turmoil of 1968 . . . combined with Jimi's dependably heartfelt vocal, the song is transformed from a sentinel's warning into the desperate howl of a drowning man . . ."[42]

On January 21, 1968, Jimi and the Experience had begun recording their version of the song at Olympic Studios in London with Eddie Kramer at the controls. The traditional Experience setup was altered when Noel lost patience with Jimi's multiple retakes of the guitar part and left the session. Mitch stayed on to hold down the drum line and added tambourine and temple block parts. Dave Mason again joined the session, this time to add acoustic guitar and electric guitar parts. Both Jimi and Mason recorded bass lines for the song with the one that Jimi played making the final cut. Musically, the Experience version of the song contained multiple layers of instrumental overdubs. Jimi added a slide guitar part that was reportedly produced by using his cigarette lighter as a slide and holding his guitar in his lap.[43] The musical effect of the added parts and multitracking was that Dylan's sparse texture was replaced with a dense musical landscape over which Jimi's voice and guitar soared. In an interesting twist, after Jimi died, Dylan went on record saying that he actually favored the Hendrix version and that Jimi's take on the song changed the way he [Dylan] has played the song since.

As Jimi and the Experience continued to grow in fame, popularity, and fortune, Ed Chalpin and PPX again entered the picture. Legal posturing over who actually had the rights to Jimi's work had been going on for two years at this point and Chandler and Jeffery tried to put it to an end by offering Chalpin a $70,000 buyout deal. Chaplin said, "they offered me $70,000 to buy me out. I wouldn't take it. My lawyer insisted that I take it, but I said no."[44] Because they were unable to settle with PPX, the legal wrangling over Jimi's management and contracts continued.

The Experience spent most of the second half of April in the studio. They recorded "Long Hot Summer Night," "Little Miss Strange," "South Saturn Delta," "1983 . . . (A Merman I Should Turn to Be)," "Moon, Turn the Tides . . . gently gently away," and "Gypsy Eyes" at the Record Plant through the middle of the month. Throughout these sessions, Jimi worked at a maddening speed, outpacing the staff at the Record Plant. He was now exerting significant control over his own sound, song choice, structure, and lyric content. This ever-growing individuality and creative control often put him at odds with Chandler, whose job (as producer) had been to control these dynamics. By the end of May 1968, Chandler relinquished his creative control on Jimi and stopped working as his producer. He continued on as a comanager, but stopped being with Jimi on a day-to-day basis. While this left the door open for Jimi to fully spread his creative wings musically, it also allowed studio time, hangers-on, and drug use to steadily increase with little control. Also by the end of the month, the Experience had recorded "House Burning Down," "Tax Free," "Cherokee Mist," "Voodoo Chile," "Straight Ahead," and "Three Little Bears." Steve Winwood from the band Traffic and Jack Cassidy of Jefferson Airplane made guest appearances in the studio for "Cherokee Mist" and "Voodoo Chile."

As the May recording sessions progressed, the band continued to play live shows. Through the middle and end of the month the Experience played several live shows beginning with a gig at the Fillmore East, with Sly and the Family Stone on the 10th. They then traveled to Miami for *The Underground Pop Festival*, with Eire Apparent, Arthur Brown, Blue Cheer,[45] Frank Zappa, and John Lee Hooker.[46] The band then made a quick sweep through parts of Europe with dates in Milan, Rome, Bologna, and Zurich. The Zurich shows were part of a festival called *The Beat Monster Concert* and included Traffic, the Small Faces,[47] John Mayall's Bluesbreakers, and the Move.

As the summer of 1968 dawned, the Jimi Hendrix Experience continued to struggle with legal difficulties caused by Jimi's early contract with Chalpin and PPX. This was compounded by the ever-growing number of managers and lawyers who entered the fray. In early June, the group was warming up to mount an extended United States tour that kept them on the road in America until the end of the year. On June 8, the Experience played a show at the Fillmore East in New York with the group Electric Flag.[48] At this show, Jimi jammed with drummer Buddy Miles and, as a bit of foreshadowing, it was noted by the writer Richard Kostelanetz that " . . . in cahoots [they] could well emerge as one of the sparking talents of the new bluesy rock."[49] In fact, Jimi asked Miles into the studio for a jam session at the Record Plant on June 11.

As Jimi continued jamming with a host of people at various locations around New York in preparation for the United States tour, a deal was finally struck with PPX which ended the years-long drama between Chalpin, Chandler, and Jeffery. As a result, Jimi was freed to sign with Warner Brothers and a new era began with Chalpin finally out of the contract picture. To replace

Yameta, a new company was created called Are You Experienced? This gave Jimi greater control over his money, but Jeffery was still taking 40 percent. By the end of the summer, the Experience had signed legal documents moving their assets from Yameta to the new company.

Just prior to the official launch of the United States tour, the Experience were called to Europe for a pair of important dates. On July 6 they played the second Woburn Music Festival with T-Rex,[50] Geno Washington,[51] and the Family.[52] The concert was a sellout and an enormous success with approximately 14,000 audience members. The second special European show was on July 18 at a new club called the Sgt. Pepper's Club in Palma, Majorca, Spain. The Experience was the first band to play the new venue as it was opened by Chandler and Jeffery. The band was back in New York by the end of the month as the shows for their American tour were all booked. The support acts for the first half of the tour were Soft Machine and Eire Apparent.

The tour began in earnest on July 30 with a show at Independence Hall in Baton Rouge, Louisiana. After several other Louisiana dates, the tour moved on to Texas for four shows. The Experience then played Illinois, Iowa, and Maryland. Prior to the August 17 show at Municipal Auditorium in Georgia, the band Vanilla Fudge was added to the package. According to several reports from the time, Vanilla Fudge was not a welcomed addition to the tour.[53] Instead, they were brought on by the demands of the Mafia. The Fudge was connected to the mob and through this essentially forced their way on to the tour for the southern and West Coast legs.[54] Although Vanilla Fudge was on the tour through August and early September, they had little to do with the other bands and were kept separate by their handlers.

With the package now including four bands (the Jimi Hendrix Experience, Soft Machine, Eire Apparent, and Vanilla Fudge), the tour continued. The bands next moved to Florida, Virginia, New York, Connecticut, and Massachusetts. These dates included several stadium shows and the *New York Rock Festival* on August 23 with the Chamber Brothers, Janis Joplin with Big Brother and the Holding Company, and the other packaged bands. By the end of the month, the tour moved west through Utah and Colorado. In early September the bands played six venues in California, and shows in Arizona and British Columbia. On September 6, Jimi was able to again return home with a tour stop in Seattle for a concert at the Seattle Center Coliseum. In the midst of all this, "All Along the Watchtower" with B-side "Burning of the Midnight Lamp" was released on September 2 as a United States single. The package aspect of the tour broke down September 15 as Soft Machine disbanded. Vanilla Fudge also left the tour never to open for the Experience again.

By early October 1968, Jimi and the Experience were showing signs of wear in the wake of an aggressive touring and recording schedule. It was now obvious that Noel was chaffing under the control that Jimi exerted over the band's sound. In fact, at the end of the summer, Noel had begun to form his own band with a group of players that he knew from his pre-Experience days. Noel's new band would go on to play under the name Fat Mattress.[55] With Noel's time now progressively being split between the two groups, the end of the Experience began to seem imminent. This situation was exacerbated by Jimi continually jamming with non-Experience artists—even bringing them into the studio to record with the group. The Experience unwound slowly over the next six months. During that period, Fat Mattress even served as an opening act for the Experience. Jimi was aware of the distance desired by Noel and commented on it saying that " . . . he had already agreed with Noel and Mitch that they needed a rest from each other."[56] Although it seemed like the beginning of the end, the anticipated separation was considered by the group to be a positive move geared toward reinvigorating the band and allowing them to come back together later at even greater potency.

The creation of Fat Mattress began as an attempt to improve the relationship between Jimi and Noel. This was attested to by Jimi's involvement in the Fat Mattress recording sessions. Jimi even played percussion on the Fat Mattress song "How Can I Live?" Chandler took Fat Mattress on and got them a record deal through Polydor as another sign that this musical diversification was originally intended to benefit the Experience and its members and not to lead to the group's ultimate demise. Even as the bedrock foundation of the Experience was being tested, Eddie Kramer wrapped up the session tapes for the *Electric Ladyland* album and sent them off to mastering. The new album was issued on September 17 in the United States and on October 25 in the United Kingdom—with a different cover design. Of the record Jimi said "every little thing on there means something . . . it wasn't just slopped together."[57]

The Experience continued to tour through October 1968. On the 5th, they played a concert in Hawaii at the Honolulu International Center. They then returned to the mainland for three dates at Winterland, in San Francisco, with Dino Valenti[58] and the Buddy Miles Express.[59] The Winterland shows were scheduled for two appearances per night and Jefferson Airplane's Jack Cassidy stood in for Noel. The Winterland concerts included other guests as well, such as Virgil Gonzales on flute and Herbie Rich on organ (from the Buddy Miles Express). These shows exhibited the Experience at full strength—even without all of the members of the group present (a selection of fifteen songs from the concerts was issued as *Live at Winterland*). The sets included the group's standards, plus less often performed or newer tunes like "Tax Free," "Lover Man," and "Sunshine of Your Love" (Cream cover). Jimi decided to cover "Sunshine of Your Love" as a tribute to Cream, having just been made aware that the band was splitting up—their final show was October 19. Though little was made of it at the time, it was ironic that both bands were composed of three members and both were essentially disintegrating simultaneously. The rest of October was filled with continued record sessions. During the end of the month, the band laid down tracks for "Messenger," "Calling All the Devil's Children," "Hear My Freedom," "Look Over Yonder," "The New Rising Sun," "Peace in Mississippi," "Everything's Gonna Be Alright," and "Lover Man."

In November, the Experience kicked back into the concert mode and played shows in Kansas City, St. Louis, New York, Cincinnati, Boston, New Haven, Jacksonville, Tampa, Miami Beach, Providence, Detroit, and Chicago. They ended the year back in New York with a jam session at the Fillmore East with the James Cotton Blues Band.[60] For most of the dates in November and December, the group was supported by Cat Mother & the All-Night News Boys.[61]

ELECTRIC LADYLAND

The *Electric Ladyland* album was released separately in the United Kingdom and the United States, as were the band's first two records. The United States version was released on Reprise with a gatefold album sleeve. Unlike with *Axis: Bold as Love*, the new record needed the gatefold sleeve as it was a double album. The United States cover was a head shot of Jimi in midperformance with red and orange coloring on a black background. The inside of the gatefold listed the name of the band, the name of the album, the track list for each record, the musicians who appeared and their instrument specialization, and the production credits—Jimi was listed as producer and director. Also included were the credits for the songs on the release not written by Jimi and a lengthy letter penned by Jimi on September 2, 1968, called "Letter to the Room Full of Mirrors." Jimi also included a dedication on the inside of the album that read, "We dedicate this album to acoustic and electric women and men alike, and to the girl at or from or with the button store, and Arizona, and Bil of some English town in England, and well, EVERYBODY." Around all of this, creating a black and white border, was a selection of photos by Linda Eastman.[62] The photos included images from the stage, in the studio, and several candid shots showing the members of the Experience with the women in their lives. The back cover was a photo of the Experience arranged in a triangle posing for the camera. It also included the album title and track list.

The United Kingdom version of *Electric Ladyland* was similarly released in a gatefold cover. However, on the Track Records version, the outside of the album was a photo of twenty-one nude models provocatively looking into the camera. Several of the models held copies of previously released Experience albums. The overall appearance was striking, but according to contemporary reports, Jimi had not given permission for this album artwork and he also did not like it. A possible reason for all of this was that Jimi had taken to calling the group's hanger-ons (groupies) "electric ladies" and the United Kingdom album art put a fine point on this. Rather unfortunately, the full-color nude images on the United Kingdom release at first achieved greater media attention than the music on the records. Several stores banned the album as pornographic and others sold it with the gatefold turned inside out to hide the offending image.

Even with the controversy over album art, the United Kingdom version of the album topped out at number five during a twelve-week run on the charts. In the United States, *Electric Ladyland* made it to number one and spent thirty-seven weeks on the charts. The material on the two albums clocked in at an astonishing seventy minutes. Even more incredible was that it reached that overall length with only sixteen different songs. Both versions listed the session engineers as Gary Kellgren and Eddie Kramer. Jimi knew that with Kramer in the control room he would be able to achieve any number of subtle nuances of sound that had become an Experience trademark. Even with Kramer's assistance, the final product was not completely satisfying to the band. In the mastering process, changes had been made to the phasing that altered the resulting sound. Jimi and Kramer were wary of this and had included a note on the tape box saying "Special phase effects on this tape. Do not change phase!"[63] Sadly, the effect was changed so the released product did not reflect Jimi's truest vision for the album's sound.

The first song on the double-record set was titled ". . . And the Gods Made Love." Jimi said of the song that he wanted to create a ". . . sound painting of the Heavens."[64] He went on to say that "it's typifying what happens when the gods make love . . . or whatever they spend their time on."[65] Here there were no standard song sections, but instead a pastiche of sounds meant to evoke an otherworldliness not imagined by most. The song was built of a layering of a variety of atypical sounds. It opens with Jimi playing the tympani, the sound of which was subjected to alteration by tape speed manipulation. An additional part came from Jimi on bass. The song included some vocal sounds, but these vocals were played backward at half speed and were thus rendered unintelligible. The overall effect was quite stunning and served as a jumping off point for the rest of the material on the album.

The second song on record one of the set was a complete contrast to the opening track. Song two was the title track, "Have You Ever Been (to Electric Ladyland)," and cast the Experience as the Impressions with Jimi taking the role of Curtis Mayfield and finally putting the title track in a traditional album position. Here Jimi sang in his falsetto range and the Experience played like a quasi-psychedelic soul trio. In contrast to many songs in the soul style, Jimi penned this tune in a narrative manner with two verses separated by a short guitar solo containing the repeated lyric "make love." Noel was also missing from the recording of this song so Jimi recorded guitar, vocals, and bass parts. Mitch was in for the drum and tambourine lines and the drum track was subjected to the phasing effect. Lyrically, Jimi imagined that Electric Ladyland was a place that one could reach on a "flying carpet" over a "love filled sea." Images of angels, peace, and love permeated the song as Jimi imagined a utopian land for him and his "electric woman." The song was another of Jimi's musical paintings with "a scenario conspicuously removed from real life, Jimi's music being about as close as many of his fans (or Hendrix himself) could come to actually experiencing it."[66]

Track three was the third different side of the Experience displayed in as many songs. "Crosstown Traffic" was recorded with all three members of the Experience in the studio, plus added harmony vocals by Dave Mason (of the band Traffic).[67] Here the Experience unleashed a blast of psychedelic funk that rode a wave of solid vocals and guitar playing.

For years of live performance and jam sessions, Jimi had been working with the chords of Muddy Waters' classic "Catfish Blues"—the group often covered the song live in 1967. For "Voodoo Chile," Jimi spun out a new song based on the essence of Waters' tune. Significantly, "Voodoo Chile" on the first side of record one and "Voodoo Child (Slight Return)," the last song on the second record of the set form ". . . the twin pillars of *Electric Ladyland*."[68] For "Voodoo Chile," Jimi enlisted Jack Cassidy to play bass and Steve Winwood for organ, along with some overdubbed crowd noise. Creating an update on the electric blues sound, Jimi and the band built a dense texture with Jimi's guitar punches countered by Winwood's sustained organ lines.

Lyrically, the song was psychedelic blues. The words that began each verse were repeated as per the standard in the blues style (see "Red House"). The content of the lyrics also contained the spirit of the blues. In the first verse, Jimi described being born under a red moon and the terror of this causing his mother to "[fall] down right dead." The song then progressed into the second verse without being interrupted by the chorus. In verse two, Jimi paid homage to a longstanding blues tradition of animal symbolism in the lyrics (see Waters' "Catfish Blues" lyrics). Jimi referenced a series of animals and their deeds. The song then moved into its first chorus statement which boiled down to two statements of its title.

In verse three, Jimi evoked the image of lovemaking, but not in the conventional sense. Here he described his lovemaking taking place in his woman's dreams while he was a "million miles away." After the third verse the band launched into the second chorus which built into the bridge/solo comprising the middle section of the song. The bridge was not typical for Jimi as he was matching skills with Winwood's organ playing. As the exchange progressed, Jimi name-dropped Winwood with the statement "go 'head on little Stevie." There followed a volley of call and response between the guitar and organ, which was made even more incredible by the knowledge that, according to Winwood "there were no chord sheets, no nothing."[69] Verses four and five continued the general sentiment of verse three with animal images mixed with mentions of various planets of the solar system. The song ended with further exchanges between guitar and organ as it winded around to its close.

In this manner, the Experience ended side one of the first record from the *Electric Ladyland* double album. They presented four songs each of which cast the group in a different style, mood, speed, and lineup. Further, Jimi had included a wide variety of "love" songs each of which took on a different perspective from the ethereal love made by gods to the straight-ahead blues sentiment illustrated in the animal symbolism.

Side two of record one began with a song written by Noel. "Little Miss Strange" sounded much different from the material on the A-side of the album. For this track, Noel took over the lead vocals and Mitch provided high vocal harmony. The song was a short blast of sound in alternating verse and chorus statements.

It opened with Jimi playing a guitar lick in octaves which led into the first verse. Noel's lyrics commented on various qualities of the unknown woman about whom the song was written. Twice during the song, Jimi took extended solos, building musical tension that was released during the closing section. Unlike the other songs on the album, "Little Miss Strange" changed meter from four beats per measure to three in the closing. The song then faded out on a cymbal roll. Of the song Doggett said, ". . . 'Little Miss Strange' did little more than repeat the ingredients of 'She's So Fine' from *Axis*, and *Electric Ladyland* would have been a stronger album without it."[70] While Doggett's comment was likely correct and straight to the point, Jimi was still trying to smooth Noel's increasingly ruffled feathers and maintain some type of working relationship with his bandmates. It is noteworthy that Noel only appeared on five of the sixteen songs on *Electric Ladyland*.

Jimi wrote the lyrics for "Long Hot Summer Night" on January 17, 1968. One of his notebooks contained the song in complete form with markings for where the bridge and guitar solos were supposed to take place.[71] "Long Hot Summer Night" was another song on which Jimi covered Noel's bass part. In fact, Jimi was credited with playing guitar and bass as well as providing lead and background vocals. An added musician on the track was Al Kooper who was responsible for the piano part.[72] Mitch was in on the session for this track in his standard role on the drums. Musically, the song was a blues-tinged psychedelic jam with Jimi describing his feelings about a lover who ran away from him "down cross the border." The song kicked off with Jimi laying down a bluesy guitar lick that led directly into the first verse. Here Jimi began the main sentiment of the song which had him sweltering in the heat, but with a cold and frozen heart because his lover was gone. He established these contrasting temperatures with mentions of "cold winter storms," "snow," and "blizzards" set against images of "fire" and "summer." Jimi divided the song in half with an extended guitar solo in the middle which led into the direct narrative of him getting a phone call from his baby. The second half of the song held the resolution to Jimi's frozen heart with his lover coming back to rescue him. The theme of redemption through love was one that Jimi touched on in the lyrics of several songs and here it was done to expert effect.

"Come On (Part I)" was written by New Orleans blues guitarist Earl King.[73] For the song, the Experience was again its usual three-piece crew and flew through this rollicking version of the song. Also known as "Let the Good Times Roll," the song was straight-ahead guitar-driven electric blues. "Come On (Part I)" started out with an aggressive opening statement by the band that led into the first verse. The overall sentiment of the song was that the singer and his baby were out for having a good time and little else mattered. The three verses of the song were presented by Jimi in a half-sung, half-spoken manner very common to the style. Further, while the lyrics were being stated, the band dropped out so it was Jimi's voice alone. Two-thirds of the way through the song, Jimi took a solo that displayed his immense virtuosity and speed. The solo was further extended by a guitar repetition of the music of the opening verses. The song ended with Jimi again taking an extended guitar solo that eventually faded out. Detractors of this song's inclusion on the album note that as a cover and in the blues style it added little to the overall product. That notwithstanding, Jimi did an excellent job of asserting his roots with the song and also created a solid update to the New Orleans blues style. Doggett pointed out that ". . . [the song] was pleasant but undemanding, its last-minute addition to the album was strange, in view of the fact that Jimi left out-takes from these sessions like 'South Saturn Delta' and 'My Friend' unreleased."[74]

"Gypsy Eyes" was another song on which Jimi played both the guitar and the bass parts in addition to supplying the vocals. This allowed him to match the three parts masterfully. Mitch laid down the drum part and started the song with a solo drum lead-in with alternating bass drum and high hat. The guitar then entered to lead into the first chorus statement. The music of the song was a minimalist combination of Mitch's drumming and Jimi's guitar and bass playing a repeated riff that stayed constant throughout. Lyrically, the song was an open letter to Jimi's mother who had had little contact with him and who had died in 1958 (reportedly of cirrhosis of the liver).[75] Jimi began the song with a direct profession of his love for his mother who he referred to by the title of the song. In this opening chorus, Jimi played the same notes on his guitar that he was singing, which added depth and further emotion to the words. In the opening two verses, Jimi described missing his mother and wondered if she still thought about him. As he described his dilemma he tied together the lost love of his mother with a sense of his own soul. The third verse described a meeting between him and his mother during which her eyes were full of tears when she related how strongly she felt about him but still had to make her "getaway." The second chorus was the same as the first with Jimi continuing to declare his love for his mother. The final verse described Jimi searching for his mother and then being saved by her return-redemption through love. The song winded down with him continuing the chorus sentiment and then coming to an abrupt stop. While the timeline Jimi used in the song was not historically accurate to his life, the strong and emotive language he used made it clear exactly how he felt about his wayward mother.

The Jimi Hendrix Experience, shown center: Jimi Hendrix (Courtesy of Photofest)

The final song on the first record of the *Electric Ladyland* double record was "Burning of the Midnight Lamp." Although the song had been released previously as a single, the sound and emotion of it fit well with the rest of the material on the album. Through blasts of wah-wah pedal guitar, Jimi again made clear his thoughts with the lyric "loneliness is such a drag." With the song's grand flourishes and wall of sound-style arrangement, record one of the pair came to a close.

The second record began with the song "Rainy Day, Dream Away." Just as "Voodoo Chile" and "Voodoo Child (Slight Return)" made an excellent set of bookends for the entire two-album set, "Rainy Day, Dream Away" and its sister song "Still Raining, Still Dreaming"—on the B-side of record two—created cohesion within the second record. In fact, the two songs were generated in the same jam session and then divided for presentation on the album. As a testament to the jam-style nature of the song, one of the first sounds heard on the recording is Jimi coughing to clear his throat before he started to sing. The origin of the song came from a combination of events in Jimi's life. It was likely penned in response to a long drive that Jimi had endured through a south Florida rainstorm in May 1968. The principal lyric was actually lifted from one of the many albums that Jimi collected. The lyric " 'Hey man, it's raining' (by Jimi in a funny voice) came from a Bill Cosby story which was on the Bill Cosby LP (*Revenge*)."[76] It was known that Jimi had this record in his collection and there was little other explanation for him adopting a different voice to state those lyrics.

In on the jam session were a host of players from outside the Experience. In fact, Noel and Mitch do not play. Instead, Jimi invited a wide range of other instrumentalists in to jam. Buddy Miles covered the drum part, Larry Faucette played congas, and Freddie Smith played saxophone. Mike Finnigan was the organist and Jimi himself covered the guitar and vocal lines and he also likely supplied the bass part.[77] Recorded as a one-off jam session, the song still came together as a tight interplay of all the instruments.

The organ, drums, bass, and congas laid down a slow and comfortable groove over which the other instrumental lines were spun. The song began with the rhythm section establishing the groove and then the guitar and the saxophone entered into a short call and response in which Jimi was matching Smith note-for-note. Verse one was then stated and it was here that Jimi imitated Cosby's line and established that in the face of rain all that was left to do was groove, jam, and dream. The break after the first verse again had the lead instruments in a call and response, this time between Jimi on guitar and Finnigan on organ. In verse two, Jimi described the delight of children, flowers, and ducks enjoying the rain without a care. The interlude after the second verse began with Jimi playing a fuzzed-out guitar line that built into an extended solo. The third verse continued the notion that the rain would wash away worries and faded out leading into "1983 . . . (A Merman I Should Turn to Be)."

The next song on the second album was among Jimi's most grand in scope and duration. Not a jam session like "Rainy Day, Dream Away" or "Still Raining, Still Dreaming," "1983 . . . (A Merman I Should Turn to Be)" illustrated Jimi at his most avant-garde. Clocking in at nearly fourteen minutes, here Jimi painted a musical portrait of a world torn by war in which he had to seek refuge in the sea. Likely in response to his background in science fiction reading, Jimi imagined a world that had been destroyed leaving only the ocean as a place of escape. In the underwater world, Jimi described scenes of Neptune and Atlantis. The overall musical design of the song has been described as "[an] opening mixture of gorgeous folk-rockish balladeering and martial drum patterns, the track soon melts into rather mucky, swampy, eerie noise—like the soundtrack for a psychedelic journey to Atlantis—which, indeed, Jimi hears 'full of cheer' by the end of the track."[78]

In pursuit of painting this otherworldly landscape, Jimi supplied vocals, guitars, bass, and percussion parts. Mitch laid down the drum track and Chris Wood (of the band Traffic) supplied the flute line. The sounds of the instruments involved were manipulated through a variety of means including the slowing down and speeding up of the tape and the use of backward parts for the guitar and the flute. Additionally, the sound of seagulls was approximated by feedback coming from Jimi's headphones with added effects.[79] The style of the music itself has been described as an attempt by Jimi to create a rock and jazz fusion (for those who think that Jimi was pushing in the direction of free jazz as his style evolved). As the music of the track spun out seemingly endlessly, Jimi and his love descended into the sea to escape a ravaged world and were greeted by smiling sea creatures. While improvisatory in sound and scheme, Jimi's notes for the song were quite explicit. Penned in January 1968, Jimi's handwritten accounting for the song included specific chord changes, changes in tempo, and the complete lyrics.

"Moon, Turn the Tides . . . gently gently away" was not truly a freestanding song in its own right. The final track on the A-side of the second album was actually a continuation of "1983 . . . (A Merman I Should Turn to Be)." Separated from the body of the previous song by an extended and distorted instrumental break, the final track on the side finished the sentiment of "1983." The lyrics of the two-song suite ended with Jimi and his lover reborn as undersea creatures. Now a mermaid, she greeted him with a smile and together they descended into Atlantis. The song gradually spun to a close with "space" sounds informed by Jimi's fascination with science fiction. The texture of the music on the song was filled with "multi-dubbed guitar motifs [that] restored the psychedelic jazz feel . . . the familiar theme of '1983' reemerged, to guide the suite to its conclusion, and complete 20 minutes of stunningly complex and beautiful instrumental tonalities."[80]

The final side of the two-record set began with the continuation of "Rainy Day, Dream Away" called "Still Raining, Still Dreaming." Again, the Experience lineup was altered with Noel and Mitch absent for this song. Jimi played guitar, bass, and provided all the vocals. Miles was back on drums and Mike Finnigan returned to supply the organ part. The song was really a vehicle for Jimi to jam some more with the above-listed musicians. Loosely constructed, the lyrics for "Still Raining, Still Dreaming" were a repetition of the third verse from "Rainy Day, Dream Away." The basic sentiment was the same as in the original song; the clouds were not going to get Jimi down because he was going to spend the day laid back and grooving in the studio. It was a shame that " . . . Jimi didn't devote more attention to developing the lyrical side of 'Still Raining, Still Dreaming' . . . [as] his jubilant singing at the track's outset is delightful, as is his unflappable why-worry attitude toward the rain, so often the signifier of sad and troubled times in popular music, yet celebrated here as something that should be allowed to 'groove its own way.' "[81] Of note, Jimi used his guitar to interesting effect in this song. In spots, Jimi seems to be making the guitar talk—approximating the sound of the human voice. This was done during sections of the song that did not have vocals. The result was that the guitar seemed to take over the vocal part and superseded Jimi's own singing.

Next up was the blistering track "House Burning Down." Unlike many of Jimi's songs, this one was constructed in a fairly straightforward alternation of chorus and verse sections. The opening of the song "twisted through several key changes in its tight, swirling intro, and then shifted again as the strident chorus moved into the reportorial verses."[82] For the track, Jimi covered the guitar, bass, and vocal parts and Mitch laid down the drum line. Jimi's guitar was put through the phasing effect which resulted in it achieving the sound of being scorched or on fire. Jimi said, "we made the guitar sound like it was on fire . . . constantly changing dimensions, and up on top that lead guitar is cutting through everything."[83]

The lyrics of the song likely referenced the increasingly violent urban landscape as an exponent of the civil rights movement and the death of Martin Luther King, Jr. The opening chorus set up the scenario in which Jimi described that the sky was red from the flames coming from a house fire. In the first verse, Jimi asked around to find out where the fire was coming from. The respondent was cast as someone who did not want to get involved and told Jimi that the sky was black because "it might snow." Jimi then immediately knew what had actually happened—black on black violence. After a second chorus statement, he moved into a guitar solo during which his guitar screamed in terror over the scene. Also during the solo, Jimi created the impression of two guitars passing a riff back and forth through studio trickery. The third verse offered the lessons of the song. First, Jimi cautioned that people had to "learn instead of burn" in an effort to put an end to the violence. As was the case with several of Jimi's songs, the final verse ended with a savior and a chance for redemption—in this case the savior came from space. Much like the protection of the sea sought in "1983 . . . (A Merman I Should Turn to Be)," the space traveler who came to Jimi's aid at the end of this song was another image likely informed by his science fiction reading. The song ended with a section of fuzzed-out and distorted guitar work that eventually faded out.

The next to the last song on the album was Jimi's cover of Bob Dylan's "All Along the Watchtower." Jimi had already released this song as a single that went to number five in the United Kingdom and broke the top twenty in the United States.[84] The final track on the *Electric Ladyland* release was "Voodoo Child (Slight Return)" which created the twin pillar effect of bookending the album with "Voodoo Chile" on the first side and this track at the end. Jimi, Mitch, and Noel were back together for this song and each took their usual roles with the only added part being a maraca line played by either Jimi or Mitch.

Structurally, the song alternated two verse and chorus statements, but the core of the track was not as much in the lyrics as it was in the guitar playing. Jimi opened with a blast of wah-wah effected guitar work that led the rest of the band into the song. He then basically took a solo before the first verse even arrived. The lyrics of the first verse describe destruction and rebirth all the while tempered by the immense presence of the guitar part. While Jimi was singing he was at times doubling himself on the guitar matching each pitch note-for-note. These were further enhanced when he stated a line of lyrics and then answered with a blast of guitar creating an impromptu call and response between the vocals and the guitar. The chorus stated the title of the song twice before launching into another frenetic guitar solo during which Jimi's guitar wailed and groaned furiously. The second verse was among the most telling of any that he wrote. Here he described leaving this world and meeting on the next one—and "don't be late." This thread of impending death ran through several of Jimi's songs and could be interpreted as autobiographical or even a statement on the coming end of the band.

Another common theme in Jimi's lyrics was ". . . references to voodoo here and in other songs (including of course, another cut on *Electric Lady-land*, 'Voodoo Chile') and could be seen as evidence of some kind of belief in supernatural powers, it should be remembered that voodoo was often referenced in blues and R&B before Hendrix came along, notably on another song popularized by Waters, 'Got My Mojo Working' . . . [thus] Hendrix can be fairly viewed as continuing a long and venerable R&B tradition, though with far more heavy-metal thunder than any of his predecessors."[85] The song, and album, ended with Jimi again displaying his finely honed guitar playing virtuosity with subtle returns to the sound of the tracks opening to create a fitting close.

Summer turned to fall in 1968 with the future of the Jimi Hendrix Experience uncertain. Jimi continued to play with a wide ranging lineup under the Experience name, Noel directed most of his time and creative energy toward Fat Mattress, and Mitch ended up running interference. "How much this was self-delusion is difficult to say—like a 'trial separation' in marriage as a way of postponing taking [sic] a decision about the inevitable."[86] One way or another, the period of separation was not likely to pan out as planned. However, the group soldiered on for the first six months of 1969.

At the beginning of the year, the group again returned to London and Jimi settled in with Kathy Etchingham at 23 Brook Street—coincidently "next door to the classical composer George Frideric Handel's previous residence at number 25."[87] The group had an existing run of shows booked as well as an appearance on the television show *Happening for Lulu*. They played the TV show on January 4. They were not alone on the bill as the Iveys (who would go on to be the group Badfinger) also appeared. The Experience was slated to play "Hey Joe" but Jimi made an abrupt change—on live television—and sent the band into Cream's "Sunshine of Your Love." This caused some confusion on stage and pushed the producers of the show into a fit. Afterward, Jimi and Lulu had the following exchange: Jimi "Lu, I'm really sorry if I messed your show up." Lulu "Listen, don't even worry about it. It was fabulous television."[88] With this, the Experience kicked off 1969 in England.

The Experience began another swing through Europe on January 8 at Lorensberg Cirkus in Göteborg, Sweden, with support from Amen Corner and Burning Red Ivanhoe.[89] Chandler turned up to see the group play and Jimi asked him to return to the band's management.[90] Chandler declined the offer, but the olive branch had been extended. The tour then played in

Stockholm with Jethro Tull, and in Copenhagen before moving on to Germany.[91] In Germany the band played a series of dates supported by Erie Apparent, which included Hamburg, Düsseldorf, Köln, Münster, Munich, Nuremburg, Frankfurt, and Stuttgart. While in Germany, Jimi met Monika Dannemann who according to Jimi "managed to turn my life upside down, and it would never be the same again."[92] Next the Experience moved into France for a show in Strasbourg, then Vienna, and Berlin before a two-night stand at the Royal Albert Hall in London—supported by Fat Mattress, Van der Graaf Generator,[93] and Soft Machine. Beginning with these shows, Fat Mattress was the support group for the Experience for the next month.

In early March, Jimi returned to New York and again spent time jamming at clubs such as Ronnie Scott's. At this same time, Kathy Etchingham turned up in New York looking for Jimi. He had left her in England after he met Monika Dannemann in Germany. Etchingham had paid her own way back to the states for the purposes of reuniting with Jimi. However, by the end of the month the two had split for good. Depending on which version of the story was to be believed, either Jimi left Etchingham for Dannemann, or Etchingham got scared off by the ever-increasing drug culture surrounding Jimi.

March also included more work for Jimi in the studio. He recorded at Mercury Sound Studios, in New York, tracking "Blue Window" and "Message to Love." At the Record Plant he tracked "The Star Spangled Banner" and "Hey Gypsy Boy." Also at the Record Plant, with John McLaughlin, Jimi worked up "Drivin' South" and "Everything's Gonna Be Alright."[94] Of this session McLaughlin said, ". . . Buddy Miles [was] playing drums. I didn't know Buddy at the time; I just saw this guy who was playing some boogaloo. So I played, and then Jimi came and joined in. Dave Holland (Miles Davis' bassist) was there, and we played all night—it was really nice."[95] At the end of the month, Jimi made a trip to pursue one of his few nonmusic passions: the Corvette Stingray. On March 29, Jimi flew to Los Angeles to take delivery of his latest Corvette.

In April, Jimi resumed recording by tracking "Ramblin" at Olmstead Studio Sound, in New York. Of the Olmstead session, Eddie Kramer said "the sessions didn't go very well, as things were pretty crazy. There was a lot of partying going on."[96] Other songs that were recorded at Olmstead were "Hear My Train A Comin'," "Midnight Lightning," and "Trash Man." With the Olmstead sessions complete, Jimi returned to the Record Plant. Through mid-April, Jimi recorded a series of other songs at the Record Plant including "Ships Passing in the Night," "Stone Free," and "Earth Blues."

Also during the first half of April, the Experience played live with Fat Mattress serving as an opener. They played Dorton Arena in Raleigh, the Spectrum in Philadelphia, Ellis Auditorium in Memphis, and Sam Houston Coliseum in Houston. This set of shows marked the kickoff of another extended United States tour. In Houston, the Experience was backed by Fat

Mattress and Chicago Transit Authority—who would later become the band Chicago. During the end of the month, the group played the Forum in Inglewood, California, and the Oakland Coliseum. For these shows the openers included Chicago Transit Authority, Cat Mother & the All-Night News Boys, and Jefferson Airplane. Amid the opening concerts of the new tour, Jimi continued to record at the Record Plant as he could. He also made a formal offer to Billy Cox to come on board as his bass player—another signal that Jimi did not believe that his professional relationship with Noel could be repaired even as they toured and Noel's band served as opener. Additionally, plans for Jimi's Electric Lady Studio also got underway. By this time, Jimi was already authorizing the purchase of equipment to outfit the control room.

May began with more touring through Detroit, Toronto, Syracuse, Tuscaloosa, Charlotte, Charleston, and Indianapolis. Cat Mother & the All-Night News Boys served as support for this series of shows. An unfortunate turn of events transpired with the border crossing for the Toronto show. Jimi's bag was searched and a small quantity of heroin was found. There had been rumors of the possibility of planted items in Experience bags just prior to the find. Jimi took responsibility for the bag but not its contents, saying that he had no knowledge of the drugs. Regardless, he was arrested and released on $10,000 bond. It was conventional wisdom in the group and its entourage at the time that it was a plant, but no one knew by who or why.

Regardless of the drug arrest, the tour continued, although Jimi had to return to Toronto on May 5 to appear in court where a hearing was set for June 19. After the hearing, which determined his court date, Jimi went directly to Toronto's Maple Leaf Gardens where he appeared before a house of nearly 12,000 fans. The following night, the Jimi Hendrix Experience played the War Memorial Auditorium in Syracuse, New York. During the show, "Hendrix improvised a verse or two of new lyrics for a new song. The words came out something like '. . . and I was in this room/full of light and a thousand mirrors . . .' "[97] Certainly, this was a telling description of Jimi's time with the Royal Canadian Mounted Police, as well as a bit of an insight into the genesis of the song "Room Full of Mirrors."

Mid-May tour stops included Baltimore, Providence, and Madison Square Garden in New York. The Buddy Miles Express came on the bill as support. Simultaneously, Billy Cox arrived in New York gearing up to begin work with Jimi. With Miles and Cox in Jimi's immediate orbit, he was prepared in the event that the original Experience should suddenly fold. Jimi's attempt to surround himself with musicians who were willing to work with him—according to his rule—did not go unnoticed by those already surrounding him. Cox sensed friction with Jimi's management as soon as he came on the scene. This was made worse by Noel's reaction to the appearance of a new bass player. According to Noel, "Jimi had been 'advised' to get somebody else and just employ them . . . that [somebody] was Billy Cox."[98]

Also during mid-May, Jimi continued to work in the studio as he was able. He recorded "Villanova Junction," "Hallelujah," and "Ships Passing in the Night" at the Record Plant. Next, he tracked "Power of Soul" followed by "Valleys of Neptune," "Hear My Train A Comin'," "Bleeding Heart," and "Earth Blues." The sessions at the Record Plant ended for the month with the recording of "Message From Nine to the Universe."

The end of the month again found Jimi back in his birthplace. On May 23, the Experience played the Seattle Center Coliseum with Fat Mattress opening. Next the group moved on to the San Diego Sports Arena followed by an appearance at the *San Jose Pop Festival* in Santa Clara, California. This was a large outdoor concert with several other heavyweights on the bill including Taj Mahal[99] and Eric Burdon, along with openers Loading Zone[100] and Fat Mattress. The Experience spent the end of the month in Hawaii where they played a series of three shows. The first concert was cancelled due to a variety of problems, some with the sound system and some with Jimi's unwillingness to work with the extra noise coming through the amplifiers. The second and third shows went off without a hitch, although the venue was overfilled due to honoring the tickets for those who had come to the first night's cancelled show. Jimi and the Experience tore through sets in Hawaii that included "Lover Man," "Hear My Train A Comin'," "Fire," "Stone Free," "Foxey Lady," and "Spanish Castle Magic."

June began with the Experience completely worn out from the road, recording, and internal band strife. Jimi continued to pursue his dream studio with work on Electric Lady Studios continuing as money allowed—strange for an internationally renowned recording artist, but an indication of the problems Jimi was having with his management. In an effort to recharge, Jimi booked himself into a room in the Beverly Rodeo Hotel, Beverly Hills, where he spent time working out songs, doing interviews, and occasionally leaving to jam with various local musicians.

On June 19, Jimi returned to Toronto for his preliminary hearing on the border-crossing drug bust. The judge set a trial date for December 8 and Jimi traveled to San Fernando Valley State College to be part of the *Newport 69 Pop Festival.* The Jimi Hendrix Experience was scheduled along with other acts like Albert King, Ike and Tina Turner, Joe Cocker, Taj Mahal, Booker T and the MGs, and the Byrds—quite a group of serious performers. The Experience was scheduled to perform on the first night of the two-day event. The group was reportedly paid $125,000 for their appearance, which was the largest single-act sum paid to date in the United States. According to contemporary reports, Jimi was given excessive drugs without his knowledge before the Experience set. The result was a mess. The group got through fewer than ten songs before Jimi had to leave the stage. In an effort to redeem himself, Jimi came back out on the second night of the concert for an unscheduled appearance. Instead of Noel and Mitch, Jimi brought Buddy Miles (drums), Brad Campbell (bass), and Eric Burdon out on stage and satisfied the crowd with "Train Kept A Rollin'," "Power of Soul," "Hear My Train A Comin'," "Voodoo Child," "Sunshine of Your Love," "Come On," an onstage jam, "We Gotta Live Together," and "Things I Used To Do." Jimi's second set was a high-water mark for the festival and far overshadowed the mishap of the night before.

The 1969 American tour concluded with the *Denver Pop Festival* at Mile High Stadium, in Denver, Colorado, on June 29. The thirty thousand people in attendance witnessed the final concert by the Jimi Hendrix Experience in its original incarnation as Jimi had announced the day prior that he was expanding the band. An oddity of this was that Jimi did not formally remove Noel. Instead he made public that, "his bassist will be former Army buddy Billy Cox, but Noel Redding and Mitch Mitchell are not necessarily out of the band."[101] Although, Jimi did not formally remove Noel, he also did not make all of his intentions clear to his original bassist. The Experience took the stage and during their set the crowd came through the barriers. The police intervened and tear gas was deployed into the crowd. A riot ensued and the band was rushed off stage and whisked away in the back of a truck.

When clouds of the noxious gas begin to waft across the stage, the gig is quickly abandoned, before Hendrix's road manager bundles him and the band into the back of a U-Haul rental van. As they begin to inch their way through the rioting mass, fans clamber onto the top of the vehicle in an attempt to escape the fumes. Those trapped inside the van feel it begin to rock, its sides appearing to buckle.[102]

After the group got to safety, Noel told Jimi that he was leaving the band. With the chaos of the *Denver Pop Festival*, the Jimi Hendrix Experience, as the collective of Jimi, Noel, and Mitch, came to an end. Noel quickly departed for London while Mitch stayed on to work with Jimi in whatever capacity that he could.

4

New Horizons

Amid the tumult of the summer of 1969, Jimi recognized that he still had a great deal of work to do. His dreams of building his own studio were slowly coming to fruition, but the construction was often slowed by lack of a direct money stream. Further, Jimi now needed to build a new band. He had Mitch waiting in the wings and Miles and Cox were ready to work with him on short notice—regardless of how his management felt about it. In addition, Jimi had been jamming with a percussionist named Geraldo "Jerry" Velez, who Jeffery did not like but who Jimi enjoyed due to the Latin flavor that Velez brought to the overall sound.[1] In fact, Jimi was looking to make his new expanded band quite large—with two percussionists. The other was Juma Sultan who brought more of a traditional African approach in his drumming.[2]

On July 7, Jimi appeared on the *Dick Cavett Show* where he performed "Hear My Train A Comin'," followed a few days later with an appearance on Johnny Carson's *Tonight Show*. In the middle of the month, Jimi sent for his old friend guitarist Larry Lee. Although Jimi had been used to playing both rhythm and lead guitar parts, he had begun to feel that having a dedicated rhythm guitarist in the band would give him greater flexibility. Lee had just returned from Vietnam and was quickly immersed in Jimi's new musical world. On July 23, Jimi and his new bandmates relocated to Traver Hallow Road, Shokan, New York, where they spent the next month working up new songs and trying to create a new musical core around Jimi.[3] The move to New York and the Shokan location was part of the run-up to the *Woodstock Music and Art Fair—An Aquarian Exposition: 3 Days of Peace and Music* which Jimi had committed to playing.

The month that the band spent in Shokan was filled with creating new music and rehearsing to get used to each other's playing styles. This was also a very creative time with Jimi writing several new songs. Additionally, Jimi spent time in Woodstock jamming with various musicians at the Tinker Street Cinema. He also wrote new songs at the house on Traver Hallow Road that would continue to surface for the next several months. The atmosphere in Woodstock in the period leading up to the festival was pure 1960s psychedelic renaissance. Notable musicians of all kinds were around town including Janis Joplin as well as Rick Danko and Levon Helm (both of the Band), and others.

On August 17, Jimi relocated closer to the farm on which the Woodstock music festival was going to take place. Eddie Kramer was already at the venue and upon his arrival was shocked at the condition of the stage and the sound system. The logistics of the show were all handled poorly. Every act got progressively more and more behind schedule and the (now famous) rain came down soaking everyone's gear. The group of musicians who were supposed to go on with Jimi included Mitch, but he was the last to arrive. There had been some question if Miles would play instead, but he never committed to the show and did not perform. The group that surrounded Jimi as the sun came up in Bethel, New York, was Mitch (drums), Billy Cox (bass, backing vocals), Larry Lee (rhythm guitar), Juma Sultan (percussion), and Jerry Velez (percussion).

Woodstock was scheduled for three days, but due to delays from rain and long change-of-act periods the entire event was stretched out. Beginning on Friday the bands that performed were Richie Havens, Swami Satchidananda, Sweetwater, the Incredible String Band, Bert Sommer, Tim Hardin, Ravi Shankar, Melanie, Arlo Guthrie, and Joan Baez. On Saturday the festival continued with Quill, Keef Hartley Band, Country Joe McDonald, John Sebastian, Santana, Canned Heat, Mountain, the Grateful Dead, Creedence Clearwater Revival, Janis Joplin and the Kozmic Blues Band, Sly and the Family Stone, the Who, and Jefferson Airplane. The Sunday acts were the Grease Band; Joe Cocker; Country Joe and the Fish; Ten Years After; the Band; Blood, Sweat, and Tears; Johnny Winter (with his brother Edgar); Crosby, Stills, Nash, and Young; Paul Butterfield Blues Band; and Sha-Na-Na. By Sunday night, it looked like Jimi's band would not be able to go on until midnight. Since it appeared that there would be some music on Monday (although the festival was only scheduled for three days), Jimi instead opted to perform Monday morning.

BAND OF GYPSYS

Jimi's group was the last to go on. Many of the people who had come to the festival on Max Yasgur's 600-acre farm had already left, but those who remained in the mud-covered field were treated to the highlight of the entire weekend. Just before taking the stage, Jimi said to Cox " . . . there's a lot of people . . . sending a lot of energy toward the bandstand . . . so we'll take that energy, absorb it and send it back to them."[4] As the group came on stage, they were announced as the Jimi Hendrix Experience. Jimi and the group walked out on stage and as they were preparing to play Jimi said to the crowd (many of whom were screaming "we love you")

> We got tired of the Experience—it was blowing our minds too much
> So we decided to turn the whole thing around—we call it
> Gypsy Sun and Rainbows—for short it is nothing but
> A Band of Gypsys.

He then flashed the crowd the peace sign and started warming up his guitar. The backing band was positioned around Jimi in a vague semicircle with Mitch's drum kit in the middle. Jimi was wearing a cream-colored shirt with some thin blue stripes that was open in the front and had fringes hanging from the arms and down the front and back of the torso. He also wore blue bell-bottomed pants, a bright pink headband, and a silver necklace with a turquoise pendant hanging from it. He had a tie-dyed scarf wrapped around his left leg and was wearing tan suede shoes.

Jimi began the Band of Gypsys' set with a blazing take on "Message to Love." The original sound of the song was significantly enhanced with the additional players added to the texture. The group then went into "Hear My Train A Comin,'" which changed up the sound of the set from the more psychedelic opening to driving blues.[5] Next, the group tore into a fairly straightforward take on "Spanish Castle Magic." Of note, Jimi's guitar solo was lengthy, virtuosic, and contained several brief sections where he repeated notes and let the percussion players shine. Throughout the performance, Jimi often half-turned toward the band and away from the audience as he led them through each song. A slow-burning take on "Red House" came next with an extended guitar-driven opening. Always a perfectionist in guitar sounds and tuning, Jimi winced at the end of this song and was clearly unhappy with how out of tune his guitar was becoming.

"Lover Man" was next up and the band threw themselves in for a spirited take on the song. An interesting aspect of this version was that Larry Lee actually took the first solo while Jimi danced a short jig on stage and kept pace as the rhythm guitarist. Jimi soon took over the lead guitar role and released a barrage of guitar bombs through the course of an extended solo. The song ended with Jimi working over his guitar with use of the whammy bar, some single-handed playing (right hand only), and a final flourish created by running the microphone stand against the neck of his guitar. The band next launched into "Foxey Lady," which was presented with an especially dirty and distorted guitar by Jimi. Jimi kept this song pretty close to its original, but with added guitar work at the end of the song.

The psychedelic sound returned with "Jam Back at the House," the opening of which often rang with guitar feedback. Clocking in at just under

Jimi Hendrix at Woodstock with Jerry Velez and Juma Sultan
(Courtesy of Photofest)

eight minutes, this song took the audience on several musical twists and turns
with changes in groove and speed. At the midpoint Mitch took a drum solo
during which the whole rest of the band took a short break. Jimi lit a cigarette and returned to his forward position on the stage. He then led the
group back into a guitar playing tutorial during which his soloing was so liq-
uid and seamless that it seemed to be pouring from his guitar.

Jimi took a moment to dispense with his cigarette before addressing the
crowd. He commended them for their patience ("three days worth") and then
dove into "Izabella." The guitar solo in the middle of this song illustrated
how lost in the music Jimi could become. He played for several minutes with
his eyes tightly shut and the solo reached a climax with Jimi returning to his
old trick of playing with his teeth. The song again ended with an extended solo
during which Jimi put on another clinic of guitar virtuosity. Next the Band of
Gypsys went careening into an up-tempo version of "Fire." Throughout the
show, Jimi was essentially directing the other members of the band with his

guitar, small gestures, and eye contact. This was very true when he shot members of the group a nasty look as the band made a musical misstep during the first minute of the song.

Working his wah-wah pedal, Jimi pushed the group into an over twelve minute–long version of "Voodoo Child (Slight Return)." An interesting aside was that although Jimi was quite animated during his performance, most of the other members of the band largely stood still throughout the nearly two-hour set (save for perhaps some animation on the part of Velez). The midsong solo here illustrated Jimi again lost in the music. His mouth hung open; he played with only his right hand while his left windmilled in the air, and all the while he kept his eyes screwed shut tight. For an added twist, Jimi also worked in a piece of the song "Stepping Stone"—both words and music—into the middle of the song. Coming out of the solo, Jimi again turned toward the band and bobbed his head as he prepared to return to the microphone. Instead of singing the rest of the song's lyrics, Jimi took the opportunity to introduce the members of the band to the crowd—again calling them a Band of Gypsys. Through the rest of the song, Jimi continued controlling the band with little more than the look in his eyes and the massive weight of his guitar sound. The song wound to a close with Jimi returning to its opening riff and again playing with his teeth.

Without stop, the group then moved into "The Star Spangled Banner." Jimi's performance of this song was considered by most as the climax of the entire festival. During the opening of the song, Jimi played with just his right hand while flashing the peace sign with his left (made that much more interesting bearing in mind his own military background coupled with the fact that Lee was just back from Vietnam). He then tuned two strings while still playing before altering the middle of the song to include extremely realistic guitar impressions of "bombs bursting in air." He then further altered the song to include a brief reference to "Taps" before returning to a fairly straightforward rendition of the end of the song—although with a good dose of feedback added. During the performance of the song, Jimi employed the Uni-Vibe effect pedal to enhance his sound. Additionally, he relied heavily on feedback, the whammy bar, and other pedal effects to create a programmatic depiction of war. Although Jimi never went on record in opposition to the Vietnam War—in fact several times he seemed to be in support of the war effort—many people have subsequently chosen to interpret Jimi's version of this song as an anti-Vietnam statement.

Again without stopping, Jimi melted the end of "The Star Spangled Banner" into the opening of "Purple Haze" with its characteristic opening dissonant tritones. Although an outstanding live performance of an Experience standard, little sets the Woodstock version of "Purple Haze" ahead of other solid live takes of the song. Jimi did end the song with some ferocious guitar playing that kicked off the "Woodstock Jam." At just under five minutes, the "Woodstock Jam" was Jimi airing out a series of guitar improvisations with the band pacing him as best they could. During the jam, Jimi changed styles several times from psychedelic to a Spanish-flavored groove. Throughout he illustrated how much impact his right thumb made on his playing. Several times during the jam he actually changed notes with his thumb instead of just using it to help play bar chords. "Woodstock Jam" moved directly into "Villanova Junction." An instrumental, "Villanova Junction" made a wonderful contrast to the furious playing in "Woodstock Jam."

It seemed that Jimi was slowing down his set to draw it to a close. He had played "Voodoo Child (Slight Return)," "The Star Spangled Banner," "Woodstock Jam," and "Villanova Junction" as a medley without stops between songs. The crowd was chanting for more as Jimi was winding down to the end of nearly a half hour of playing without a break. Jimi walked off stage, came back, the band was again announced as the Jimi Hendrix Experience, Jimi warmed up for a minute and went into what can only be described as an encore. They moved into an extended version of "Hey Joe" with Jimi making expert use of the blues medium along with the call and response between his voice and guitar. At the end of the song, Jimi made eye contact with Lee and signaled him to play the characteristic closing lick of the song while Jimi stepped up to the microphone and again slid the neck of his guitar against the metal of the stand. The announcer then said "Ladies and gentlemen, thank you so very much" and Woodstock was over. The Woodstock performance was the only show that Gypsy Sun and Rainbows, with that lineup, would ever play.

While Jimi was at Woodstock, he authored "500,000 Halos: an Unfinished Rough Sketch of Woodstock Fest." The opening stanza of the work was:

> 500,000 Halos
> Outshined the mud and history
> We washed and drank in
> God's tears of joy,
> And for once . . . and for everyone—
> The truth was not a mystery

Since Woodstock, a great deal has been written about the festival, but Jimi's sentiments stand among the most prophetic.

The pre-Woodstock atmosphere of jokes and partying at the house in Shokan masked a great deal of tension on the part of Jimi, the other musicians around him, and Jimi's management. Subterfuge was undertaken by the management that made the new musicians surrounding the guitar superstar feel less than welcome. Little care was taken of anyone's gear but Jimi's and money was often withheld. The principal problem was that Jeffery saw Jimi Hendrix as a moneymaker only as part of the Jimi Hendrix Experience (with Noel and Mitch). Minus one or both of these original cohorts or with the inclusion of other musicians, the formula changed and it became clear that Jeffery felt that would adversely affect the bottom line. This, coupled with the general paranoia caused by the drugs that most of the musicians in the new band were doing, only amplified the problem. Sultan, Velez, Cox, and Lee all went on record after Woodstock saying that they felt like they were being pushed out by Jimi's management and that the front office was looking for the return of the original Jimi Hendrix Experience. These external tensions only served to amplify Jimi's own internal struggles to reinvent himself into a musician no longer defined by the Experience.

The Gypsys: Part II

After Woodstock, Jimi remained in New York for a time. Some of the rest of the band headed out in opposite directions, but Jimi stayed in Shokan. He was often spotted in and around Woodstock in his flashy Corvette Stingray as it was the only one of its kind in a part of the state largely dedicated to farming. After continuing to rehearse at the Shokan house for about ten days, Jimi decided to move to the Hotel Navarro in New York.[1] This came on the heels of a meeting with Jeffery that took place in Shokan during which Jimi was pressed into a gig at the Salvation Club in New York. The club and its scene were known to be mob connected at the time and it was unclear whether Jimi was "muscled" into the gig. What was clear was that Jimi again needed access to a studio so the move into the metropolitan area made sense from a work standpoint.

Back in New York City, Jimi got down to work in the studio. He put down tracks for several new songs at the Hit Factory, including "Message to Love," "Easy Blues," "Izabella," and "Beginning." By the end of August he also had worked up "Machine Gun," "Stepping Stone," and "Mastermind." As summer dragged into fall, Jimi began to identify more directly with his black roots. Through the run-up to Woodstock, the Black Panthers organization had frequently visited with Jimi and talked with him about being one of the "brothers." However, Jimi purposefully chose not to identify people by color and instead focused on his music. He had been gaining a greater affinity for those who were less fortunate and had direct experience with the urban black underclass in New York City. To that end, Jimi signed on to play a concert to benefit the United Block Association.[2]

The group that Jimi had on stage with him for the benefit included both black and white musicians and this did not go over well with the Black Panthers at the show. Jimi attempted to maintain his neutrality by saying ". . . . I want to show them that music is universal—there is no white rock or black rock."[3] The concert was officially called the *Jazz Street Festival* and during their set Jimi and his group played a seven-song set. The songs that they played were "Fire," "Foxey Lady," "The Star Spangled Banner," "Purple Haze," "Red House," "Voodoo Child (Slight Return)," and "Machine Gun." This set, along with the set at Woodstock, illustrated Jimi's desire to showcase his most recent songs once they were worked out in the studio. Other major acts were also recruited for the benefit including Sam and Dave[4] and Big Maybelle.[5]

In addition to playing the Harlem benefit, Jimi was still spending time in the studio. He returned to the Hit Factory and recorded "Burning Desire," "Lover Man," "Valleys of Neptune," and "Lord I Sing the Blues." Another aspect of early September was the enormous publicity that Jimi received in the wake of Woodstock. Although Jimi was already an international star, his Woodstock performance had rocketed him to superstardom and everyone wanted a piece. On September 8, Jimi returned to the *Dick Cavett Show* where he was interviewed and performed "Izabella" and "Machine Gun." The band that backed Jimi on the show had been pared down by his management to include only Mitch, Cox, and Jimi—again a power trio. Sultan, Velez, and Lee were omitted as Jeffery tried to strong-arm a "consistent image" for Jimi's backing band. While this was Jeffery's image for the band, Jimi continued to try to bring the players from Woodstock back into the fold—along with other players whose talents Jimi respected.

The September 10 show at the Salvation Club was next on his performance itinerary. Jimi was still locked in a battle with his front office over who he should be playing with and Jeffery's increasing stranglehold was taking its toll on the legendary guitarist. Drug use had long been a part of Jimi's life, but it began to seem to those around him that Jimi's use had escalated from recreational to medicinal to avoid the reality of his contractual agreements. The Salvation Club gig made things worse. Jimi had asked a wide variety of players to join him for the show. Some of these musicians had history that kept them from playing together and soon enough the whole scene blew up. This was made much worse by the alleged mob connections of the club. The core issue at hand was that everyone, especially Jeffery, wanted to control Jimi's new post-Experience direction and Jimi seemed increasingly unable to stop their interference.

Shorty after the Salvation Club gig, Jimi came face-to-face with the fallout of Jeffery's bad choices. From the outside, it seemed that Jeffery had lost control of Jimi's career and with that the seemingly never-ending money that was associated with it. Additionally, through the Salvation Club show, Jeffery seemed to have allied himself with some rather unsavory people in the New York underground and these people now took a vested interest in what Jimi decided to do next. The result of this was completely astounding.

In mid-September, Jimi Hendrix was abducted by four men. According to Jimi himself "[I] was blindfolded and gagged and shoved rudely into the back of a car . . . [and] taken to a deserted building and made to believe that they really intended to hurt me."[6] The purpose of the kidnapping was to try to wrestle control over Jimi's contract away from Jeffery and to make a show of force. As it turned out, Jeffery's connections could be quite persuasive as well and after a while Jimi was rescued by men sent by Jeffery. An oddity of the whole thing was the identity of the original offenders. Upon reflection, Jimi began believing that the whole thing had been a setup by Jeffery to try to get Jimi to trust him again. The basic premise being, Jimi would have to trust Jeffery after Jeffery "saved" him from this ordeal.

Amid this absolute chaos, Jimi returned to the studio. However traumatizing the whole abduction had been, it did not stop him from continuing to record. It was likely the case that the studio was the only place where Jimi truly felt safe and in control of his own destiny. The run-in with the kidnappers did cause Jimi to return to his house in Shokan where he had greater freedom to jam with whoever he chose to surround himself. Unfortunately, it was during this same period that members of the group that played with Jimi at Woodstock started leaving one-by-one. Lee left after beginning to feel like he was in the way and could not take all the outside pressures, bearing in mind that by mid-September he had only been back from Vietnam for two months. Velez also quit. Cox had left; Jimi tried to persuade him to return but he quit anyway. Miles was still with Jimi, but Mitch was fed up and returned to England.

As the confusion only increased, Jimi again headed into the studio. This time he enlisted the assistance of Alan Douglas.[7] Douglas was not sure at first what Jimi expected him to do. However, after watching Jimi jam in the studio for a while Douglas realized that what he could offer the guitar legend was a credible ear in the control room (much as Chas Chandler had provided in the early days). With Douglas in the booth, Jimi went on to record several more tracks at the Record Plant. Douglas' work on Jimi's behalf infuriated Jeffery who saw it as another person trying to serve as the producer and confidante of his talent. The result of all of this was that Jimi began to feel the confidence to sever ties with Jeffery.

BAND OF GYPSYS

As the confusion and level of absurdity increased between Jimi, Jeffery, and Douglas, an old problem again reared its ugly head. Ed Chalpin and PPX resurfaced with a demand for a record to fulfill Jimi's commitment to his original contract. It was decided that a group called the Band of Gypsys would record a live record to give to Chalpin and end the whole mess. By the middle of October the Band of Gypsys were jamming together with Douglas serving as de facto producer. Another addition to the setup was Stefan Bright who had worked with Douglas on several other recordings around 1970. The Band of Gypsys was not the same outfit that played Woodstock; by October it was Jimi, Miles, and Cox. The end of the month was spent rehearsing and preparing to record.

While Jimi felt that the addition of Douglas to the studio would facilitate the creation of a good record, he did not anticipate how much more trouble it would cause him. Jeffery and Douglas immediately clashed over the control of Jimi's work and Jeffery demonized Douglas as someone looking to take his power. In November, Jimi moved again—which is to say that he took up residence elsewhere; he never really moved in the traditional manner because he did not accumulate material belongings in the same way as most people. Also in November, Jimi spent long hours in the studio. He worked with Miles and Cox as well as with other musicians who he was introduced to by Douglas, such as the Last Poets.[8]

Throughout the month of November, Jimi and his new rhythm section tracked the songs that would become the next chapter of his musical journey. Recording of the songs "Izabella," "Ezy Ryder," "Shame, Shame, Shame," and "Room Full of Mirrors" took place at the beginning of the month. As part of Douglas' input on the sessions, he enlisted the help of engineer Tony Bongiovi who ran the "Izabella" recording.[9] The result for the session was that Bongiovi gave Jimi's sound an updated appeal that was more on the funk than the psychedelic side. By the middle of the month, Jimi's unhappiness with the loss of control over his own creative direction really began to show. Although he was still recording, he was not playing live (at least in concert) and his troubles were mounting. He still had an open drug case in Toronto and PPX was becoming increasingly demanding about another record. This was exacerbated by his ongoing feud with Jeffery, the presence of Douglas, lost revenue from cancelled shows, and his ever-increasing outgoing money flow for legal fees. And to make matters even worse, the Warner Brothers label was also waiting for Jimi to send them a marketable product.

Unfortunately, Jimi turned inward during this period of crisis. Instead of letting his music do the talking the way that he had in previous years, he began to escape into his own world through the increasing use of drugs. While he was not alone in this type of behavior, Jimi's drug use was gradually building a wall around him with everyone else on the outside. He did manage to continue to record, although many of the songs he worked on were left temporarily "unfinished"—as he wanted to endlessly woodshed tracks in his quest for perfection. In mid-November he tracked "Look Over Yonder," "Lonely Avenue," "Power of Soul," "Burning Desire," "Cherokee Mist," "Stepping Stone," "Further on up the Road," and others. Sessions toward the end of the month included work on "Burning Desire," "Hear My Train A Comin'," "Lover Man," and "Them Changes." As November dragged to a close, Jimi continued to struggle with life inside and outside the studio. Although he was recording a great deal of material, he felt that little of it was finished.

As December dawned, Jimi had to go back to Toronto for the next stage of his trial. Incredibly, on the way back into Canada Jimi got caught for drug possession again. He was placed back into police custody. On December 10, Jimi was acquitted of all charges—for this particular run-in with the law. While on trial, Jimi was frank and open about his drug use but maintained that the drug possession that he was currently standing trial for was a setup. His honesty won the day, but his problems continued. In fact, behind the scenes Jeffery was working to dismantle the Band of Gypsys for the purpose of reintroducing the original Experience. For reasons only Jeffery knew— which he took to his grave—he did not want Jimi on stage with Miles and Cox. The most direct possibility was that the other two Gypsys were old friends of Jimi's and this was seen by Jeffery as a wedge pushing him out of the picture.

While this was going on in Toronto, Noel's band Fat Mattress began a tour to try to promote their most recent work, their eponymous first album. However, five shows into a scheduled thirty-show run, Noel abruptly left the band and the tour was cancelled. Although the band did release another album (*Fat Mattress 2*), they quietly broke up in early 1970.

Jimi seemed ready to step back into the footlights and signed on for two dates at the Fillmore East, two shows per night. He also continued working in the studio building up a massive amount of recorded material. The December sessions were also at the Record Plant and included tracking for "Message to Love," "Ezy Ryder," "Bleeding Heart," "Power of Soul," "Earth Blues," and several others. While recording at the Record Plant began to slack off, rehearsals for the Fillmore shows began to heat up. The trio worked at Baggy's in New York honing the Fillmore content. Jimi also took a renewed interest in the Electric Lady Studio project. He rededicated himself to being a major financial backer of the studio. This resulted in a great deal of concern on the part of his money handlers and attorney Henry Steingarten who warned Jimi that the new money commitment meant that he had to go back to releasing albums and playing paying live shows.

On New Year's Eve of 1969, the Band of Gypsys (Jimi, Miles, and Cox) took the stage at the Fillmore East for a two-night stand. An interesting side note to these Band of Gypsys shows was that this was the first all-black group that Jimi had staged since he met Chandler several years earlier. Both nights were recorded and subsequently released as a six-song live recording (taken from an amalgam of both nights).[10] The first show exhibited Jimi back in his showman form with all of his guitar-slinger gimmicks coming back into use. He played with his teeth, behind his back, and everything else for which he had become known. According to Cox, Jimi also had a full retinue of guitar effects pedals on stage with him including a Fuzz Face, wah-wah, Uni-Vibe, and Octavia.[11] After the first show Jimi and Bill Graham discussed the performance and Jimi realized that he had not played up to his own standards—regardless of how well it was received by the audience. For the second show, Jimi did not use any of the flash of the first night. Instead he held electric church for a set during which he moved very little, but had everyone in the place, including Miles and Cox, mesmerized.

Although the release was not a "studio" album, it did contain the first releases of the songs played that night. Contained on the *Band of Gypsys* album were the songs "Who Knows," "Machine Gun," "Changes" (credited to Miles), "Power to Love," "Message of Love," and "We Gotta Live Together" (also credited to Miles). The group played a wide range of other songs during the two-night stand at the Fillmore East. However, live versions of songs such as "Izabella," "Fire," and "Foxey Lady" did not make the final cut for the release. The material on the live album was recorded by Wally Heider and remixed and engineered by Eddie Kramer.

A rather disheartening aspect of the only live record that Jimi released during his lifetime was the slight framework, with the inclusion of only six songs. Most reviewers and critics discuss the album as lacking the potency of the Experience and cite the fact that Jimi and the band got thrown into the live recording scenario before they were really ready. Jimi was known for his meticulous studio work, which often frustrated all those around him, but the material released here was not up to his usual standards. "Who Knows" was the first song on the record and found the group in a slow burning and bluesy mood. Jimi had originally written the lyrics of this song on stationery from the Beverly Rodeo Hyatt House.[12] The song itself was really more of a groove that spun out for almost ten minutes with Jimi alternating between singing and taking solos on his guitar. Approximating the standard blues form, Jimi began the song as the group was introduced by laying down the song's signature guitar lick. Once the lyrics begin, the twice-stated vocal couplets do smack of the blues style even if all of the playing far exceeded the style of even the electric blues. The basic topic of the words was Jimi's talking about a woman who had a hold over him that no one else could recognize or understand. There were some standard blues themes in the words with talk of travel (". . . just came back from Mexicali") and a variety of takes on the pain of love and loss.

Possibly the most attractive aspect of the song was the guitar work. Jimi hit his stride about halfway through the song and unleashed electric guitar pandemonium that weaved the opening lick around an extended jam that mixed elements of the blues and Jimi's breed of psychedelia with use of guitar effects including the wah-wah pedal. Of particular interest was that after the midsong solo, Miles took over the singing duties for the rest of the lyrics while Jimi dropped out completely. After Miles sang the final set of words, Jimi again joined the fray with another extended solo during which he essentially let his guitar do the "singing" for him. To end the solo and the song, Jimi brought the opening guitar lick back and used it as an ending.

Before moving on to the second song, Jimi wished the crowd a happy New Year and also dedicated the next song to all of the soldiers fighting in Vietnam (along with those he said were fighting in Chicago, Milwaukee, and New York). He then launched into the opening of "Machine Gun." An easy standout on the album, the song's propulsive and guitar-soaked opening was given greater weight by Miles' rat-a-tat drumming what openly smacked of the sound of gunfire. Grounded in the blues, Jimi's playing on the song was amped up to incredible volumes and levels of guitar mayhem. The lyrics smacked of foreboding and impending death. The whole sentiment of the song was pure fatalism that ". . . doesn't just apply to the lyrics, which bewail evil forces shooting Jimi down repeatedly and tearing his 'family' apart—perhaps a veiled reference to his African-American brothers, dying in Vietnam in numbers hugely disproportionate to their share of the US population."[13]

Jimi's guitar playing on the song was his musical attempt at depicting war through music done to a shockingly convincing effect. He painted a musical portrait of bombs dropping, bullets flying, and senseless death. Just as was the case with "Who Knows," Jimi again let Miles take the vocals for the final words of the song, which clocked in at twelve and a half minutes. The lyrics of the song certainly describe the pain of war controlled by evil men pitting one group against another—another possible meaning could be an autobiographical glimpse at the war raging within Jimi himself for the control of his music. However, the words in the middle of the song discussed a woman of whom Jimi would no longer be afraid as he expected her to cause him pain and then leave. As in several other songs, Jimi seemed to here use the concept of war and its realities to also discuss the torment in his heart.

"Changes," also known as "Them Changes," was the first of the two songs that Miles contributed to the six-song live release. Here Miles took the lead vocal role and controlled the action with both his voice and his drum kit. Essentially describing the negative effects that a woman had on his emotions, Miles offered ". . . little more than a lightweight Stax [Records] R&B riff, to be honest, topped with a melody line that stretched Buddy's voice to the limit."[14] In addition to describing his own personal struggles, Miles reached out and mentioned that everyone had gone through a great number of changes over the past year and specifically pointed to Jimi and Cox as sharing in the struggle. Miles' singing pushed his voice to its outer reaches with the inclusion of some Little Richard–esque hollers. Through the course of the song, Jimi's contributions added some lyrical weight to the overall texture but in general it was Miles who was the centerpiece for the song.

After finishing "Changes," Jimi took a moment to retune his guitar and name-dropped the Southern California Trojans who had, he noted, "beat the hell out of Michigan."[15] He then took off on the extended opening of "Power of Soul," which was also called "Crash Landing" or "Paper Airplanes." With this song, Jimi again took charge of the proceedings and unleashed some howling guitar work that was really the showcase of the number. Again penned on stationery from the Beverly Rodeo Hyatt House, "Power of Soul" had one foot in the blues and the other in the great wide openness of Jimi's mixture of psychedelia and early funk. The lyrics were as straightforward as Jimi got; "with the power of soul, anything is possible." The opening verse discussed a love interest that had been flying her airplane too low and needed to come back to earth with Jimi for a little taste of reality. The chorus followed and was a terse bit of philosophy courtesy of Jimi's individual outlook on the world. Leading out of the first chorus statement, Jimi flexed his guitar skills for a brief statement before diving back into the lyrics. The second verse spoke of a jellyfish that was groovily floating about, but without a backbone it was not going to get anywhere. It is impossible to say if Jimi cast himself as the groovy jellyfish or it was just a convenient metaphor for the freewheeling decade that had just come to a close. Regardless, the song was not the typical guitar showcase that could match up with "Machine Gun." Instead, Jimi and the rhythm section just let the song spin out with the vague image of boundless possibilities. Although the Band of Gypsys have been criticized for having been loose or unrehearsed, this song featured a spot-on, locked-in rhythm section that Jimi was simultaneously part of and also adding layers to.

"Message to Love" began with an impressive ascending opening riff that led straight into the lyrics. Another of Jimi's free-flowing narrative style songs, "Message to Love" unfolded without a traditional verse/chorus arrangement. Overall, the song was much more guitar driven than "Power of Soul." Here Jimi again cast himself as a traveler who was on a quest to set a woman free from her chains. His message of love was summed up about two-thirds of the way through the song when he described men and women as being equal, talented, and children in the eyes of God. Packed with this refreshing sentiment, the song ended in the same way as it had begun with the propulsive ascending opening riff. A notable addition to this song was the three-part harmony that Jimi, Miles, and Cox supplied. The tight layering of the vocals was not part of the standard Hendrix style, but was done to great effect. Stylistically, the song again bridged the gaps between electric blues, psychedelia, soul, and R&B.

The final song on the album was another of Miles' offerings called "We Gotta Live Together." According to Doggett, "Hendrix gifted this second Buddy Miles tune (again, later a minor hit for its composer) with some astonishing guitar playing, as free-flowing and ambitious as anything on the album."[16] The core lyrics of the song were of much less significance than the guitar work. Here Jimi unleashed a series of superb guitar flourishes that really made the piece into a showcase for his playing, more so than a Miles composition. After a first-rate solo during which Jimi burned up and down the neck of his guitar with reckless abandon, the song picked up speed into a power trio free-for-all until unwinding with a series of repeated notes to create an ending.

With this, the Band of Gypsys' one-off live release ended. Jimi had fulfilled his contractual obligations to Chalpin and PPX. What Chaplin had done was parlay the contract that Jimi had signed in 1965 into a one-album deal with Capitol Records. Although Capitol probably wanted a Jimi Hendrix and the Experience album, they settled for the six-song *Band of Gypsys* album. Finally, after all of the legal wrangling and years of trouble, Jimi was no longer beholden to Chalpin, PPX, or Capitol.

What the Gypsys may have lacked in studio-based refinement, they certainly made up for with a direct connection between the three musicians. Jimi knew and trusted Miles and Cox and he had selected them, unlike Mitchell and Redding who Chandler had selected. While the Jimi Hendrix Experience had gone a long way toward defining the 1960s psychedelic music movement, the Band of Gypsys had established a new pocket of style that included elements of psychedelia, electric blues, R&B, soul, and the dawning of funk. Jimi's audience was expanding as were his musical horizons.

In the wake of the Fillmore East shows, Jimi and the band went back in the studio. They continued to record at the Record Plant and jam at Baggy's. In addition, Jimi and Kramer began working on paring down the four shows (two per night) from the Fillmore East with the purpose of turning them into the record that they gave to Capitol. The Band of Gypsys' lineup was interesting insomuch as Jimi and Miles were both used to leading a band—Miles had been running the Buddy Miles Express. This created some friction but also afforded Jimi some freedom that he had not experienced in a while. With Miles in the band, Jimi did not have to emphasize his singing as much since Miles was already an accomplished singer. Jimi himself even admitted that he was more comfortable on stage without having to handle all of the singing duties. He was already playing rhythm and lead guitars, so letting Miles sing more was not such an issue. That said, Jimi did begin to feel that Miles was taking too many liberties with the inclusion of his own material. Through the middle of January, the Band of Gypsys continued to work at the Record Plant and it seemed that Jimi had again caught his stride as he worked with a renewed sense of purpose.

Even as the musical side of Jimi's world was blossoming in fresh and new directions, he had another run-in with his management. By the end of January, Jeffery was again trying to get Jimi to reform the original Experience. Jeffery had already contacted Noel about again working with Jimi, and Mitch was still part of Jimi's inner circle. On January 28, 1970, the Band of Gypsys played the *Winter Festival for Peace* at Madison Square Garden. Although it seemed that Jimi did not know, Noel was now back in New York with the Jeffery-inspired notion that Experience was reforming. Unfortunately, just before the show someone slipped Jimi a tab of acid and he quickly lost his ability to focus on the performance. His longtime roadie Gerry Stickells was trying to convince him to go on stage and carry on with the performance. The band took the stage and tried to get their set started. After about ten minutes of playing,

Jimi simply took off his guitar and sat down on the stage saying that he just could not get it together. Jimi was led off stage and did not return. The Band of Gypsys came to a bittersweet end at the Garden that night. After the show, Jeffery fired Miles and Cox quit the band and with this the Band of Gypsys dissolved.

In the wake of the end of the short-lived Band of Gypsys, Jimi announced in early February that the Experience was reforming. In the statement announcing the return of the Experience, Jimi was careful to note that there would still be time for side projects and that he intended to continue to work with other musicians. Also at this time, work on the Electric Lady Studio construction again halted. Hampered by lack of money, the studio was creating a great financial drain which was made much worse by the fact that Jimi had basically stopped playing live shows. By early 1970, the work on building the studio could only progress with a loan from Warner Brothers Records guaranteed against future royalty earnings.[17] Jimi really needed his own studio as he was basically in residence at the Record Plant and was racking up enormous studio bills. Jeffery met with Warner Brothers executives and secured the loan that would allow Electric Lady Studio to be completed.

The "New" Jimi Hendrix Experience

With the now-impending reformation of the Experience, Jimi needed to somehow reconcile his situation with Noel. After the pair had parted company on such bad terms it seemed unlikely that they would be able to mend their fences. Jimi turned to Mitch for advice and it was agreed that bringing Noel back into the fold would be tricky—regardless of the fact that it seemed that Noel was game to return. Instead, Jimi again enlisted the help of Billy Cox. While the new collective was still not the original Experience, it was closer than the three musicians that had formed the Band of Gypsys or the masses that were on stage with Jimi at Woodstock. This point has led to a great deal of debate concerning what to call the band that Jimi toured with for the rest of his life. The collection of Jimi, Mitch, and Cox was sometimes billed as "the New Jimi Hendrix Experience" and on other concert announcements only Jimi's name appeared. Toward the end of the *Cry of Love* tour the group began to be informally known as Cry of Love.[1] Further complicating matters, Jimi continued to work with other musicians in the studio that he had increasingly surrounded himself with through the later part of the 1960s.

The middle of February again found Jimi in the studio working on the tracks that would be the next album. The live record that he had recorded at the Fillmore East with Miles and Cox was completed and Capitol had the album that Chalpin had promised them. Still, Chalpin did not go away quietly and continued to gripe that the live record did not constitute an Experience release and that was what he was due based on Jimi's original contract.

By March, Noel was back in New York anticipating his return to the studio with Jimi and Mitch. He was again the last to learn that he had been replaced with Cox. The level of confusion and chaos took a direct toll on Jimi's spirits and he decided that he needed a break from all of the goings-on in New York. On March 10 Jimi left for London to reconnect with his old girlfriend Kathy Etchingham. Jimi and Etchingham spent time together during which he relayed to her that he was sick of the whole mess that surrounded him and who he played with. He was also worn out with the idea of being a rock star and just wanted to be a guitar player.

While in London, Jimi also reconnected with Stephen Stills. The pair jammed together and Jimi even overdubbed a guitar part of Still's solo song "Old Time, Good Times."[2] He also spent time with Arthur Lee from the band Love. While it seemed upon his arrival that Jimi wanted to restart a romance with Etchingham, he ended up spending time with Devon Wilson—who was coincidentally also Lee's girlfriend at the time. While in London under the guise of limiting the confusion in his life, Jimi only managed to make it more complicated with promises to several artists to record that never came to fruition. In mid-March, Jimi flew back to New York and returned to the Record Plant with Mitch and Cox. In New York, little had changed in his absence. He was still struggling with Jeffery over how he was being managed and who should be in the group—in addition to what it should be called.

In April, Jimi began gearing up for a United States tour with Mitch and Cox backing him on stage. Several months of dates were scheduled and the tour was to kick off in Los Angeles on April 25. The tour commenced at the Forum in Inglewood, California. Jimi's band was the headliner and the Buddy Miles Express and Ballin' Jack were the openers.[3] The outing was dubbed the *Cry of Love* tour and opened to twenty thousand fans at the Forum. Although technically not the Experience, since Noel was not on stage, Jimi tore through a host of gems from the Experience days along with a healthy dose of newer songs. The set list for the Forum show was "Spanish Castle Magic," "Foxey Lady," "Lover Man," "Hear My Train A Comin'," "Message to Love," "Machine Gun," "Ezy Ryder," "Room Full of Mirrors," "Hey Baby," "Villanova Junction," "Freedom," "The Star Spangled Banner," "Purple Haze," and "Voodoo Child (Slight Return)." Jimi's mood on stage was that of the consummate guitar god. He made little use of the gimmicks for which he had become famous, instead preferring to stand and deliver with furious and scorching guitar power.

The next day the tour moved on to the Cal Expo on the State Fairgrounds in Sacramento, California. The Buddy Miles Express and Blue Mountain Eagle opened for Jimi's group for the Cal Expo show.[4] For the second show of the tour, Jimi changed up the order of the songs from the concert at the Forum. However, he stuck with the same set list and the crowd loved it. The centerpiece of the performance was "Machine Gun" with Jimi using his guitar to amazing effect. The band then moved on to shows at the Milwaukee Auditorium and the Dane County Memorial Coliseum in Madison, Wisconsin. From Wisconsin the group went on to a show on May 4 at the St. Paul Civic Center in St. Paul, Minnesota. Jimi was still not varying the set list much, other than changing the order of the songs. Audience members at these shows did note that he had stuck with the removal of most of the gimmicks in the set and instead choose to stand still and let his performance speak for itself.

On May 4 Jimi made an appearance at the Village Gate in New York as part of a benefit for Timothy Leary. The Village Gate, a famous New York club at the corner of Thompson and Bleeker Streets in Greenwich Village, had a storied history of live performances of a variety of musical styles. For the Timothy Leary benefit, notable artists turned out including Jimi, Jim Morrison, Noel Redding, Johnny Winter, and the poet Allen Ginsberg. Jimi again stuck with the same basic set list for the tour thus far. The next show, on May 8 at the University of Oklahoma, was dedicated to the victims of the shootings at Kent State which had occurred on May 4.

The group next rolled on to Will Rogers Auditorium in Fort Worth, Texas. The show in Fort Worth was backed up by the band Bloodrock.[5] Next the group made an appearance at the HemisFair Arena in San Antonio, Texas. At the San Antonio show, the group was backed by one of the earliest country-rock outfits, a band called Country Funk.[6] The tour then moved on to Temple Stadium in Philadelphia, Pennsylvania, where they were backed by the Grateful Dead, the Steve Miller Band, and Cactus.[7] Of note, Jimi chose to start off this show with two covers, "Sgt. Pepper's Lonely Hearts Club Band" and "Johnny B. Goode." On the heels of the Temple Stadium show, the tour had a week-long break. Jimi and the band returned to New York and the studio where they recorded "Keep on Groovin'" and "Freedom."

The *Cry of Love* tour was scheduled to play in Ohio, Missouri, and Indiana next, but these shows were cancelled as Jimi's health was not good. The tour got back on its feet at the end of the month and on May 30 the band rolled into the Berkeley Community Theater. The Berkeley appearance was for two shows in one night and Jimi again covered "Johnny B. Goode" during the first show. At these shows, Jimi was again in showman mode with all of his guitar tricks of old back in play. The opening act for the Berkeley sets was the group Tower of Power. Interestingly, this was Tower of Power's first professional show and Jimi had them set up their gear and play in front of the curtain, which was less than a desirable situation.

As the summer of 1970 began, Jimi was in the middle of the tour. He was surrounded by a host of hangers-on including Devon Wilson. Wilson was unofficially Jimi's girlfriend at the time, though her groupie reputation put her with several other famous musicians simultaneously. Also at this time, Jimi had enough recorded material in the can to release several albums. He was increasingly interested in what songs to release, how (single album, double album, even triple album), and under what title. The tour launched again in early June with a series of concerts in Texas and Oklahoma backed by Ballin' Jack. On June 9, the tour pulled in to the Mid-South Coliseum in Memphis, Tennessee. Back in Jimi's old stomping grounds, Larry Lee showed up at the concert and met with Jimi. Next the tour swung out to Evansville, Indiana, for a date at Roberts Municipal Stadium. Here Jimi altered the fairly standard tour set list with a performance of the song "Getting My Heart Back Together." Although he had performed this song live in the past, it was not one of the eleven or twelve songs per night that he had been playing from the beginning of the tour.

The June leg of the tour then pressed on to Maryland for a show at the Civic Center in Baltimore with support from Cactus. On June 15, Jimi made his first use of the Electric Lady Studios in New York. The Electric Lady setup was two studio spaces, A and B. While Jimi jammed with Steve Winwood and Chris Wood of the band Traffic in Studio A, work continued on Studio B to make it operational.[8] Once the studios were open, Jimi was very involved in every facet of the recording process. He even enlisted the talents of the legendary guitar pioneer Les Paul.[9] In an interview from 2009, Paul recounted his experiences with Jimi. "Back when Jimi Hendrix opened Electric Lady Studios, he was on the phone all the time, we talked about how to mike a guitar amplifier and where he should place the mike in the studio."[10] Also in the mix at Electric Lady was Eddie Kramer, Jimi's longtime engineer of choice. Kramer assisted with the construction of the studio space and once it was complete he did much to keep it a professional recording space.

After the June 15 jam session, Jimi got right down to work in his new studio. On June 16, Jimi recorded "Night Bird Flying" at Electric Lady and this track was the first official material generated at the new recording space. There followed other Electric Lady recording sessions for tracks including "Straight Ahead," "Drifter's Escape," "Blue Suede Shoes," "Come Down Hard on Me," and "Astro Man." Although he wanted to stay at the new studio, the ongoing tour beckoned Jimi back to the road. On June 19, Jimi, Mitch, and Billy were back on stage—this time at the Civic Arena in Albuquerque, New Mexico. The group next played the Swing Arena in San Bernardino, California, where Jimi started the set with "All Along the Watchtower." The next stop on the tour was the Ventura, California Fairgrounds where the band was backed by Ballin' Jack and Grin.[11] The western leg of the tour ended with a show in Denver, Colorado, at Mammoth Gardens. The group did not have another show until June 27, so they went back into Electric Lady Studios and got down to the work of recording.

From June 24 to June 26, Jimi and the band worked at Electric Lady Studios. They laid down tracks for several more songs, including "Earth Blues" and "Cherokee Mist." The group then played live at the Boston Garden in Massachusetts with Cactus and the Illusion as openers.[12] The group then went back in to Electric Lady Studios and tracked "Drifting," "Dolly Dagger," "Beginning," "Pali Gap," and "Ezy Ryder."

On July 4, 1970, Jimi and the band appeared at the *Atlanta International Pop Festival* at the Middle Georgia Raceway. Other notable artists on the bill for the festival were B. B. King, Mountain, Procol Harum, the Allman Brothers,

Jethro Tull, and Johnny Winter. The set list was much the same as it had been for the tour, but there were several additions. The group played "Fire," "Lover Man," "Spanish Castle Magic," "Red House," "Room Full of Mirrors," "Hear My Train A Comin'," "Message to Love," "All Along the Watchtower," "Freedom," "Foxey Lady," "Purple Haze," "Hey Joe," "Voodoo Child (Slight Return)," "Stone Free," "The Star Spangled Banner," "Straight Ahead," and an instrumental version of the song "Hey Baby (New Rising Sun)." The festival was similar to Woodstock in that it took place outdoors, in a pecan grove and at the race track, and was attended by as many as 350,000 people.

The next night, Jimi and the band played two shows at the Miami Jai Alai Fronton before returning to New York. On July 17, the group played the *New York Pop Festival* at Downing's Stadium on Randall's Island. The concert was a benefit for the Young Lords—a group of Puerto Rican nationalists who fought gentrification in Chicago and subsequently formed regional chapters in cities such as New York, with special interest in Spanish Harlem. Along with Jimi, the bill included acts such as Steppenwolf, Grand Funk Railroad, and Jethro Tull. Jimi's set was a disaster as he had reportedly taken too many drugs waiting to get his turn on stage.

The middle of July was spent back in the Electric Lady Studios. Jimi, Mitch, and Cox cut the tracks for songs such as "Night Bird Flying," "Lover Man," "In From the Storm," "Hear My Train A Comin'," "Drifting," and "Angel." On July 25, Jimi and the group played a show at the International Sports Arena in San Diego. Back out on the West Coast, the group then went to Seattle to play a concert at Sick's Stadium. It was an outdoor concert that was hampered throughout by rain. Regardless, it was another homecoming for Jimi and he spent time during the day with his family. Although the rain was oppressive at times, Jimi still played a solid set showcasing his talents for his father and family members in attendance. The set list that Jimi led the band through on that rain-soaked outing was the same basic collection that he had showcased throughout the *Cry of Love* tour.

Also in attendance at the show was a figure out of Jimi's childhood, Freddie Mae Gautier. She had looked after Jimi when he was a baby and continued to take a vested interest in his happiness as his career blossomed. After the concert, Jimi ended up back at her house where he stayed sequestered from his tour manager.[13] With the Seattle show complete, Jimi's touring for the summer came to an end.

JIMI HENDRIX: *RAINBOW BRIDGE* ORIGINAL MOTION PICTURE SOUNDTRACK

At this same time, Jeffery had concocted a plan to make a movie in Hawaii that involved Jimi. Although Jimi did not have any interest in Jeffery's project, he ended up becoming an unwilling participant. Jeffery knew that the next album that Jimi released was already promised to Warner Brothers, but in his typically wily business fashion Jeffery knew that he could release a "soundtrack" that would not be part of the existing contractual agreement. On July 28, Jimi and his crew embarked for Hawaii. Oddly, the lion's share of the early financing for the movie was procured from Warner Films, which was another mark of Jeffery's business savvy.

The actual filming process was a mess that involved Jeffery, filmmaker Chuck Wein, the Warner Films' crew, and Jimi and the band. Those active in the creation of the film titled *Rainbow Bridge* were Chuck Wein (director), Michael Jeffery and Barry De Prendergast (producers), Charlie Bacis (writer), Pat Hartley (starring actress), and Villis Lapenieks (cinematographer). Also present for the shooting were Mitch and Cox to back up Jimi for his performances along with their basic road crew. The premise of the movie was the spiritual awakening of the Pat Hartley character upon journeying to the Rainbow Bridge location on Maui. Jimi was not taken by the idea at all and wanted little to do with the entire project. However, with Jeffery calling the shots Jimi ended up agreeing to do a performance as part of the filming.

On July 30, Jimi and the band (which went unnamed in the film credits) played a free concert as part of the film process. The concert was staged at the top of the Haleakala volcano in a pasture. The audience numbered in the hundreds and the performance was hampered by high winds. The sound engineer on hand, Mike Neal, had to do his best to shelter the microphones from the wind in order to get any usable audio—a goal that he ultimately failed to achieve. For the film, Jimi and the band played "Dolly Dagger," "Villanova Junction," "Ezy Ryder," "Red House," "Freedom," "Jack Back at the House," "Straight Ahead," "Stone Free," and "Hey Joe." However, there were licensing issues with the majority of this material and little of it ended up appearing in the film.

Ultimately in 1971, Reprise—as a division of Warner Brothers Music—issued an album called *Jimi Hendrix: Rainbow Bridge Original Motion Picture Soundtrack* with a completely different track list. The songs that appeared on the album were culled from recording sessions at Electric Lady Studios, the Record Plant, and TTG Studios from 1968 to 1970. The tracks on the album were "Dolly Dagger," "Earth Blues," "Pali Gap," "Room Full of Mirrors," "Star Spangled Banner," "Look Over Yonder," "Hear My Train A Comin'," and "Hey Baby (New Rising Sun)." In fact, several of the musicians that appeared on the release were not even in Hawaii with Jimi at the time of the taping for the movie.

Two days after the original set in Hawaii, Jimi and the band again performed. This time they took the stage at the International Center Arena in Honolulu. Although unknown to all at the time, this was the last time that Jimi would take the stage for an American concert appearance. The Honolulu show again found Jimi in top form. The group played the fairly standard set list for the *Cry of Love* tour. Their performance marked the end of the American leg of the tour and afterward they all returned to the mainland. Jimi headed back into Electric Lady Studios where he continued to work on the mixes of newer songs. Jimi, Mitch, Cox, and Kramer all worked on tracking and overdubs on songs such as "Dolly Dagger," "Room Full of Mirrors," and "Belly Button Window."

August 25 marked the official opening date of the Electric Lady Studios. The opening coincided directly with the band's planned departure for the European leg of the tour and Jimi was reticent about appearing at the studio so close to having to leave for Europe. He was eventually persuaded and the opening party was a big affair. Various rock and roll luminaries were in attendance including "Yoko Ono, Johnny Winter, Noel Redding, and members of Fleetwood Mac."[14]

The Electric Lady Studios was officially opened in 1970 and remains a fixture in Greenwich Village to this day. Since 2000, several other New York City studios have closed their doors, including Legacy Recording's Studios A509, Philip Glass' Looking Glass Studios, and LoHo Studios in the Lower East Side, as well as upstate's Allaire Studios.[15] Electric Lady Studios' continued presence remains a testament to the care that went into its creation. While Jimi enshrined himself in the space during the last year of his life, many other artists have used these studios to create masterworks of American popular music, including Chuck Berry, Curtis Mayfield, Stevie Wonder, Lou Reed, Guns and Roses, Dave Matthews Band, the White Stripes, Foo Fighters, Bob Dylan, Frank Zappa, and many others.[16]

The studio itself had been built to Jimi's exacting specifications and included his own eclectic views of art and music. Located at 52 West 8th Street in New York City, where it is still, the state-of-the-art studio's façade was a unique outward curving brick wall that immediately distinguished it from the surrounding architecture. The interior of the space was further individualized by a large mural of a mythical woman at the controls of a spaceship. The construction of the space cost more than a million dollars and was supervised by both Eddie Kramer and John Storyk. At Electric Lady, Jimi felt at home and this allowed his creativity to further blossom.

With Electric Lady Studios officially open, Jimi and the band again turned their attention to touring. The European leg of the *Cry of Love* tour was already scheduled and the group left for London at the end of August. After a series of press interviews, the European leg kicked off with an appearance at the *Isle of Wight Festival* on East Afton Farm, Isle of Wight. The festival on the Isle was already legendary from two previous years of well-attended shows and the 1970 show was meant to be even bigger—in fact, this concert reportedly drew around six hundred thousand audience members. Jimi's band was booked along with a litany of other popular recording artists of the day including Kris Kristofferson, Chicago, Free, Donovan, the Moody Blues, Jethro Tull, Joan Baez, the Who, Leonard Cohen, and many others.

As Jimi and the band were among the most famous of those that played the festival that year, they ended up being the final act of the concert. This was a rather difficult position to fill as those in attendance had been watching the previous artists perform for a long period of time. After a delay during which it was uncertain if Jimi would even go on he finally took the stage. Although the concert was technically part of the *Cry of Love* tour, the group performed a series of songs that were not part of the standard tour play list. At the *Isle of Wight Festival*, Jimi and the band played "God Save the Queen," "Sgt. Pepper," "Spanish Castle Magic," "Machine Gun," "Lover Man," "Freedom," "Red House," "Dolly Dagger," "Midnight Lightning," "Foxey Lady," "Hey Baby (New Rising Sun)," "Ezy Ryder," "Hey Joe," "Purple Haze," "Voodoo Child (Slight Return)," and "In From the Storm." The set was a crowd-pleasing success and Jimi and his entourage left for Sweden.

The group was set to play their next show at Tivoli Gardens in Stockholm on August 31. Jimi met with several old friends at the show including his original producer Chas Chandler. Also in attendance was one of Jimi's old flames, Eva Sundquist, with whom Jimi had a child that he inquired about.[17] Although the concert proved to be a nice reunion of sorts, Jimi's performance was off par and overall the show did not go well. The next day the tour rolled on to the Stora Scenen in Göteborg, Sweden. For this concert, the group was supported by Cat Mother & the All-Night Newsboys. Again, the show did not go as well as planned and the European leg of the tour was off to a difficult start.

The tour then moved on to Denmark for a show at the Vejiby-Risskov Hallen. As was the custom, Jimi did press interviews prior to the evening's concert. Although out of sorts, Jimi shocked interviewer Anne Bjorndal with the statement "I don't think that I will live to be 28."[18] The concert that night was a disaster as Jimi only managed to play "Freedom," "Message to Love," and "Hey Baby (New Rising Sun)" before collapsing on stage. With this, the show ended. Jimi's long mistreatment of his body with drugs and drink, coupled with his seemingly constant psychological turmoil, were catching up with him. A week before this concert, Jimi had met Danish model Kirsten Nefer and she had become his companion during the opening set of European concerts. After a disastrous Demark show, he made a momentary escape with her from the rigors of the road.

The next tour date was the following day at the K. B. Hallen in Copenhagen, Denmark. Here the group was supported by the band Blue Sun and it seemed that Jimi had gotten his touring legs back under him.[19] The show was lauded as one of their best in recent memory and Jimi even entertained an encore coming back on stage and playing "Hey Joe" and "Fire." The set for the show lasted almost two hours and included sixteen songs. The group was then scheduled to play at *Super Concert '70* at the Deutschlandhalle, in Berlin, Germany. This was the sixth concert appearance in six days in four different countries.

The *Super Concert* appearance was with several other major acts of the period. Others on the bill that night included Canned Heat, Procol Harum, Ten Years After, and Cat Mother & the All-Night Newsboys. Again, Jimi put on a clinic of guitar mastery while Mitch and Cox locked in the rhythmic grooves. For reasons only known to Jimi, he significantly altered the *Cry of Love* tour play list. For the *Super Concert* show, the band played "Straight Ahead," "Spanish Castle Magic," "The Sunshine of Your Love," "Hey Baby (New Rising Sun)," "Message to Love," "Machine Gun," "Purple Haze," "Red House," "Foxey Lady," "Ezy Ryder," "Hey Joe," "Power of Soul," and "Lover Man." The band was next scheduled to play the *Open Air Love and Peace Festival* on the Isle of Fehmarn on September 6.

Jimi and the band were originally scheduled to play on September 5, but bad weather had delayed several of the other performers and pushed Jimi's set onto the following day. Tension at the concert was high with the delays and Jimi's roadie, Gerry Stickells, was assaulted while at the concert grounds. The audience in attendance on Sunday was unruly and because of this the band was on edge. All of which was exacerbated by Cox, who was becoming increasingly paranoid as the tour wore on. Even with these distractions, Jimi and his rhythm section took the stage in the midafternoon and led those in attendance on a thirteen-song odyssey that encompassed most of the guitarist's career which culminated with "Room Full of Mirrors," "Purple Haze," and "Voodoo Child (Slight Return)."

After the concert, Jimi and his entourage barely escaped the grounds with their equipment intact. Jimi returned to London and booked himself into the Cumberland Motel to recover. Over the course of the next several days, Jimi spent time with several of his female acquaintances who were in the city. On September 14, Jimi relaxed with his old flame Monika Dannemann who was helping shield him from all of the stress and tension of the tour, his management, and business dealings. At the same time, Kirsten Nefer fell out of Jimi's scene. Jimi and Dannemann spent time together for the next few days including putting in a couple of appearances at Ronnie Scott's club. By mid-September, Jimi was visibly strung out from the road and various drugs. This was made worse by the fact that Cox had gotten so paranoid that he had to return to the United States to get himself back together.

Jimi was briefly reunited with Chas Chandler and the two spoke about Jimi's career and the direction that his most recent recording sessions had taken. Jimi remained dissatisfied with his own work and again tried to enlist Chandler to come on board to help him achieve the type of sound he desired. The pair agreed to meet again to further discuss their future plans.

Although he maintained a room at the Cumberland Hotel, Jimi began staying with Dannemann at the Samarkand Hotel. Together the pair visited with friends and business acquaintances including Alan Douglas. With Douglas, Jimi decided that he needed to sever all business ties to Jeffery and make a radical change in his career direction. On September 16, Jimi turned up again at Ronnie Scott's and wanted to play with Eric Burdon, who was jamming there that evening.

The following day, Douglas headed back to New York to put into play the plan of removing Jeffery from Jimi's management. Jimi spent the day with Dannemann and they began to make plans for a future together. During the afternoon, Jimi connected with Mitch who informed him that Sly Stone was coming to town. With excitement, Jimi asked if there was a chance that everyone could get together and jam and Mitch told him that there was already a session set up for that evening at the Speakeasy.[20]

Jimi never showed up for the Sly Stone jam session at the Speakeasy. He was staying with Dannemann at the Samarkand Hotel where the two had spent the evening together. This location was where Dannemann took the last known picture of Jimi, standing in a garden. The Samarkand Hotel was located on Lansdowne Crescent in the Notting Hill area. On the morning of September 18, Dannemann woke before Jimi and went out for cigarettes. When she returned Jimi had vomited in bed and she was unable to wake him. She called an ambulance. The paramedics on the scene tried to revive Jimi without success. He was taken to St. Mary Abbots Hospital where doctors cleared his airway and attempted to resuscitate him. It was reported that Jimi's stomach contents contained quite a bit of red wine (he and Dannemann had shared a bottle the prior evening) and that he had taken sleeping pills before bed. At age twenty-seven Jimi Hendrix was pronounced dead by Dr. John Bannister at 12:45 p.m. The official cause of death was inhalation of vomit due to barbiturate intoxication.

The circumstances surrounding Jimi's death remain uncertain. Like much rock lore, everyone who surrounded Jimi at the time had a different take on exactly what happened. Reports by Dannemann, the paramedics who came to the hotel, and the attending physician created a haze that has yet to be completely lifted.

The rumors swirling around Jimi's death did a great disservice to the life of the legendary guitarist. Many papers printed stories about his final days that were filled with misinformation. To make matters worse, the police in both the United States and England seemed to help perpetuate myths about Jimi's character and drug use. Both Warner Brothers and Michael Jeffery had substantial insurance policies out on Jimi and with the stories circulating that his death was drug related the insurers were remiss to settle—as they would consider a drug-related death a suicide and therefore not have to honor the policy.

On September 21, Jimi's body was subjected to an autopsy. The official findings of the examination were not immediately made public. The inquisitor, Professor Donald Teare, first needed to question key people about Jimi's state of mind just prior to his death. After questioning Gerry Stickells, Monika Dannemann, and coroner's officer Station Sergeant John Shaw, Professor Teare concluded the following:

> [The sleeping pill Jimi took was] . . . identified as Vesparaz [sic-actually Vesperax], a German compound barbiturate containing a fairly high dose of

short-acting quinalbarbitone (150 mg) and a smaller dose (50 mg) of intermediate-acting Brallobarbitone. The normal dose was half to one tablet to be taken half an hour before retiring. However, Monika stated that at times she took a whole tablet and on that basis, the coroner concluded that Jimi had taken nine times the normal dose. Teare also estimated Jimi had 100 mg per 100 ml of alcohol in his blood at the time he took the pills. Of itself the amount of alcohol was not significant—enough to fail a breathalyzer test, but only the equivalent of about four pints of beer. However, the forensic literature showed that this amount, taken with the (at least) 1.8 gms of barbiturate that Jimi took, would potentiate the effects of the drugs enormously. In addition, Professor Teare identified 20 mgs of amphetamine and cannabis.[21]

With this, the conclusion was drawn that there was no evidence that Jimi committed suicide—he had in fact accidently overdosed on sleeping pills, vomited while unconscious, and suffocated.

On September 28, Jimi's body was flown to Seattle for a private family funeral. In addition to Jimi's family, several of his most intimate friends also attended the service. On hand were the original members of the Experience, John Hammond, Johnny Winter, Miles Davis, Buddy Miles, Eddie Kramer, and several others. The funeral was held at the Dunlap Baptist Church during which family members and close friends spoke on Jimi's behalf often marveling that someone with such a difficult early life had gone on to such great success. After the service, Jimi's coffin was taken to Greenwood Cemetery in Renton, Washington. With his passing, Jimi joined a number of rock luminaries who suffered untimely deaths under mysterious circumstances between 1969 and 1971—Brian Jones, Janis Joplin, and Jim Morrison (Joplin and Morrison were also both twenty-seven when they died). As an unofficial memorial to Jimi, Mitch, Noel, Miles Davis, and Johnny Winter staged a jam session at the Seattle Arena after the funeral.[22]

Jimi Lives On: Selected Posthumous Albums

When Jimi died, he had not released a studio album in almost two years. The vault of unreleased material that he, and various other musicians, had recorded during that period represents a substantial catalogue. He had spent countless hours in the studio with a host of musicians and he left behind a treasure trove of unreleased material. Progressively, since his death, these songs have been gradually coming to light. Immediately following his death, a host of albums were released—some sanctioned, most not. Since then, new songs and new versions of previously released material have continued to surface. As a true testament to Jimi's songwriting and performing skills, the world continues to wait for future releases. To satisfy this insatiable appetite for all things Jimi, further releases continue to trickle out of the vaults.

Almost immediately after his death, Track Records released "Voodoo Child (Slight Return)" as a single that climbed to the number one spot on the United Kingdom charts. Much behind-the-scenes wrangling ensued concerning what would become of the unreleased material that Jimi had left on tape. Jeffery enlisted Eddie Kramer—who clearly had the most direct connection to Jimi in the studio after serving as his longtime engineer—to construct the first album to be released after Jimi's death. Toward the end of his life, Jimi had been envisioning making his next record at least a double album. However, when the first posthumous album came out it was released as a single album—possibly a move to milk as much money out of a now finite amount of material.

CRY OF LOVE

The *Cry of Love* album was issued in March 1971 by Reprise Records as a division of Warner Brothers Music. Jimi, Eddie Kramer, and Mitch Mitchell were all listed as producers on the album. Michael Jeffery was listed as the executive producer and the album's material was all recorded at Jimi's Electric Lady Studio. Mitch went on record at the time as saying that he had no doubt that had Jimi lived the record would have been quite different, but that every effort was taken to make decisions about the album based on his and Kramer's shared experiences with Jimi. The musicians on the album were Mitch on drums, Cox on bass, the Ghetto Fighters (Albert and Arthur Allen) as backing vocals on "Freedom," Buzzy Linhart on vibes (vibraphone) for "Drifting," Stevie Winwood and Chris Wood on backing vocals for "Ezy Ryder," Miles on drums for "Ezy Ryder," Gers on harp for "My Friend"—there does not in fact seem to be a person called Gers; instead the proper credit should have been given to Paul Caruso—Noel Redding on bass for "My Friend," and Emeretta Marks on backing vocals for "In From the Storm."

The liner notes for the release describe the album as among Jimi's "most personal and revealing albums in the Jimi Hendrix catalog." The album consisted of ten original songs by Hendrix including "Freedom," "Drifting," "Ezy Ryder," "Night Flying Bird," "My Friend," "Straight Ahead," "Astro Man," "Angel," "In From the Storm," and "Belly Button Window." Although Jimi was already gone, Kramer and Mitch mixed the record to sound as close as it could to what they believed Jimi's intentions had been for each track. That said, it should not be forgotten that at the time of his death Jimi was envisioning his next release as a double album. Upon its release, the album reached number three on the American charts and number two in the United Kingdom.

The album began with the cut "Freedom." Here Jimi laid bare his feelings about the basic right for autonomy. Even more so, the song was about freedom from heroin addiction. As Doggett stated, "[I]ts lyrical theme was not just political, but romantic, with a chilling reference to his girlfriend's heroin addiction in the first verse (widely quoted as referring to Devon Wilson)."[1] In the second verse Jimi directly stated that his girlfriend was hooked by the drugstore man and that all he could do was try to "slap it out of her hand." The third verse contained the sentiment that Jimi was calling for freedom by having the "dagger" stuck into someone else so that he could get away. The three verse statements reiterated this feeling with the lyric "freedom, so I can live." Musically, the song was a funky romp with an active bass part. Jimi engaged in significant call and response between his vocals and his guitar lines. The core of the performers on the song was Jimi, Mitch, and Cox with the addition of Arthur and Albert Allen (the Ghetto Fighters) as background vocalists, and Juma Sultan on congas.

Track two was the song "Drifting" which used the same core trio as listed above with only one addition. Buzzy Linhart was brought in to overdub a vibes part. "That was [recorded] posthumously, it was very emotional for me . . . most of the things had been done, but he was telling Eddie and Mitch that he didn't know whether to add on 'Drifting' another rhythm guitar or vibes. We rented some vibes and there were no charts written out."[2] The song was a slow grooving ode to sadness with very few words. It was primarily a wordless pastiche of guitar and vibes that painted a picture of redemption through love—one of Jimi's more oft-visited song topics. Here Jimi used the image of being adrift in an ocean of sadness from which he could be rescued by a lifeboat of love. An interesting effect used during the recording was playing one of Jimi's rhythm guitar parts backwards which produced an almost organ or electric pianolike sound.

Jimi's guitar muscle was in full force on the next track, "Ezy Ryder." Often described as overcrowded with multiple guitar parts, the frenzied nature of the song expertly painted the desperation of its central character. The biker life that the song described was filled with the freedom of the road coupled with the double-edged sword of despair. Jimi posed questions about how long the rider could last and what would become of him—was he riding off to his own death? The result was that the rider (maybe an autobiographical reference to Jimi himself) was free to chase his own path for the day. Lyrically, Jimi set the two verses of the song between an opening and closing chorus statement that smacked of wild abandon.

Musically, Jimi began work on "Ezy Ryder" with the Band of Gypsys at the Record Plant in December 1969. Cox had come up with a basic bass pattern that Jimi layered his myriad guitar lines over. ". . . I had [the bass pattern] and didn't know what to do with it. Jimi built on it from there and it became a living, breathing, song, rather than just a combination of patterns."[3] The musicians on the track harkened back to the Band of Gypsys days with Jimi, Miles, and Cox as the core group. To this was added Juma Sultan on congas, and Steve Winwood and Chris Wood on backing vocals.

On "Night Bird Flying," Jimi went with a more stripped-down band setup. The core trio of Jimi, Mitch, and Cox was only augmented by Juma Sultan on cowbell. According to Doggett, "it [was] built on the foundations of a piece called 'Ships Passing Through the Night,' introduced into Hendrix's repertoire in 1968."[4] Further, it was a tribute to the Alison Steele whose on-air persona was "the Night Bird." Steele was born Ceil Loman (1937–1995) and was a Manhattan DJ on WNEW-FM. Her show was broadcast in high fidelity and became a bastion of 1960s and early-1970s counterculture. She championed the music of the psychedelic and progressive rock bands like Yes, Jefferson Airplane, and Jimi Hendrix. Her nightly introduction included words that Jimi adopted for the lyrics of this song. Lyrically, Jimi painted a picture of a benevolent female figure who carried him through the night, wrapping him in her protective wings, until he was safely delivered to the next morning. Jimi again presented the lyrics of this song with chorus statements to begin and end, thereby bookending the two internal verses.

"My Friend" was a steady talking blues during which a lengthy story unfolded. Musicians on the song were numerous with Jimi and Cox as the main players along with drummer Jimmy Mayes. Added to this were Paul Caruso on harmonica, Stephen Stills on piano, Kenny Pine on 12-string guitar, and members of Mitch Ryder's Detroit Wheels who lent various cheers and applause. The rollicking and free-flowing tale that Jimi told in the story was about a series of events from encounters in his life. He began by recounting his running into a woman on the street in Harlem who asked him up to her room to which he is meant to bring "a bottle and a president." He then moved on to an episode in Los Angeles, which was followed by a verse begun by the account of getting busted in Scandinavia and spending time in jail. The form of the song was classic Jimi, with long and rambling verse statements each of which ended with a short recurring chorus statement.

Track six on the album was "Straight Ahead," the title of which sounded like it was drawn straight from the end of the lyrics of "Freedom." "Straight Ahead" again cast Jimi as the master of 1960s psychedelia. Tracking for the song began at Electric Lady Studios on June 16, 1970, and (at the time) constituted Jimi's first concerted effort to put together a fourth album. Here Jimi, Mitch, and Cox were at full force with driving rhythms and scorched earth guitar work. The song's working title had been "Pass It On" but this lacked the force and potential that the song actually contained. Jimi penned "Straight Ahead" as his contribution to the civil rights movement in 1970. With lyrics such as "power to the people" and "freedom of the soul," Jimi was calling people together to lift up their voices and be heard. He also put a fine point on the sentiment that children needed to be told the truth and loved as they were the leaders of the future.

"Astro Man" again tapped into Jimi's fascination with superheroes and cartoons. He reportedly loved Mighty Mouse and Rocky and Bullwinkle to the extent that he actually began the song with Mighty Mouse's famous herald "Here I come to save the day." Jimi's interest in cartoons actually encompassed the creation of a pair of his own superheroes: Astro Man and Strato-Woman. The original lyrics of the song included the subtitle "The Cosmic Lovers of the Universe and Everything." In the song itself, Jimi fashioned himself into Astro Man, a figure who could outdo Superman, Donald Duck, and all the rest.

Musically, Jimi's guitar smacked of the surf guitar styling of Dick Dale or the Ventures. In fact the opening guitar sounded like it could be the beginning of "Wipe Out." The middle of the song separated the two halves with an extended guitar solo during which the rest of the band was content to mark time. The song itself was Jimi indulging in his comic book fantasies of superstrength and the ability to fly. The guitar work on the track was playful, but still up to the solid quality of much of Jimi's other work. The song ended by fading out with swirling guitar as Astro Man took to the sky and he blew "out the rest of your mind."

According to Billy Cox, the inspiration for the bass line in "Angel" came from "an old record we loved called 'Cherry Pie.' That gave the record the feel of those great 1950's R&B ballads."[5] The song "Cherry Pie" was written by Marvin and Johnny and popularized by Skip and Flip. Much of the basic material for the song had been around since 1967, but Jimi never felt comfortable enough with it to include it on an earlier album. Jimi created the song in the mold of the classic rock and roll ballad—a type of song that he did not seem to favor. The genesis of the lyrics reportedly came from a dream that Jimi had about his mother, Lucille. Jimi continued to work on the song until just a few months before his death. That said, Jimi's own sketchbooks reflect that he had fully realized the lyrics by January 14, 1968. In 1972, Rod Stewart famously remade the song and scored a hit.

Musically, the version that appears on the *Cry of Love* album was pretty sparse. The only instrumentalists that appeared on the track were Jimi, Mitch, and Cox. Further, the only significant effects used on recording were an echo on Jimi's voice which added an ethereal quality and a guitar effect that produced an organlike sound. The song was not characteristic of Jimi's output in a variety of ways—which does not diminish its quality in any way. First, it was a ballad of which Jimi wrote few. Second, Jimi's vocals are pushed forward in the mix which was not a customary position of them on most of his tracks. Lyrically, the song comprised two alternations of verse and chorus material. The verses were professions of love between Jimi and the "Angel" character and the choruses were glorious and ". . . as graceful as his more celebrated rockers were hard-driving."[6]

"In From the Storm" was classic electric blues with a psychedelic tinge. Jimi opened the song with a two-line lyric which was immediately repeated—in the standard blues style. The first two-thirds of the song was heavily blues related. After a solo and a tempo change the song kicked into high gear for the final third. Musicians on this track were Jimi, Mitch, Cox, and Emeretta Marks who supplied all of the high vocal harmonies. Back in the mold of his earlier blues-based hits, Jimi's vocals were perfectly counterbalanced by his guitar and the rhythm section.

Cry of Love ended with the track "Belly Button Window." The song was written about Jimi's impressions of what it must have been like for Aysha, Mitch and Lynn Mitchell's daughter, while she was still in her mother's womb. The content of the lyrics were the thoughts of the unborn child. Issues discussed included Aysha's process of deciding whether to be born or return to spirit land, her experience that it was dark in the womb, and her hope that she would not be born late. Clearly, Jimi's imagination took hold and this was exemplified when he laid down his vocal tracks during which he periodically giggled into the microphone. One version of the lyrics, penned in Jimi's own hand, was titled "Mr. and Miss Carriage."

Musically, the song was a soft-spoken blues with very light instrumentation. Jimi recorded the song without backing vocals or rhythm section. The sparse texture included only Jimi singing and playing guitar. His guitar part was akin to the electric blues players such as B. B. King. There were some moments where the guitar took center stage, but for the most part he used it to mark time behind his vocals. He chose to end the song by whistling a short riff instead of singing. The final recording of this song was made at the end of August 1970, on a four-track recorder and is generally believed to be the last song that Jimi recorded.

EXPERIENCE—MORE EXPERIENCE—THE LAST EXPERIENCE

The next Jimi Hendrix product that surfaced was a slapdash live recording of the show at Royal Albert Hall from the concert recorded there on February 24, 1969, called *Experience*. The record was issued on the Ember imprint in England and never made the charts. Four songs were included on the release with only one of them an actual Jimi original. Track one was Jimi's take on the Cream's hit "Sunshine of Your Love." While Jimi, Mitch, and Noel did a wonderful send-up of the popular song, the concert actually began with the song "Lover Man." Track two was "Room Full of Mirrors" with guests Dave Mason on guitar, Chris Wood on flute, and Rocki Dzidzornu on bongos. Next the recording moved on to Jimi's take on the Elmore James standard "Bleeding Heart." The less-than-pleasing release ended with the sounds of the band smashing their equipment at the end of the show. With the market progressively getting flooded by material of this sort, those who would protect Jimi's legacy began getting worried. In fact, two more similar albums—*More Experience* and *The Last Experience*—along with several singles did little more than begin to erode the high levels of quality that Jimi had always strived for in his releases.

RAINBOW BRIDGE

On the heels of the *Experience* and *Cry of Love* releases, many fans wondered if there were still more unreleased gems that had been held back. This had been a strategic move which was substantiated by the release in late 1971 of the *Rainbow Bridge* album. According to its name, this release should have been the soundtrack associated with the *Rainbow Bridge* film project. Quite the opposite, the *Rainbow Bridge* record contained a strange mixture of studio recordings which Jimi had made over the period of 1968 to 1970. The album also included one live cut and seemed to be a money-grabbing effort as the material on the record did not have the internal cohesion that marked much of Jimi's earlier work.

The *Rainbow Bridge* album was a true compilation. It seemed that little effort had been made to create an album that worked as a unit. Further, the wide range of dates and sessions from which the songs on the album were collected involved multiple different band lineups. It also spanned the majority of Jimi's career—almost like a greatest hits album. The release seemed to reflect an interest on Jeffery's part to milk as much money as possible out of Jimi's legacy on the heels of his untimely death—in fact, Jeffery had already set into motion plans to release a series of live-show recordings that started with Jimi's performance at the *Isle of Wight Festival*.

The tracks collected on the *Rainbow Bridge* album were "Dolly Dagger," "Earth Blues," "Pali Gap," "Room Full of Mirrors," "Star Spangled Banner," "Look Over Yonder," "Hear My Train A Comin'," and "Hey Baby" which is now more commonly known as "Hey Baby (New Rising Sun)." The credited producers for the record were Jimi, Mitch, Kramer, and John Jansen. Jeffery took executive producer credit for the project.

Track one was the first official appearance of "Dolly Dagger" on a Jimi Hendrix record. Jimi had played the song live for some time but it failed to appear on any previous studio release. The recording of "Dolly Dagger" that appeared on this album was made with Jimi, Mitch, and Cox, plus Juma Sultan on congas and Arthur and Albert Allan (the Ghetto Fighters) on backing vocals. Jimi's guitar sound was modified through the use of the Uni-Vibe pedal and Cox used a fuzz effect on his bass. The sound of the song illustrated Jimi taking the band to the next level—in fact, Jimi intended to make this song his next A-side single before he died.

The story of the lyrics of "Dolly Dagger" has long been a topic of discussion. Toward the end of the song, Jimi called out one of his girlfriends, Devon Wilson, who was in the control room during the recording with the line "Watch out Devon, give me a little bit of that heaven." The original rough tracks for the song had been laid down at the Record Plant, but those were replaced with the material cut at Electric Lady at the beginning of July 1970. The overall feel of the lyrics was one of genuine affection. Although Jimi did make it sound at times like Dolly/Devon was getting the best of him, he remained playful and committed. Again, Jimi's interest in comic book heroes surfaced with a reference to Superman in the second verse.

Musically, the mood of the song was a combination of blues and funk with a psychedelic edge at times. The inclusion of the Ghetto Fighters on high male harmonies gave the song an interested funk leaning but much of Jimi's guitar work was straight-ahead electric blues. The overdubbed guitar lines had a more psychedelic edge which created an interesting musical stew. Add to that the sound of the drum cadence and the overall band sound in the final third of the song and it seemed that Jimi and the group were right in step with Curtis Mayfield and his work on the songs like "Shaft." The strength of tracks like "Dolly Dagger" pushed *Rainbow Bridge* to number fifteen in the United States and number sixteen in the United Kingdom.

"Earth Blues" had much in common with the sound of "Dolly Dagger." Here the core group was Jimi, Miles, and Cox. To this was added the Ronettes (Veronica Bennett, Estelle Bennett, and Nedra Talley) on harmony vocals along with Juma Sultan on percussion. Jimi again ran his guitar through the Uni-Vibe. The recording for this track came from January 20, 1970.

Another of Jimi's electric blues send-ups, "Earth Blues" was a rock solid example of Jimi at full potency. Doggett described the lyrics of the song as ". . . a careful combination of political and gospel motifs, while only hinting ('don't get too stoned, please remember you're a man') at a more personal subtext."[7] An interesting mixture of civil rights call-to-action, '60s flower power love fest, and cautionary drug use warning, Jimi still managed to get the whole thing to hang together. Even with the seemingly scattered lyrics, the music of the track was pure psychedelic blues mastery.

The next song on the album was "Pali Gap," which was an artful and wordless exploration of the guitar. Mitch and Cox took a back seat and let Jimi hold court with ever-higher runs up the neck of his guitar. Juma Sultan was again along for added percussion instrument playing, but the whole track served to highlight Jimi's playing ability at the height of its power. The track was recorded in early July 1970 and still stands as a testament to Jimi's ability to paint a musical picture without words. The various overdubbed guitar parts intermingled as Jimi built tension toward the end of the song. Apparently, Jeffery had given the song a Hawaiian-sounding name for purposes of the movie. Pele (as per Jeffery "Pali") is the Hawaiian goddess of the volcano and fire and Jeffery used this to his own marketing advantage. During recording, the song was known to its players as "Slow Part."

"Room Full of Mirrors" was next up with Jimi, Miles, and Cox back as the core group with the addition of Juma Sultan on various percussion parts. Like "Pali Gap," this song was also recorded in early July 1970. Musically, the song was another of Jimi's hard-driving blues explosions with plenty of psychedelic guitar leanings thrown in for spice. Jimi again employed guitar effects including the Octavia pedal for the track in addition to creating a slide effect.

The lyrics of the song were described by Jimi himself as trying to end what he saw as his own self-centeredness. He was essentially talking about trying to get out of a mode of living where no matter where you looked all you saw was yourself looking back—a true room full of mirrors. Two-thirds of the way through the song's lyrics it seemed as though Jimi had found his redemption—again through love—and that the sun finally replaced his own image. Toward the end of his career, Jimi repeatedly engaged with the notion of redemption of a broken figure (presumably himself)—redemption through love, music, drugs, almost anything.

Next up was one of the many renditions of "The Star Spangled Banner" that Jimi recorded in the final years of his life. This particular version was quite far removed from Jimi's more famous performance from Woodstock.

Here, Jimi's playing of the national anthem was "a multi-dubbed studio concoction, taped during his first ever 16-track session in March 1969."[8] Unlike Jimi's version of Francis Scott Key's work at Woodstock, the *Rainbow Bridge* album version was an experiment in the creation of new sounds on the guitar, both with the use of the Octavia pedal and through the combining of multiple guitar overdubs.

"Look Over Yonder" was also known as "Mr. Bad Luck." The roots of the song ran deep with Jimi as it was a tune that he had been performing in some form since the earliest days of his career with Jimmy James and the Blue Flames in 1966. Musically, the track included parts provided by Jimi, Mitch, and Noel that were recorded at TTG Studios on October 22, 1968. "Look Over Yonder" was a bit of early electric blues with a driving psychedelic tinge. The middle of the song was a pounding chorus that repeated the song's title words. However, the lyrics of the two verses of the song were evocative of a few images from Jimi's life. The lyrics began with Jimi singing about the blues. However, he changed his tack quickly from the blues style to the emotion of the blues. He then parlayed that into a reference to the police in their blue uniforms. Jimi went on to discuss himself getting harassed by the police to the extent that they even broke his guitar strings. During the second verse, he turned the prism and his woman became the subject of the police's attention. He detailed this woman getting picked up for holding his smoking pipe. The second verse ended with Jimi warning the police (or in general, the blues) to stay away from him unless they wanted a fight.

After "Look Over Yonder," the album moved on to a twelve-minute version of "Hear My Train A Comin'." This was the single live track on the album. It was recorded at Berkeley Community Center by Wally Heider Recording on May 30, 1970. The band was Jimi, Mitch, and Cox and the majority of the song was composed of extended guitar jams as the lyrics were not numerous. The song began in the electric blues model with the band beginning and then the lyrics kicking in with the opening line being repeated twice. Jimi then moved into an extended guitar solo before properly getting into the first verse. Verse one was about Jimi's desire to leave a lonesome place and his desire to hop a train to escape his feelings of isolation. The second half of the first verse placed Jimi as a sad figure with tears in his eyes over lost brothers (presumably from Vietnam or the civil rights movement), loneliness, and lost love.

The second chorus statement was again followed by an extended guitar solo. The solos grew more effects laden and psychedelic in sound as the song progressed. The second verse reiterated Jimi's desire to escape his troubled circumstances to return to the freedom of the road. The language of the second verse began to sound like Jimi was referencing Seattle, his birthplace. Verse two progressed with Jimi discussing getting out on the road and making enough money to buy the town and give it to his lover. Jimi's adult life left several documents that attested to his disfavor for Seattle. He rarely returned and usually when he did he had to be coerced. Jimi's childhood in Seattle was filled with sadness as his father was away in the military and his mother often left him in the care of others. After another chorus statement, Jimi soloed over light beat keeping by the rhythm section for several more minutes before the song ended as he repeated the title words, just like the song began. Arguably Jimi's finest blues number, "Look Over Yonder" remains a timeless example of Jimi's guitar playing mastery in the line of blues guitarists that was begun with Robert Johnson.

The final song on the album was "Hey Baby (New Rising Sun)." This song appeared under a variety of different titles including "Hey Baby (The Land of the New Rising Sun)," "Gypsy Boy (New Rising Sun)," and simply "Hey Baby." The musicians on the track were Jimi, Mitch, Cox, and Juma Sultan on percussion. Jimi's guitar playing on the track was extremely strong and began with him exploring an opening riff that moved experimentally through a host of different keys before settling into a groove that was similar in sound to his take on "All Along the Watchtower." The record that was used for this album was made "live in the studio" on July 1, 1970, at Electric Lady Studios. The impromptu nature of the recording was made clear when Jimi asked "Is the mic even on?" That alone would have prevented Jimi from ever using this version as a studio release, but did not stop Jeffery.

Throughout the song, Jimi's guitar work was an exhibition of his skills at full strength. He made use of the Uni-Vibe guitar effect to enhance his sound and put some teeth into his guitar work. Lyrically, Jimi's lyrics again focused on one of his principal topics: him chasing or interacting with a female relationship interest. The first half of the song cast Jimi as the pursuer who was working to convince the woman to take him with her "for a ride." The second half of the song was separated from the first with an extended guitar solo. After the solo, the woman agreed to take Jimi with her and he peppered the lyrics with some of his favorite images—like science fiction with a reference to Jupiter's sands. The song wound down with Jimi continuing to riff to the woman with both his voice and guitar about the two of them getting together.

ISLE OF WIGHT

In the wake of the release of the *Rainbow Bridge* album, Jeffery continued to flood the market with Jimi's material with little to keep him in check. One month after the release of *Rainbow Bridge*, Jeffery released Jimi's *Isle of Wight* performance as a live album in the United Kingdom and other parts of Europe. The record topped out at the seventeenth position on the United Kingdom charts. Recorded by the Pye Mobile truck on August 3, 1970, Jimi's backing band for the concert was Mitch and Cox. Jimi and the band had not taken the stage until about two in the morning and although exhausted they put in an inspired set with a long list of songs. The tracks that were included on the release were "God Save the Queen," "Sgt. Pepper's Lonely Hearts Club Band," "Spanish Castle Magic," "All Along the Watchtower," "Machine Gun," "Lover Man," "Freedom," "Red House," "Dolly Dagger," "Midnight Lightning," "Foxey Lady," "Message to Love," "Hey Baby (New Rising Sun)," "Ezy Ryder," "Hey Joe," "Purple Haze," "Voodoo Child (Slight Return)," and "In From the Storm."

The flood of 1971 continued with the release of several singles in addition to two films. Jeffery released the *Rainbow Bridge* film and also the live film *Jimi Plays Berkeley*. Added to this were three bootleg albums under the title *Jimi at His Best, Volumes 1, 2, and 3* and it seemed that the floodgates had been torn from their hinges.

HENDRIX: IN THE WEST

The year 1972 saw little that would contradict the overexposure of 1971. In January 1972, Jeffery issued *Hendrix: In the West* on Polydor in England. As was the custom with most of Jimi's material, this album ran up the charts to the seventh position where it stalled. This album contained material recorded at one of the Royal Albert Hall shows, this one from February 24, 1969; here Jimi, Mitch, and Cox were in fine form. In his rush to put out Jimi's material, Jeffery ran afoul of Steve Gold and Jerry Goldstein who owned the production company responsible for recording Jimi at that venue. In fact, most of the tracks on the album were actually taken from other concerts, which did not prevent the nasty legal action that ensued.

Hendrix: In the West was remixed by Kramer and John Jansen at Electric Lady Studios and the pair shared the production credits. The album cover depicted Jimi in the ecstasy of the moment playing his guitar. Another of Jimi's gatefold offerings, the inside of the album contained additional concert stills along with the track list and production credits. The eight tracks on the album were a compilation of material recorded at Royal Albert Hall, Berkeley Community Theater, the Sports Arena in San Diego, California, and the *Isle of Wight Festival*. The album contained the following tracks: "Lover Man," "Johnny B. Goode" by Chuck Berry, "Blue Suede Shoes" by Carl Perkins, "Red House," "God Save the Queen" by Dr. John Ball, "Sgt. Pepper's Lonely Hearts Club Band" by Lennon and McCartney, "Little Wing," and "Voodoo Child (Slight Return)." Jimi addressed the audience intermittently to talk about issues of tuning and volume levels.

WAR HEROES

At the end of 1972, the album *War Heroes* was released on the Polydor label. The album was sanctioned by Jeffery, and Kramer and Jansen were the producers of record. *War Heroes* was an interesting collection of songs culled from a host of recording sessions from 1967 to 1970. As the result,

Noel and Cox both appeared on the record. Recordings used for the album came from the Record Plant, Olympic Studios, Olmstead Studios, the Hit Factory, and Electric Lady Studios. The cover of the album was a black and white close-up of Jimi's face that depicted him in a pensive mood. The back of the album was again in black and white and caught Jimi in midsolo while including the track list and the recording information.

The tracks on the album that were contributed by the Jimi, Mitch, and Cox collective were "Bleeding Heart," "Peter Gunn Catastrophe" (by Henry Mancini), "Three Little Bears," "Beginnings" (aka "Jam Back at the House"), and "Izabella." The songs on which Noel appeared were "Highway Chile," "Tax Free" (by Bo Hansson and Janne Karlsson), and "Midnight." The release again charted and reached number twenty-three on the English charts. Juma Sultan supplied a variety of percussion on several of the above-listed tracks, but appeared without credit on the release. *War Heroes* was released in the United States on Reprise in December 1972 and topped out in the forty-eighth position.

The end of 1972 and the beginning of 1973 brought several changes to Jimi's recorded output. The first, and possibility most significant, was that Eddie Kramer dissolved his association with Michael Jeffery and stopped mixing and mastering Jimi's releases—at least for a time. The second was that Jimi's contract with Warner Brothers Music ended, which left Jeffery free to manipulate Jimi's catalogue at will. The third was that on March 5, 1973, Michael Jeffery was killed in a midair plane crash on a flight from Majorca. Some have speculated that Jeffery staged his own death in an attempt to disentangle himself from a great deal of bad blood, ill will, and legal troubles. However, this was unlikely given the fact that he was reaping enormous financial benefits from Jimi's catalogue at the time of the crash.

As a new era of Jimi's music dawned in the wake of Jeffery's death, a film about Jimi's life and a subsequent two-album set were released. The Warner Brothers communication group and producer John Boyd went to great lengths to realize the project, which included multiple interviews with most of the key figures in Jimi's life. The two albums released under the title *Soundtrack Recordings From the Film Jimi Hendrix* were again packaged in a gatefold cover. The front cover was a painting of Jimi by Nigel Waymouth while the back was a close-up photograph of Jimi's hands while he played. The inside of the gatefold was filled with family photographs of Jimi from his earliest days through his meteoric climb to stardom. Also, included in the inside of the album were credits and track lists for the four sides including some film credits and a list of interviewees for the film that included the Ghetto Freedom Fighters, Paul Caruso, Eric Clapton, Billy Cox, Monika Dannemann, Alan Douglas, Al Hendrix, Mick Jagger, Buddy Miles, Mitch Mitchell, Fay Pridgeon, and many others.

Each album side contained three or four songs, but more importantly concluded with a series of interviews. Side one contained the songs "Rock

Me, Baby," "Wild Thing," and "Machine Gun" along with interviews with Freddie Mae Gautier, Dolores Hall, Jimi himself, and Al Hendrix. Side two included "Johnny B. Goode," "Hey Joe," "Purple Haze," and "Like a Rolling Stone" and interviews with Jimi, Little Richard, Pat Hartley, and Fay Pridgeon. Side three contained the songs "The Star Spangled Banner," "Machine Gun," and "Hear My Train A Comin'" and interviews with Fay, Jimi, and Paul Caruso. The final side held the songs "Red House" and "In From the Storm" along with interviews of Pat Hartley, the Ghetto Fighters, Alan Douglas, and Fay again. The recordings were compiled from the live shows *Monterey Pop* in 1967, *Woodstock* in 1969, *Isle of Wight* in 1970, and the Fillmore East in 1969—thus, there were a wide range of musicians employed and both Noel and Cox appeared as Jimi's bassist.

More and More: The Douglas Releases, Dolly Dagger Records, and More Modern Releases

DOUGLAS RELEASES

The labyrinth of Jimi's posthumous releases continued unabated in the wake of Jeffery's death. With Jeffery and Kramer out of the picture (Jeffery permanently and Kramer temporarily), the road was cleared for Alan Douglas to step back into the light. The material that Douglas had of Jimi's was little more than "jams, demos, and scraps."[1] That said, Douglas dove headlong into the idea of releasing "new" Jimi albums in any way that he could. His efforts to reshape Jimi's music were mindboggling to many at the time. Douglas' reworking of Jimi's music was so heavy handed that he actually replaced original parts with overdubs done by studio musicians years after the fact. With that in mind, the Douglas material cannot be considered as original Jimi music, but still must be accounted for in some way. The truly unexplainable aspect of all of the Douglas work was his steadfast assertion that he somehow had a clearer picture of Jimi's intent than Jimi himself did. Regardless of Douglas' intent, the material that he issued under Jimi's name was overdubbed, remixed, and remastered in a very heavy-handed manner.

Crash Landing

The first record that Douglas put out as a Jimi Hendrix album was called *Crash Landing*. The record surfaced in 1975 and was billed as containing previously unreleased material. Unlike the other Douglas releases, *Crash Landing* actually did quite well. For a compilation of overdubbed songs by an artist who had been dead for five years, the fact that the album made it to number five on the United States charts spoke volumes for the timeless nature of Jimi's musical genius. The album contained eight songs including "Message to Love," "Somewhere Over the Rainbow," "Crash Landing," "Come Down Hard on Me," "Peace in Mississippi," "With the Power," "Stone Free Again," and "Captain Coconut." The cover of the album was a drawing of Jimi soloing with his guitar and the back was a dark, black and white image of the guitar hero's face along with the song list and album credits. Douglas and Tony Bongiovi were listed as producers.

The first song on the album was "Message to Love." The basic tracking was done by Jimi, Miles, and Cox. Added to this was overdubbed percussion by Jimmy Maeulen. That said, it was very difficult to account for who actually supplied which parts on this release as the general information on the creation of the album indicated that Douglas removed/erased the majority of the original backing tracks leaving only Jimi's voice and guitar work intact. The song itself left a rather incomplete feeling as it ended prematurely and the dubious authenticity of the backing band was problematic to many Jimi enthusiasts. What was unmistakable was the solid performance put in by Jimi both on vocals and guitar. Jimi's masterful songcraft and guitar playing must have been the principal reason for the album's initial chart success.

The second song on the album was mistakenly listed as "Somewhere Over the Rainbow" and should simply have been called "Somewhere." Here Jimi's guitar and vocal parts were overdubbed with additional guitar work by Jeff Mironov, a bass line by Bob Babbit, and drums by Alan Schwartzberg. The overdubbing notwithstanding, "Somewhere" was another excellent example of Jimi's musical prowess. The vocals and guitar work weaved a masterful tapestry of top-flight Hendrix performance. The lyrics again keyed in on many of Jimi's favorite themes including apocalyptic images of the Earth, science fiction, and pleas for redemption. Interestingly, toward the end of the song Jimi sang "sell me, brother, sell me," and that was just what Douglas did. The song again came to a rather unfulfilling conclusion as it faded out while Jimi was still soloing after the lyrics had ended.

The third track was the namesake of the record, "Crash Landing." Again stripped down to little more than Jimi's guitar and vocal tracks, Douglas added dense layers of overdubs with a host of other musicians. Mironov again supplied guitar work, Babbit and Schwartzberg were back on bass and drums respectively, and Maeulen again added percussion. To all of this was also added female backing vocals by Linda November, Vivian Cherry, and Barbara Massey. Again, the song was a solid effort by Jimi who infused his parts of the recording with the fire that his fans had become accustomed to with blazing solos. Lyrically, Jimi again focused on science fiction–based imagery and the discussion of a personal relationship—assumed to have been his relationship with Devon Wilson. Here Jimi implored Devon to cut him free as he could no longer live in her world. Regarding the Wilson connection, Jimi referenced her heroin habit and his general feeling that she did not love him, but rather loved who he was. Here Jimi repeatedly mentioned her general disregard for his feelings as well as her ability to deceive him. Additional lyrical content directly referenced her true love affair with the needle.

"Come Down Hard on Me" came next with Jimi's basic tracking again supplemented by Mironov, Babbit, and Schwartzberg. The song itself was a funky jam on Jimi's desire to not only be loved, but also for the physical manifestations of love. Jimi repeatedly called out to his love interest for the pair to be together and to remain that way. In the style of classic electric blues, Jimi repeated the entire opening set of lyrics twice. The song then chugged through a closing set of words in which Jimi recognized that the relationship would not last. The conclusion of "Come Down Hard on Me" was a blazing guitar solo that strangely, and uncharacteristically for Jimi, led back into a restatement of some of the earlier lyrics. Again, the song faded out leaving the listener with less than a sense of finality.

"Peace in Mississippi" was as heavy and hard driving as any song Jimi ever cut. Originally recorded in 1968, the version here was wiped clean of all parts but Jimi's solo and rhythm guitar work. Douglas' usual studio overdubs were done and one can only imagine how much more appropriate and driving Mitch's original drum line worked. The hugely powerful instrumental was still pure Jimi—at least in the guitar work. Overdriven guitar solos and a massive wall of sound were complemented by some limited feedback and echo effects.

Listed as "With the Power," track six on the release was more properly known as "Power of Soul." The song was known under other titles such as the original working title "Paper Airplanes." Jimi's guitar and vocal lines were again overdubbed. However, here the relatively chopped-together tracks included work by Cox, Miles, and Sultan. To that was added Maeulen on percussion. The overall impression of the track was that it was somehow left incomplete and it faded out in a relatively unsatisfying manner.

"Stone Free Again" was the next song listed on *Crash Landing*. The song was in fact Jimi's original "Stone Free" given the Douglas treatment. Again taken down to bare guitar and vocal tracking, Douglas added overdubs to the original 1969 material by Mironov, Schwartzberg, Babbit, and Maeulen. The original version of the song was much stronger and lacked the compression inserted on Jimi's voice which amounted to him sounding like he was singing into an inexpensive microphone.

The album ended with the song listed as "Captain Coconut." In the studio, this track was actually known as "M.L.K." for its dedication to Dr. Martin Luther King, Jr. The material contained in this track was a relative hodgepodge of several different tracks—which may have been the reason why the beginning of the song was so out of tune. The song on the album was actually cut together from three separate song versions, cleaned of the original backing material, and then rebuilt with Douglas' crew of overdubbed musicians. The result was a strangely interesting electric guitar instrumental cast in a setting that does not seem to match the innovation or intensity of the solo line. For all of the rush and fire of Jimi's guitar work, the backing material lacks any of the propulsive fury that Mitch and Noel or even Cox and Miles supplied.

Midnight Lightning

Although quite uneven as a "studio" album, the success of *Crash Landing* encouraged Douglas to release a second compilation of Jimi's material later in the same year. With his regular studio trick in play, Douglas again removed the backing tracks that Jimi had originally recorded with and replaced them with new material by musicians who never actually worked with Jimi during his lifetime. The second release of this type was titled *Midnight Lightning* and met with much stronger opposition than did the first release. *Midnight Lightning* did not even chart in the United Kingdom and did not crack the top forty in the United States. Further, public opinion on the second release was filled with the bile of an audience who was now heartily sick of those who would continue to degrade Jimi's work only to cash in on his legacy. This was only made worse once Jimi's fans realized that Douglas had actually taken coauthorship credit for five of the songs on the *Crash Landing* release.

The *Midnight Lightning* album cover depicted Jimi soloing on the front with his signature white Fender Stratocaster amid a stormy sky with bolts of lightning descending behind him. The back contained another image of Jimi's face in close-up along with all of the production credits for the album which again listed Douglas and Bongiovi as producers. The eight songs on this release were "Trashman," "Midnight Lightning," "Hear My Train A Comin'," "Gypsy Boy (New Rising Sun)," "Blue Suede Shoes," "Machine Gun," "Once I Had a Woman," and "Beginnings."

The album opened with another of Douglas' incorrect titles and listed track one as "Trashman" when the song was known as "Midnight." The song was an extended instrumental meant to showcase Jimi's ever-evolving guitar style. The guitar part was originally recorded in 1969 and in 1975 the overdubbed parts by Mironov, Schwartzberg, and Babbit were inserted. While Jimi's playing was outstanding, the track lacks the urgency of much of his work with the original Experience, which had been in the studio with Jimi at the time of the initial recording.

The second song on the album was the one for which the entire work was named, "Midnight Lightning." Oddly, the version of this song that appeared on the Douglas release was not the same song that would appear under this title on other Jimi albums. The chopped-together "Midnight Lightning" here contained different lyrics than the original with Jimi riffing on snippets of nursery rhymes, as opposed to the actual tale of a nighttime storm that Jimi recounted in the proper song of this title. Jimi said of the original words, "I like to watch the lightning . . . especially on the fields and flowers."[2] For the Douglas version, even more overdubbing was added with the inclusion of guitar work by Lance Quinn and female harmony vocals by Maeretha Stewart, Hilda Harris, and Vivian Cherry.

"Getting My Heart Back Together" was track three on the album. The song was more popularly known as "Hear My Train A Comin'." Here, Douglas left Jimi's vocals and guitar intact along with Mitch's drum part. To this was added the Douglas treatment of overdubs by Mironov, Babbit, and Schwartzberg. However, nothing could diminish the potency of Jimi's work on this track. The original tracking for the song was done in early 1969 and Jimi performed the song live multiple times. In his own words, the song was a "slow blues about this cat who feels kinda down, 'cause his old lady put him down, and his people and family don't want him around, so he had this big old frown, and had to drag his ass down to the railroad station, waitin' for the train to come take him away on the road . . . [then he] comes back, do it to his old lady one more time, give her a piece because she's all nice to him again."[3]

"Gypsy Boy (New Rising Sun)" was again a mislabeled song on the album. The song was best known by the title "Hey Baby (New Rising Sun)." The version of this song that appeared on *Midnight Lightning* was again given the Douglas overdub treatment and additional female vocals were added. Still present were Jimi's original guitar and vocals from a session in 1970 with the use of the Uni-Vibe intact. The Carl Perkins hit "Blue Suede Shoes" was up next. The Douglas remake presented here was a chopped-together version with the expected overdubbing. The result was a somewhat unsatisfactory cover version with a general feeling of incompleteness.

The next song listed on the album jacket is "Machine Gun" when in fact it was a medley of "Izabella" and "Machine Gun" run together. A less than satisfactory version, the typical overdubbing was in play with the inclusion of Lance Quinn on additional guitar parts. Possibly more blasphemous than adding guitar overdubs to Jimi's music was the adding of a title to the next track. "Once I Had a Woman" was originally recorded in 1970 and was not given a title at the time. However, Douglas applied his normal heavy-handed treatment and even supplied a name. The final song on the release was titled "Beginning," although Jimi listeners knew it as "Jam Back at the House." With this, the second Douglas release of Jimi's music came to an end. Public opinion was no longer mixed on the Douglas material and he did not issue any further overdubbed recordings of Jimi's music.

In the wake of *Midnight Lightning*, Douglas temporarily abandoned releasing material from Jimi's back catalogue for several years. It seemed, though, that he had learned his lesson about coauthorship credit and overdubbing as he discontinued these practices permanently. He did eventually revisit Jimi's work in the form of several additional releases. In 1980, Douglas issued the compilation *Nine to the Universe*. Unlike his previous efforts, this album was a true compilation with no overdubbing and far less intrusion by the producer. He followed this with a series of live recordings that, while uneven in overall quality, did represent Jimi with the least amount of intrusion. The albums that Douglas issued after *Nine to the Universe* included titles such as the *Radio One: The BBC Sessions* and *Stages* (one live concert for each year from 1967 to 1970).

Nine to the Universe

Nine to the Universe was released in 1980 and included a series of relatively loose jams with Jimi. None of the jams on the record were given titles by Jimi except the opening cut which was called "Message From Nine to the Universe." The album contained five jam session recordings that Jimi completed in a series of adventures in the studio over the course of 1969. He was a notorious improviser and also often welcomed almost all comers into the studio with him. The album did chart in the United States, but failed to crack the top one hundred.

The album began with the track "Message From Nine to the Universe." Here Jimi was joined by Buddy Miles and Billy Cox. Devon Wilson also appeared on the original recording supplying harmony vocals which did not make the final cut. Of note, according to Shapiro and Glebbeek, none of the tracks on this release were really considered complete—as was the custom with the loose, jamming style that Jimi sometimes used to work out riffs or song ideas in the studio. The second track was labeled "Jimi/Jimmy Jam" and included several other musicians without proper credits. Jam number three was called "Young/Hendrix" and featured Larry Young on an added organ line. The fourth song was "Easy Blues" with Jimi, Mitch, and Cox as the core performers and Young again. The final track on the album was called "Drone Blues" and was recorded in early 1969. The accompanying musicians were not known, but were either Mitch and Noel or Miles and Cox.

Radio One: The BBC Sessions

Jimi's BBC sessions had a long history. As was the custom at the time, artists who appeared on BBC radio were often required to make essentially live-in-the-studio recordings. The first collection of these was issued in 1989 by Douglas on behalf of Jimi's estate (then operating under the name Are You Experienced Ltd.) under the title *Radio One*. While this release thrilled listeners and again hyped the fervor for Jimi's material, the collection turned out to be incomplete in light of the fact that Douglas had essentially created a compilation of only the tracks that he wanted to release. That said, in 1998, the true BBC collection of Jimi's material was released by his estate without Douglas' interference. The second collection contained all the material that the Experience had recorded while in the BBC studios and was produced by the trio of Janie Hendrix, Eddie Kramer, and John McDermott (under the reorganization of Jimi's estate called Experience Hendrix). Both sets were interesting period pieces for Jimi's evolutionary process, but the later set was more complete.

Stages

Possibly the most significant recordings that Douglas had a hand in releasing were contained in the four-CD set called *Stages*. Each individual disc constituted a complete live recording of Jimi's music—one for each year from 1967 to 1970. As a result, *Stages* both represented Jimi's work on stage and throughout the stages of the development of his career. The sonic quality of these releases was good for live recordings and little was done to them in the release process. The first disc was an early performance by Jimi, Mitch, and Noel in Stockholm, Sweden. A live-in-the-studio recording from Radiohuset, here the Experience were fairly dutifully reproducing the sounds heard on *Are You Experienced?* The songs on that album were "Sgt. Pepper's Lonely Hearts Club Band," "Fire," "The Wind Cries Mary," "Foxey Lady," "Hey Joe," "I Don't Live Today," "Burning of the Midnight Lamp," and "Purple Haze."

The second disc of the set was taken from an Experience performance at L'Olympia in Paris on January 29, 1968. Although this performance was not long after the set in Sweden, here the group was at greater potency and opened the set with two electric blues covers that had Jimi playing to his strengths. The set included "Killing Floor" by Howlin' Wolf, "Catfish Blues" by Muddy Waters, "Foxey Lady," "Red House," "Drivin' South," "Spanish Castle Magic," "The Wind Cries Mary," "Fire," "Little Wing," and "Purple Haze."

The disc that represented Jimi's style in 1969 was culled from one of the last concerts with the original Experience. The set was from the San Diego Sports Arena on May 24, 1969, and found the group at full throttle. In California, Jimi led the group through "Fire," "Hey Joe," "Spanish Castle Magic," "Red House," "I Don't Live Today," "Purple Haze," and "Voodoo Child (Slight Return)." The final show contained in this set was from Jimi's appearance at the *Atlanta International Pop Festival* on July 4, 1970. Here Jimi was backed by Mitch and Cox and the festival atmosphere was in the air. The group tore through the set of "Fire," "Lover Man," "Spanish Castle Magic," "Foxey Lady," "Purple Haze," "Getting My Heart Back Together Again," "Stone Free," "Star Spangled Banner," "Straight Ahead," "Room Full of Mirrors," and "Voodoo Child (Slight Return)." As a unit, the live shows contained in this set were fairly uneven from the early days in Stockholm to a "new" Experience in Atlanta. However, as a testament to Jimi's musical journey, few sets have rivaled this one as a live music document.

THE DOLLY DAGGER RELEASES

In 1995, as part of the wrangling for control over Jimi's estate, Al Hendrix finally won control over his son's music. As an exponent of this, Al and his stepdaughter Janie launched the Experience Hendrix Limited company. One of the principal goals of the new company was to regain control over Jimi's catalogue and have some semblance of order about what material was issued and in what form. By 1998, an offshoot of this was the creation of their own record label, called Dagger Records. Dagger was created as the company's official "bootleg" record operation and its sole purpose was to make Jimi's live recordings available in the best audio quality possible. Describing itself as targeting collectors, the material issued by Dagger does have better sonic quality than a standard bootleg but it still does not approach studio standards. Typically the recordings were made through the soundboard at the venue to avoid most crowd noise, but the products are generally uneven in quality. The Dagger imprint teamed with Geffen Records as part of the Universe Music Group. An interesting aspect of the Dagger imprint is that its products would only be available online through the company's own Web site, the official Hendrix online store.

Through Dagger, Experience Hendrix L.L.C. has so far issued eleven "sanctioned" bootlegs of Jimi's work. In addition, they have created what they call a Fan Pack of their bootleg release of Jimi's material from the Paris/Ottawa album which comes with a colored vinyl pressing of the Paris show, the CD of the actual release, a t-shirt, and various other pieces of Jimi-specific memorabilia. The Dagger imprint and Hendrix online retail Web site are significant in that there are few other artists who have made such a concerted effort to control such releases. Bob Marley is an excellent example of a recording artist whose musical legacy has repeatedly been muddled by unauthorized releases (from a variety of labels around the world), bootlegs, and unauthorized merchandizing. The most notable exception to this was the work of the Grateful Dead, who through their self-archiving known as *Dick's Picks* (so named for Dick Latvala, the original Grateful Dead concert archivist) somehow managed to control their own live product and make money on it in an era where such things were practically unheard of.

Jimi Hendrix Experience: Live at Oakland

The first of the Dagger releases was *Jimi Hendrix Experience: Live at Oakland,* issued in July 1998. The recording was made by a fan named Ken Koga who made an amateur recording of the concert staged on April 27, 1969. Not a through-the-board recording, Koga had "recorded the show on a portable reel-to-reel machine from the eleventh row of the stalls—pausing between songs to conserve tape and thereby missing most of the stage chatter."[4] Regardless of fidelity, Jimi, Mitch, and Noel delivered a characteristically solid West Coast performance

The set list delivered by the Experience that night was fairly standard for the 1969 tour. The group began with a brief introduction followed by "Fire," "Hey Joe," and a rambling version of "Spanish Castle Magic." There followed the blues number "Hear My Train A Comin'" and their version of the Cream hit "Sunshine of Your Love." A thirteen-minute rendition of "Red House" was next with "Foxey Lady" and the legendary send-up of "The Star Spangled Banner." The show closed with "Purple Haze" taking things to a climax that was only released through an eighteen-plus–minute version of "Voodoo Child (Slight Return)." The show itself has subsequently entered the pantheon of outstanding live performances put on by the original Jimi Hendrix Experience.

Jimi Hendrix Experience: Live at Clark University

The next Dagger Records release came one year later in July 1999. *Jimi Hendrix Experience: Live at Clark University* was recorded on March 15, 1968, at Atwood Hall on the campus of the Worcester, Massachusetts, university. The show was documented by filmmaker Tony Palmer for his BBC-TV documentary *All My Loving*, which added several significant facets to the overall set. However, the recording used for the album was not Palmer's and instead had "actually come from another unrevealed source, and [had] survived in surprisingly good stereo."[5]

Although the musical content on the album was a fine document of the Experience's life on the road at the beginning of 1968, the real interest here was the more than forty minutes of interviews preserved from the night. Jimi was interviewed before the concert and all three members were interviewed after their performance. By all accounts the Experience were even tempered and sat patiently through the interview process each adding his own thoughts on touring, stardom, and music making in general. The set that was released on the recording included only five songs: "Fire," "Red House," "Foxey Lady," "Purple Haze," and "Wild Thing."

Jimi Hendrix: Morning Symphony Ideas

Perhaps a bit strangely, Dagger decided to issue its next album from a much different source. Instead of a true live recording, *Jimi Hendrix: Morning Symphony Ideas* was a compilation of studio outtakes and home demos that Jimi had left behind. While the collection was a window into Jimi's songwriting process, this release seemed to fly in the face of the Dagger mantra of releasing live recordings. *Jimi Hendrix: Morning Symphony Ideas* was issued in July 2000, in keeping with the July release dates of the first two Dagger albums. The six tracks included on the release came from a wide variety of sources and spanned nearly two years in time frame.

The opening track was "Keep on Groovin'" which was recorded at the Record Plant on November 14, 1969. This, like the rest of the tracks on the release, provided interesting information on how Jimi worked a song out in the studio. Track two was "Jungle" from the same recording session. "Room Full of Mirrors" was recorded on September 25, 1969 and "Strato Strut" (so named for Jimi's preferred Fender Stratocaster guitar) came from December 19, 1969. All four of the opening offerings provided interesting insight into Jimi's musical behavior in the studio. The fifth track was recorded as Jimi riffed on a song idea in Maui, Hawaii, in 1970. "Scorpio Woman" may not have ever seen the proper light of day, but does appear here as a document of Jimi's late songwriting process. The final cut was an acoustic demo that Jimi made in New York in February 1970. As he was accustomed to working songs out in the studio—and miles of tape attested to this—Jimi also often recorded song ideas while playing in other locations. These "homemade" tapes were the basic information that he revisited as he worked out new songs.

Jimi Hendrix Experience: Live in Ottawa

In October 2001, Dagger returned to the live music format and issued the next of the collectors-minded show recordings. The fourth title was *Jimi Hendrix Experience: Live in Ottawa* which was recorded at the Capital Theater in March 1968. Coming just a few days after their show at Clark University, the Ottawa recording found Jimi and the group working out an extended set list with their customary energy. The group jumped out to an enthusiastic start with the Howlin' Wolf cover "Killing Floor," which was followed by Jimi's instrumental "Tax Free." There followed the then fairly standard set list of "Fire," "Red House," and "Foxey Lady" in the same order from the show at Clark. Next up were "Hey Joe," "Spanish Castle Magic," and "Purple Haze." The show ended with an incomplete version of "Wild Thing" as the tape ran out, and as it was the final song of the set there was no effort made to add a new spool.

Jimi Hendrix: Baggy's Rehearsal Sessions

For the fifth release, Dagger again turned to previously unreleased—and often unfinished—material from Jimi's work in the studio. As the Band of Gypsys trio of Jimi, Miles, and Cox were preparing for their two-night stand at the Fillmore East on New Year's Eve 1969 and New Year's Day 1970, they enshrined themselves in the New York studio called Baggy's. *Jimi Hendrix: Baggy's Rehearsal Sessions* was cut during two days of rehearsals on December 18 and 19, 1969, as the group geared up for the Fillmore shows. The Baggy's space was really less of a recording studio, as it lacked a control room, and more of an open two-story warehouse in which the Band of Gypsys could make as much sound as they chose.

The recordings themselves were made on a two-track reel-to-reel recorder. What was captured was an excellent example of Jimi and the group working out phrasings and arrangements of the ten songs housed on the release. Although the numbers lacked polish, there was excitement in the air as Jimi put Miles and Cox through their paces with a fairly fresh set of songs. Included on the release were "Burning Desire" followed by Jimi's take on the Willie Dixon hit "Hoochie Coochie Man." Next up were "Message to Love," "Ezy Ryder," "Power of Soul," and "Earth Blues." The group then changed gears and worked up a couple of songs written by Miles. Miles' song "Changes" came next with "We Gotta Live Together" following, although the pair was interrupted by Jimi's song "Lover Man." The final three tracks included different versions of "Earth Blues" and "Burning Desire," both of which were already represented on the release, and a loose rambler called "Baggy's Jam."

Jimi Hendrix Experience: Paris 1967/San Francisco 1968

The next product of the Dagger imprint returned to true live performance and the original Jimi Hendrix Experience. *Jimi Hendrix Experience: Paris 1967/San Francisco 1968* captured two of the more noteworthy Experience performances with the band at full potency. For this sixth Dagger issue from April 2003, the choice was made to combine parts of two live performances to create an extended song list with a great deal of variety. The first seven songs on the release were captured live at the Experience concert at the Paris Olympic Theater on October 9, 1967. The second half of the release was filled with six songs from the Experience concert at the Winterland Ballroom in San Francisco on February 4, 1968.

The record opened with a relatively standard collection of songs from the 1967 tour. Included were "Stone Free," "Hey Joe," and "Fire." The next track was an interesting inclusion as it documented the Experience's take on the B. B. King standard "Rock Me, Baby." The rest of the Paris set was "Red House," "Purple Haze," and "Wild Thing"—again, a series of standard live tunes. Not included from the Paris show were "Burning of the Midnight Lamp" and "Foxey Lady." Although performed, these songs could not be used as Jimi's microphone experienced technical difficulties and repeatedly cut out.

The second half of the release included several standout tracks from the Winterland Ballroom performance. The songs began with the touring standards "Killing Floor" (Howlin' Wolf), "Red House," and the less often performed "Catfish Blues." There followed two takes on the Traffic song "Dear Mr. Fantasy" penned by Jim Capaldi, Steve Winwood, and Chris Wood. Of note, Mitch called Buddy Miles on stage to sit in on the drum part for these versions. The San Francisco set ended with "Purple Haze." Overall, the *Paris 1967/San Francisco 1968* album did an excellent job of delivering high octane Experience performances and a glimpse into the future with Miles' guest spot even though the two shows were staged four months apart on different sides of the globe.

Jimi Hendrix: Hear My Music

The seventh offering from the Dagger imprint was 2004's *Jimi Hendrix: Hear My Music*. Issued as a set of instrumental jams and demos, this was another of the studio offerings from the label. As this was not one of Dagger's live records, the intention was again to cast Jimi in the light of working out new songs or song ideas in the studio with the variety of players that surrounded him in the first half of 1969. Unlike *Morning Symphony Ideas, Hear My Music* framed Jimi's song craft as a mature and world-traveled artist, and the experience that he had accumulated showed. During this period in Jimi's creative life, he was constantly on the search for new sounds and as a result there were several musicians in the studio with him who were not present in any of his touring outfits.

Hear My Music included eleven tracks and the list of credited musicians changed from one to the next. The recording dates that were represented on the album also varied from February 14, 1969, to May 14, 1969. Track one was simply titled "Slow Version" and illustrated Jimi working out some musical ideas with Mitch and Noel. The track was recorded on February 14, 1969, at Olympic Studios in London. This was also true of several other tracks on the release such as a medley version of "Ezy Ryder/Star Spangled Banner" (track three) and "Blues Jam at Olympic" (track ten). The second track on the release cast Jimi in a different light. Recorded in New York on April 24, 1969, at the Record Plant, "Drone Blues" featured Cox on bass, Rocky Isaac on drums, and Al Mark on percussion. Track four again featured a lineup change for the tune called "Jimi/Jimmy Jam." Recorded at the Record Plant on March 25, 1969, here Jimi was joined by Mitch, Roland Robinson on bass, and Jim McCarty on guitar. The final track from the Record Plant came from May 14, 1969, when Jimi created "Jam 292" with Mitch, Cox, Sharon Layne on piano, and an unknown trumpet player. "Trashman" (better known as "Midnight") was the sixth track and was cut at Olmstead Studio in New York on April 3, 1969. Here Jimi returned to his core group of Mitch and Noel, but Noel worked out his parts on the 8-string bass. The remainder of the songs on the album represented Jimi working alone in the process of crafting his songs. "Message to Love," "Gypsy Blood," and "Valleys of Neptune" were guitar alone. The final track on the release was again Jimi working alone, but this time he was playing the piano for a second version of "Valleys of Neptune."

Live at Fehmarn

For the eighth Dagger release, the label returned to the live show format with *Live at Fehmarn*. Released in December 2005, this installment in the Dagger catalogue captured Jimi, Mitch, and Cox at the *Open Air Love and Peace Festival* on the Isle of Fehmarn, Germany. Although unknown to anyone at the time, this concert wound up being Jimi's last performance live and in concert. As the story of the concert went, Jimi was scheduled to perform on September 5, but weather pushed them onto the following day. The tension at the show was high as there had been a series of fights between audience and security and the box office had been robbed.

Regardless of all the mess that the concert itself had dissolved into, Jimi took the stage and put on an epic performance that encompassed his entire catalogue. Fortunately for Jimi's fans and collectors of his music, the recording issued here was not the typical bootleg but rather an unsanctioned recording made by the promoter from two microphones positioned above the stage. The microphones fed into a reel-to-reel tape deck and the resulting recording was of surprisingly good quality.

Although Jimi was certainly unaware at the time that this was his last appearance on a concert stage, he did tear into his set with the vigor he often reserved for the studio or club performances. After a brief introduction, the group worked over Howlin' Wolf's "Killing Floor" followed by "Spanish Castle Magic." Next up was Jimi's version of the Bob Dylan song "All Along the Watchtower" with the bluesy "Hey Joe" on its heels. Moving forward in his catalogue, Jimi and the band took on "Hey Baby (New Rising Sun)" and "Message to Love" before returning to the tried and true "Foxey Lady" and "Red House." The end of the set was filled with solid live versions of "Ezy Rider," "Freedom," "Room Full of Mirrors," "Purple Haze," and Jimi's standard set closer "Voodoo Child (Slight Return)" which clocked in at a little over nine minutes.

Hendrix: Burning Desire

Sticking with material from nearer the end of Jimi's life, Dagger next released *Hendrix: Burning Desire*. Culled from sessions at the Record Plant in New York in late 1969 and early 1970, this release was another filled with studio outtakes and demo versions. Dagger issued this ninth album at the end of 2006 and with this again revisited the issue of how Jimi created music and built songs in the studio. He was accompanied by Cox and Miles for these sessions as he pushed them through working out several new songs. The first track was "Izabella," which included an uncredited keyboard player. Next was a medley of "Ezy Ryder" and "M.L.K." (aka "Captain Coconut") followed by a like version of "Cherokee" and "Astro Man" again run together. The next song was simply labeled "Record Plant 2X" and featured the trio working over a series of riffs. The final four tracks on the release were blues jams of a variety of sorts. "Villanova Junction Blues" was followed by "Burning Desire" and another pair of songs run together with "Stepping Stone" melting into another stab at "Villanova Junction Blues." The album ended with the burner "Slow Time Blues."

Jimi Hendrix Experience: Live in Paris and Ottawa

For the tenth installment on the Dagger imprint, the label returned to the successful formula of combining two solid live shows, this time one from France and one from Canada. *Jimi Hendrix Experience: Live in Paris and Ottawa 1968* paired two shows from that year. The first was Jimi, Mitch, and Noel's set at the L'Olympia in Paris on January 29 and the second was their concert at the Capital Theater on March 19. The combination was again a success as the two shows were of solid quality and featured the progress the group was making as it toured in support of its second major label release, *Axis: Bold as Love*.

Issued September 5, 2008, *Live in Paris and Ottawa* relayed heavily on the Paris performance as only three of the Ottawa tracks were included. The Paris set kicked off with the blues standards "Killing Floor" (by Howlin' Wolf) and "Catfish Blues" (by Muddy Waters). These were followed by Jimi's tune "Foxey Lady" and his own take on the blues with "Red House." Next came the R&B-tinged "Drivin' South," which had been in Jimi's repertoire since 1965. The set then moved in a more psychedelic direction with "The Wind Cries Mary," "Fire," "Little Wing," and "Purple Haze." With this, the Paris section of the release ended. The songs culled from the Ottawa set began with the Lennon and McCartney classic "Sgt. Pepper's Lonely Hearts Club Band" followed by repetitions of "Fire" and "Purple Haze."

Jimi Hendrix Experience: Live at Woburn

The most recent release from Dagger came on July 24, 2009, with *Jimi Hendrix Experience: Live at Woburn*. The concert captured here was the *Woburn Music Festival* staged in Bedfordshire, England, on July 6, 1968. The recording was made through the soundboard which resulted in reasonably good quality for a bootleg, but did little to capture the enthusiasm of the crowd. The Experience was the Saturday night headline of the festival and an estimated 14,000 people turned out to see them. The fervor for the group's appearance was the combination of enthusiasm over their studio material coupled with the fact that they had not played in England since December 1967. Their six-month absence did much to stoke the energy of the crowd. As it seemed to almost always be the case, the group struggled with extra noise from their amplifiers and Jimi did his usual best at apologizing for having to play through broken equipment.

After a brief introduction and instead of featuring the material from *Axis: Bold as Love*, Jimi launched into a spirited version of Lennon and McCartney's "Sgt. Pepper's Lonely Hearts Club Band." He then dove headlong into "Fire" which was followed by an over-ten-minute-long version of "Tax Free." Caught in the moment, Jimi upped the ante with an eleven-and-a-half-minute take on "Red House." The Experience then wound around through "Foxey Lady" and "Voodoo Child (Slight Return)" before finishing with over eight minutes of "Purple Haze." The appreciation of the crowd was captured by the onstage microphones as they called for another song. With this the current catalogue of Dagger recordings ends; however, there is every indication that the label will continue to release new, previously unreleased, material in the future.

MORE MODERN RELEASES

While Jimi's posthumous catalogue continued to grow and was filled with both sanctioned and unsanctioned releases, several studio-oriented albums have surfaced that are of significant quality and that should be accounted for here.

Jimi Hendrix: Blues

The first of these releases was the 1974 product *Jimi Hendrix: Blues*, which was issued on Polydor in the United Kingdom in 1994 and then rereleased by MCA in 1998.

Of note, Jimi's *Blues* album was actually the original idea of Alan Douglas and he was listed as the producer on the original release. It was Douglas who combed through Jimi's tapes in order to ferret out the most significantly blues-influenced tunes. In addition, Douglas has gone on record as saying that this effort was at least in part done to illustrate how deep a debt Jimi's style owed to the American blues tradition—a point that seemed little in dispute. According to Doggett, "Douglas set out to expose Jimi's roots in black music, from the acoustic blues of the inter-war period to the uptown R&B that coexisted alongside the early Experience releases in the Sixties."[6] Interestingly, *Blues* was the only Douglas product that was kept intact when control of Jimi's estate reverted back to his family.

As the blues of the American South were one of Jimi's earliest influences, it was small wonder that they had a deep impact on his playing style. It was fair to say that Jimi's more straight-ahead blues-style playing had not previously been featured on album-length releases. That was remedied with the *Blues* album which contained eleven tracks with eight of those previously unreleased. The packaging for the album was quite masterful as the front image was a collage of Jimi made by smaller photos of twenty-five of the bluesmen who influenced him. The interest in an all-blues album was attested to by the fact that the record ended up selling five hundred thousand copies in its first two years and eventually went platinum. The tracks contained on *Blues* were recorded between 1967 and 1970 and the musicians represented ran the gamut of those who typically accompanied Jimi into the studio.

In addition to being unique in its all-blues-style content, the *Blues* release began with a side of Jimi that was seldom heard. The first track, "Hear My

Train A Comin'" (aka "Getting My Heart Back Together"), was issued as an acoustic performance with Jimi alone with a 12-string acoustic guitar. In the style of the Delta blues, Jimi carried off a convincing approximation even without a well-tuned guitar.

Track two was the popular blues tune "Born Under a Bad Sign." The song was written by Booker T. Jones and William Bell and had already been a hit for Albert King in the mid-1960s. Here, Jimi spread his electric wings with backing from Mitch and Noel. Clocking in at over seven minutes, the version here was an effective attempt by the master guitarist to combine blues, soul, and rock styles in an extended instrumental.

"Red House" came next and was the fairly standard version with Mitch and Noel from the 1966 *Are You Experienced?* sessions. Still a solid blues number, this version of "Red House" was long known and the only alteration to the track that was made was to remove Chas Chandler's voice at the end. After this was Jimi's take on the blues standard "Catfish Blues." The recording used here was with Mitch and Noel from the Experience's appearance on the Dutch TV show *Hoepla* from late 1967. Although the group played the Muddy Waters hit straight for the first half of the song, Jimi then exploded with a flurry of guitar virtuosity. He brought the boys back to the more spare blues sound for another verse of the lyrics before again blasting off with another guitar solo that led into a rather interesting drum solo by Mitch. The overall tune clocked in at almost eight minutes as it blended roots electric blues with progressive whammy-bar-driven sixties psychedelia. The song ended with a full-on electric guitar assault that owed much less to the blues than it did to the guitar playing of Eric Clapton.

"Voodoo Child Blues" was a song that Douglas built out of two separate takes both recorded in May 1968 during the *Electric Ladyland* sessions. Here Jimi was backed by Jack Cassidy on bass, Mitch, and Steve Winwood on organ. Much slower than the standard version of "Voodoo Child," the blues version captured/created for this release not only helped to identify Jimi's solid blues roots but also exposed him in much stronger voice than he was typically given credit for at this point in his career. The other instrumentalists largely stayed out of the way as Jimi tore through scorching solos in the middle of the nearly-nine-minute version of the song. The musical camaraderie between Jimi and Winwood was nicely exemplified on the track as each time the guitar part swelled the organ grew to match the intensity. Without explanation, Jimi began making his guitar imitate space noises at shortly past the midpoint of the song.

Jimi launched into his take on an interesting cover selection of Muddy Waters by beginning in an opening exaltation fit for a gospel preacher. Another studio creation, either through splicing together of multiple takes or overdubbing—or both—the track actually combined Jimi's covers of Muddy Waters' "Mannish Boy" and Bo Diddley's "I'm a Man." Again backed by Cox and Miles, Jimi launched into this version with reckless abandon at times imitating or matching his guitar lines with scat-style vocals or just letting the guitar do the singing for him. The overall feel of the song was that it was left a bit incomplete as it faded out at the end.

"Once I Had a Woman" was one of Jimi's few truly slow blues numbers. Cast as a slow burner in the vein of a mythical electric Robert Johnson, Jimi's sound was frequently matched by a harmonica line throughout most of the song. At times unfolding at a snail's pace, "Once I Had a Woman" encapsulated Jimi's lifelong search for his perfect mate, a goal he seemingly never achieved. During the final minute of the nearly-eight-minute song, the band picked up the pace and the song faded out with a much more up-tempo romp begun when the lyrics were complete.

"Bleeding Heart" was the shortest song on the album and the only one that even began to approach a radio-friendly length at three-and-a-half minutes. Here Jimi took on Elmore James' blues standard "(My) Bleeding Heart" with its themes of lost love and mistrust. Backed by Cox and Miles, Jimi worked his way through this mid-tempo blues with effectiveness. The highlight of the track was the solo that came before the final verse of lyrics. Musically, Jimi's performance owned much to his own song "Red House" with the same opening guitar riff and much the same rhythm playing throughout.

The sister track to "Jam 292" from the May 1969 session, the so-called "Jelly 292," was an outtake from a Douglas-run session. Sources conflict widely on who else appeared on this track with Jimi. Glebbeek and Shapiro listed the bass as unknown but not Noel, the drummer as possibly Dallas Taylor, and the piano as possibly Stephen Stills. Other sources listed Cox and Mitch as the rhythm section and Sharon Layne as organist. As the track appeared on the album, the keyboard instrument sounded like a piano, more so than an organ, but the bass playing sounded like Cox's which left things as a toss-up. Regardless of who was playing—or even what the proper name for the track was, Jam or Jelly—the performance itself was a solid, fast-paced blues with the guitar playing off the piano and the bass matching the guitar's pace throughout.

"Electric Church Red House" was so named by Jimi himself as he spoke at the opening of the song. This track was originally recorded at TTG Studios in September 1968. Mitch and Noel backed Jimi up for the track with the inclusion of Lee Michaels on organ. The "Electric Church" version of "Red House" was possibly even more potent than the original "Red House." Here Jimi seemed slightly less interested in the blues and more focused on challenging the limits of the electric guitar over the solid bedrock rhythm of the Experience. A rarity in Jimi's studio material, the song ended with a screaming blast of feedback.

The twelve-minute version of "Hear My Train A Comin'" (aka "Getting My Heart Back Together"), which was the final track on the album, was the popular cut from the Berkeley Community Theater performance of May 30, 1970. Cut with Mitch and Cox, Jimi put forth a stunning live performance even though his guitar was gradually slipping further and further out of tune throughout. Although the release *Jimi Hendrix: Blues* was originally a Douglas product, it was unique and refreshing for listeners and caught the attention of many as a true testament to Jimi's roots in the blues and R&B of the American South.

First Rays of the New Rising Sun

First Rays of the New Rising Sun was issued in 1997 and represented the first official album prepared by Jimi's family after they gained control over the guitar player's estate. The production credits listed Jimi, Eddie Kramer, and Mitch Mitchell and as a result, the high quality of audio fidelity that was a Kramer trademark returned. The seventeen songs on the album were culled from sessions beginning in March 1968 up to Jimi's final session at Electric Lady Studios in the summer of 1970.

More so than any previous posthumous release, *First Rays of the New Rising Sun* sought to capture Jimi's vision for the double album he was unable to release before his death. That said, both Mitch and Cox readily admitted that the material on the album could not accurately capture Jimi's vision as he had not chosen the song list before he died. Some tracks that were included did seem to have been finished and preselected by Jimi, but as was his manner in the studio he would likely have continued making small changes to each song right up to the time when the album was to be sent to the label. Although Jimi himself had described lack of musical inspiration at times toward the end of his life, the album's content showed no such signs. Here Jimi was back at full creative potency. John McDermott noted in the liner notes for the release that Jimi had reworked or significantly revised all but one of the songs on the release during his final months at his Electric Lady Studios.

The majority of the tracks on the record were created in the four months of furious studio activity that Jimi undertook during the summer of 1970. The core group that surrounded him at this time was the hybrid group of Buddy Miles on bass and Mitch Mitchell on drums. Several others appeared on various tracks as the majority of the songs here included some previously recorded material with added overdubs done at Electric Lady Studios that summer.

The record opened with the song "Freedom" which also included Juma Sultan on percussion and the Ghetto Fighters (Arthur and Albert Allen) on backing vocals. Track two was "Izabella," a song that Jimi first recorded at the Record Plant in January 1970 and then overdubbed at Electric Lady (the manner in which most of the songs on this release were built). "Izabella" presented Jimi in a bit of a pensive mood lyrically, but with a locomotive rhythm track and a soaring guitar solo in the middle of the words. Much speculation has been made about the meaning of the song as here Jimi cast himself as a soldier away from his family/love interest engaged in a war—presumably Vietnam. There was also some basis for the claim that the song was actually about the relationship between Jimi and Monika Dannemann and the separation of the pair was due to Jimi's touring schedule. As Jimi referenced holding a machine gun in the lyrics it was equally possible that he was talking either of his guitar, an actual gun, or both. Of note, the lyrics of the song contained the first mention of a "new rising sun" in any of Jimi's songs.

The third track was "Night Bird Flying" followed by "Angel," "Room Full of Mirrors," "Dolly Dagger," and "Ezy Ryder." This series of songs was an intimate portrait of Jimi's personal life encompassing his relationships with women, such as Devon Wilson, and his own self-image. "Drifting," "Beginnings," and "Stepping Stone" led into "My Friend." With "My Friend," Jimi revisited the rambling lyrics, mellow blues, and interesting group of sidemen from the past. This was the only track on the release that was left in its original form without overdubbing at Electric Lady Studios. Jimi was joined by Ken Pine (originally of the Fugs) on 12-string guitar, Paul Caruso on harmonica, Jimmy Mayes (formally of Joey Dee and the Starlighters) on drums, and an opening piano gesture supplied by Stephen Stills.

"Straight Ahead" led into the almost heavy metal sounding opening descending guitar line of "Hey Baby (New Rising Sun)." With its vaguely "All Along the Watchtower" sounding groove, Jimi hit his stride. Of note for this track was that the version that appeared here was a combination of several sessions as Jimi never completed a true "studio" lead vocal. The vocal line here was from a live-in-the-studio take which was why Jimi asked if the microphone was on before he began singing. The final four tracks on the album were "Earth Blues," "Astro Man," "In From the Storm," and "Belly Button Window." Although *First Rays of the New Rising Sun* was not the fourth studio album created entirely under Jimi's supervision, it was still a very solid release that accurately captured Jimi's renewed spirit during the summer of 1970. Interestingly, the cover art on the front of the album depicted a semitransparent image of Jimi looking down from the sky amid a rising sun in the background almost as if he was keeping careful watch as his music continued to be issued.

South Saturn Delta

Also released in 1997 was the album *South Saturn Delta*, another product of the union between Jimi's estate under the care of the Experience Hendrix L.L.C. collective and MCA Records. The material on the release was a bit of a strange collection of jams, studio outtakes, live performances, and alternative versions of several of Jimi's most popular songs. On the cover of the album Jimi appeared astride a black Harley Davidson motorcycle wearing a vest and a headband—much more biker than sixties hippie. The strangeness that was this image was mirrored by some of the tracks on the album; however, *South Saturn Delta* still had a great deal of solid music contained in its fifteen tracks. The release began with the blues jam "Look Over Yonder" followed by an instrumental labeled "Little Wing," which sounded like a combination of that song and "Angel" with the drums too far forward in the mix.

"Lover Man" came next with Jimi telling the control room at the opening of the track that this one was called "Here It Comes." "South Saturn Delta" came next with its interesting blending of styles. Here, Jimi seemed to be working toward a mixture of rock and jazz through the incorporation of a set of four horns on the track. With the addition of trumpet, trombone, and two saxophones, glimpses of a new direction in Jimi's music were possible. Even more compelling was the manner in which the guitar and horns were recorded with Jimi sitting in the middle of a circle of horn players as they cut the track together.

The next two songs were issued with vocals. "Power of Love" was an interesting take with the Band of Gypsys and was followed by a track called "Message to the Universe" which was actually "Message to Love" with a particularly robust guitar solo. "Tax Free" returned to the instrumental jam-style of performance with "All Along the Watchtower" next. The previously unreleased alternate take on this song was recorded at Olympic Studios in London on January 21, 1968. On that day, Jimi and Noel had a falling out and others stepped into the studio to create this version. Dave Mason from Traffic supplied a 12-string guitar line and Brian Jones of the Rolling Stones supplied some percussion work. Jimi himself cut the bass part as an overdub once the initial tracks were laid.

"The Stars That Play With Laughing Sam's Dice" was an alternate version of the song that originally appeared on *Smash Hits* and as a B-side single. Recorded in 1967 at Mayfair Studio, what the psychedelic send-up on "LSD" lacked in lyrical cohesion was far outweighed by the shear virtuosity of Jimi's playing. Attested to by the fact that the guitar was much louder in the mix than the vocals—which could have easily been changed for this release—this song was a bit of guitar showmanship on Jimi's part. The guitar work on "Midnight" was another testament to Jimi's ability, yet it did not really constitute a completed song as it lacked vocals and the rhythm section did little more than hold down chord changes as a canvas on which Jimi painted.

"Sweet Angel" was Jimi's song "Angel" while he was still in the process of working out how it would all fit together. Here Jimi recorded guitar, bass, and vocals over a metronome beat generated by an electronic keyboard. The tempo was markedly faster than on the standard version of "Angel," but much of the actual guitar work was already present. Due to tape damage the opening of this version of the song has been lost. There followed a version of the Elmore James tune "Bleeding Heart," a fast and funky take on the blues which bore very little resemblance to the original. "Pali Gap" was the tune so named by Jeffery due to its association with the *Rainbow Bridge* movie project. The version on this album grew spontaneously out of an extended jam session during a recording session at Electric

Lady Studios on July 1, 1970. While Jimi still exhibited his prodigious guitar playing skill, he did so here without much of the sheer volume his listeners had become accustomed to in other songs.

The final two tracks on the release were quite unique, but for significantly different reasons. The penultimate song was "Drifter's Escape," another Bob Dylan cover. Unlike "All Along the Watchtower," Jimi let the guitar work take over too much of the texture on this version and with that some of the intensity of the lyrics was lost. *South Saturn Delta* ended much in the same manner as *First Rays of the New Rising Sun* had, with Jimi playing one of his original compositions alone. The lighthearted humor of "Belly Button Window" from the previous album does not transfer to Jimi's take on "Midnight Lightning" here. Jimi cut this version as a bit of gut-shot blues exhibiting a finger picking style that he rarely used. Another slow-burning blues piece, its only accompaniment for Jimi's voice and guitar was Jimi's own foot tapping time on the floor. The song faded out at the end leaving a feeling of incompleteness with this track and so ended this eclectic compilation.

Voodoo Child: The Jimi Hendrix Collection

Voodoo Child: The Jimi Hendrix Collection was issued in 2001 by Experience Hendrix L.L.C. and MCA Records. Another of the "definitive" collections of Jimi's music, the two-disc set attempted to include tracks of interest to both casual listener and collector. Several songs in the compilation were described as alternate versions, previously unreleased, or previously unavailable. The previously unavailable label was slightly misleading as these songs had been issued in the past, but the albums on which they were found had been discontinued or withdrawn.

The first disc of the set was a compilation of Jimi's tunes from the studio. There were many of his "greatest hits" with the really interesting tracks in alternate versions. Those that appeared as alternate versions included "Highway Chile" from the 1967 Olympic Studios session on April 3 and "All Along the Watchtower," also from Olympic on January 21, 1968. Two other alternate versions that were included were "Spanish Castle Magic" from Olympic on February 17, 1969, and "Stone Free" from the Record Plant in April 1969. These different versions were not wholly remarkable to the casual listener, but the version of "Stone Free" with backing vocals from Noel, Roger Chapman, and Andy Fairweather Low warranted release.

The second disc was a collection of live recordings culled from the last three years of Jimi's life. Of interest here was the ability for the listener to hear how Jimi's live sound changed over the course of his career. Additionally, Janie Hendrix and John McDermott—the listed producers for the release—did include several of Jimi's most legendary and breathtaking performances. The 1967 performance was Jimi's legendary take on "Wild

Thing" from the *Monterey Pop Festival*. 1968 was represented by "Hey Joe" from Winterland in San Francisco. The Los Angeles Forum and San Diego Sports Arena were both taped from 1969, but the real standout from that year was Jimi's performance of "The Star Spangled Banner" from Woodstock. Tracks from 1970 represented shows from the Berkeley Community Theater, the *New York Pop Festival*, and the *Isle of Wight Festival*. The gem from this year was a little-heard performance of "Foxey Lady" taped while Jimi was on Maui, Hawaii, for the filming of *Rainbow Bridge*. Another interesting inclusion in this set was the essay contained in the liner notes penned by ex–*Rolling Stone* editor and *MTV News* personality Kurt Loder.

Valleys of Neptune

In March 2010, Jimi's estate issued its latest installment from the vaults, *Valleys of Neptune*, as a collection of twelve previously unreleased studio tracks. This most recent offering from Experience Hendrix L.L.C. under the guidance of Janie Hendrix, Eddie Kramer, and John McDermott was the latest chapter to the ever-unfolding legacy that was Jimi's ravenous appetite for studio recording. The project began on the heels of McDermott uncovering a collection of studio tapes from Olympic Studios, London, from mid-February 1969. The tapes exhibited the original Jimi Hendrix Experience at full force. They were riding high on the successes of their three studio albums and although the tension between Jimi and Noel was reaching a boiling point, the group was expanding their arrangements of existing songs as well as exploring new territory. In fact, much of the material on the album exemplified Jimi's desire to move in new and experimental directions after the chart hit that was *Electric Ladyland*.

As has been the case with most of the Experience Hendrix releases, *Valleys of Neptune* was released with rich illustrations, extensive liner notes, and the highest studio quality possible. Jimi himself was listed as the producer for all of the tracks and the job of engineer was shared by Kramer, George Chkiantz, and Gary Kellgren—depending on the song. Upon its release, some considered the alternate versions of Jimi's hit songs as rehearsals or cast-off studio jams. Eddie Kramer brought this issue into tight focus in the March issue of *Mix* with his statement: "I wouldn't call them rehearsals exactly; it's a lot more than that. He's trying out stuff. He wanted to hear what some of the material would sound like with different arrangements. He's experimenting. It was a test."[7]

The cover art of the release was quite unique, even for a Jimi Hendrix release. The front of the album was a composite image. A classic image of Jimi appearing in a pensive mood as captured by photographer Linda McCartney was superimposed on top of an original watercolor painting made by Jimi himself. The watercolor, while not directly representational, does seem to suggest an otherworldly image in muted shades of blue and black. With the album title referencing outer space and other planets, this image came across as especially appropriate. The back cover continued this same basic color palette. Here though, the photograph was of Jimi playing his signature Stratocaster by James Davenport. Also on the back cover were the twelve song titles, timing for each song, and the producer credits.

The liner notes for the release were written by McDermott, as he is an expert on Jimi's life and music and also a major force behind the Experience Hendrix L.L.C. material. The material on the album itself can be divided into two sections. The first three tracks were unique from the rest of the album as bassist Billy Cox appeared. The other nine songs on the album were recorded by the original Jimi Hendrix Experience: Jimi, Mitch, and Noel. The sessions that the majority of the tracks on the release came from were recorded during the period of 1969 that Jimi and Noel were not getting along. Cox was called in to fill the gap and as such he ended up playing with Jimi for the rest of the guitarist's life.

The first song on the release was a composite of four different takes of "Stone Free." The original tracking for this song was done in April 1969 at the Record Plant. Later that month and into May, more attempts at recording the song were made and here Kramer cut all the best pieces together. The version here was a lively up-tempo take on the song about breaking free of the bonds of an unhappy relationship. Jimi's guitar solo was especially fierce and the rhythm section was locked tightly together throughout. Roger Chapman and Andy Fairweather Low were represented on the track with backing vocals.

The second track was the namesake of the entire album, "Valleys of Neptune." Over the four-minute duration of the song Jimi again referenced several of his favorite lyrical images. He talked of other planets in the solar system, mythology and the lost city of Atlantis, the waves of the ocean and other nature images, and the need to save one's soul since the future of the planet was often uncertain. The frantic manner in which Jimi spit out the words on this track was a rarity for the guitarist. "Valleys of Neptune" was recorded in September 1969 at the Record Plant with additional tracking having taken place in May 1970. Juma Sultan was the percussionist and contributed to the general funkiness of the song. Jimi had taken several stabs at recording this song over the course of almost two years as attested to by the two versions that appeared on *Hear My Music* in 2004.

"Valleys of Neptune" was released as a single a month before the album itself was issued and quickly shot to the number one spot. In fact, in an effort to market Jimi to a new—and much more technology-savvy consumer—the single was issued in a variety of different formats. Wal-Mart was the sole seller of the CD single with B-side "Peace in Mississippi." This also came with an MP3 bonus of "Red House" live from the Clark University show. In addition, a seven-inch vinyl single was issued with B-side "Cat Talking to Me." This will no doubt become a prized possession for true collectors as the vinyl release included the "definitive" version of the A-side and the B-side had never previously been available.

Elmore James was represented with the third track, "Bleeding Heart." Although technically a cover version, the "Bleeding Heart" of Jimi and the band was bluesy, loose, and expansive. Clocking in at over six minutes, the reinvention of the song's structure allowed for Jimi to pepper it with some solid electric blues solos that had a distinct psychedelic leaning. Taken from a Record Plant session in April 1969, the band on the track included Jimi, Cox, Rocky Isaac on drums, Chris Grimes on tambourine, and Al Marks on maracas. The expansive structure, virtuosic soloing, and additional instrumentation truly put Jimi's stamp on this song.

The slow building and burning blues number "Hear My Train A Comin'" came next. With this track, Noel was back in the role as bass player where he remained for the rest of the tracks included on the album. The version presented here came from the Record Plant session on April 7, 1969. The band put in a searing and extended performance that stretched out to almost seven-and-a-half minutes. Periodically on the track, Jimi matched his guitar playing with his vocals, but for the most part the song turned into a showcase for his guitar work—which exhibited searing ferocity.

The basic tracking for "Mr. Bad Luck" went back to the sessions at Olympic Studios, in London, from May 1967. Representing a relatively early Experience sound, the song was one of Jimi's oldest and the recording was the earliest represented on the release. The opening smacked of what was to come as the song was eventually transformed into "Look Over Yonder." A real peculiarity with the song was that the bass and drum parts—still supplied by Mitch and Noel—were actually overdubs from 1987. While this does seems strange, the lore of the new tracking was that during the mid-1980s Chas Chandler was in possession of the old Olympic tapes and he invited the Experience rhythm section to add the best possible accompaniment to Jimi's lines which were fixed in time by his death. While this might seem like musical cannibalism, it was/is actually quite common that Jimi's studio work invariably included overdubbing of original seed tracks with additional parts recorded later. The more modern overdubs were recorded at Air Studios, in London, under Chandler's guidance.

Jimi, Mitch, and Noel were steadfast fans and supporters of Cream and specifically of guitarist Eric Clapton. As homage to the group, Jimi worked up a cover of the song "Sunshine of Your Love," which he often performed live. Though Peter Brown, Jack Bruce, and Eric Clapton were the original creators of the song, the version that appeared here was drastically retooled. From the exceptionally fast opening tempo to the extended chocked guitar rhythm section halfway through, Jimi reimaged the tune with his own funky/psychedelic shading. Although the song did appear on other of Jimi's releases, he chose to use their live arrangement in the studio for this take with all of its associated tempo changes, including the song winding itself down to an ever-slowing close. Rocki Dzidzornu was on hand for the session to supply additional percussion to enhance the overall impression of the live-in-the-studio performance.

Track seven on *Valleys of Neptune* was another from the Olympic Studios seed tapes from February 1969, again with overdubbed bass and drum parts from 1987. The song, "Lover Man," evolved from Jimi's take on the B. B. King hit "Rock Me, Baby," but was transformed into something unique to Jimi and the original Experience. Cast as an electric blues send-up, the song featured Jimi's guitar work quite prominently as he took some extended time to solo toward the end of the song before it simply faded out.

"Ships Passing in the Night" was one of only four tracks on the album that had never appeared before in any form. Taken from the Record Plant sessions of April 1969, this number was a fairly straight-ahead electric blues piece featuring Jimi out in front of Mitch and Noel. Even though it was built on the stock 12-bar blues format, Jimi transformed the standard formula into a rather unique number for the Experience catalogue. At nearly six minutes, Jimi took his time soloing amid the basic lyrical sentiments of loneliness and travel. A particularly interesting effect in the song was the use of a Leslie speaker which gave Jimi's guitar a distinct panning quality. Unfortunately, the song seemed to essentially dissolve at its end with the rhythm section dropping out and Jimi soloing to the close.

"Fire" was another of the tracks from the Olympic session. While it was a very solid performance at a brisk tempo, there was little here that had not already been presented on countless previous releases and the overall speed brought the song to its conclusion at fewer than three minutes. Next came "Red House" in an alternate and extended version. Jimi kicked the tune off with the customary slow guitar lead-in that gradually ushered in Mitch and Noel. An interesting outtake from the early-1969 Olympic session, "Red House" was again not as remarkable as other songs on the release simply because it was already so thoroughly represented in previous recordings.

Both of the final two songs on the album renewed the spirit of tracks that had not previously been released in any form from the extensive back catalogue. "Lullaby for the Summer" smacked of "Ezy Ryder" as the two songs shared a basic rhythm pattern. The fire and anticipation built up by the opening of the song was a bit of a disappointment as it ended up without lyrics. That said, "Lullaby for the Summer" was an outstanding example of Jimi presenting a solid instrumental rocker. One can only imagine what would have been if there had been enough time in Jimi's abbreviated life for the song to have reached its full potential. This sense of incompleteness was enhanced by the disjoined manner in which the song came to an abrupt and inconclusive end.

The final track on the album was "Crying Blue Rain" which began with an introduction that recalled "Hey Joe." Originally recorded at Olympic in

1969, here Mitch and Noel again overdubbed more modern drum and bass parts. Present at the original session, Rocki Dzidzornu again supplied additional percussion to add some depth and body to the track. Here Jimi led the group through almost five minutes of tempo changes and guitar soloing in the creation of a song that although lacking lyrics did not have the missing finality of "Lullaby for the Summer." Through several interesting accelerations and decelerations of the tempo, Jimi held court with his guitar until the sounded faded out to end the release.

On the heels of the release of this most recent installment of Jimi's catalogue, little doubt was left that there was more to come. *Rolling Stone* magazine gave the album three-and-a-half stars out of five as a testament to Jimi's legacy. Further, Eddie Kramer noted: "There's a library full of stuff we haven't even touched yet . . . the good news is there's plenty more."[8] With Jimi's library of studio and live tapes in the capable hands of Experience Hendrix L.L.C., more music from the guitar legend is on the horizon. An interesting aside—which no one seems to be making much of—is that none of the songs on *Valleys of Neptune* came from Electric Lady Studios. With that in mind, the vaults must still be bursting with the work that Jimi did at the end of his life. Further, there is already a multidisc anthology of Jimi's work in the works along with DVD releases of shows at the *Monterey Pop Festival* and Royal Albert Hall.

The Legacy of Jimi Hendrix: Merchandizing a Legend and Control of the Estate

The selling of music stars has long been big business, even more so after an individual died. In Jimi's case, there has been a great deal of effort made to merchandize his image and parlay his reputation into dollars in the wake of his untimely demise. Beyond the untold numbers of t-shirts and various other sanctioned and unsanctioned products that were branded by Jimi's distinctive image, there has been a series of concerted efforts mounted to continue to immortalize the sixties superstar.

It seems to make the most sense to discuss the merchandizing of Jimi's legacy by starting with guitars that have been made and sold with Jimi's name somehow attached or associated. So far, the Fender Musical Instruments Corperation has issued no fewer than seven different Jimi Hendrix–inspired models. In 1980, they issued the Hendrix Prototype Stratocaster, in 1991 the Custom Shop '67 Reissue, in 1997 the Custom Shop Monterey, in 1997 the Tribute Stratocaster, the following year the Voodoo Stratocaster, in 2000 the '68 Reverse Headstock Stratocaster, and in 2002 the Woodstock Clone. Certainly, it stands to reason that Jimi's guitar gear legacy should rest with the Fender as he was most well known for playing their products during the height of his career—though it should be noted that he also played other guitars such as the Gibson Flying V style.

More recently, Fender has made its offerings dedicated to Jimi's legacy more specific. In 1980 they designed a Hendrix Prototype Stratocaster and in 2005 they issued a limited release Fender custom model based on Jimi's gear. Only about twenty-five of the Prototype model have been accounted for in the past thirty years with the conventional wisdom being that the guitar never went into standard production as it was meant as a promotional item. The 2005 Reverse Proto Closet Classic Ltd was designed by Fender Custom Shop master builder Dennis Galuszka and was based on exacting measurements made from Jimi's own guitar. Only one hundred of these guitars were made and it was largely at the request of guitarist-singer-songwriter John Mayer who went to the Fender Custom Shop to request that they build more.

Another major player on the guitar field where Jimi's legacy comes into play has been Gibson. In 2006, the Gibson Guitar Company began issuing instruments associated with Jimi. The most impressive of these was the Gibson Custom Inspired by Jimi Hendrix Psychedelic Flying V, which the young guitarist used on his European tour in late 1967 and into 1968. Faithful in its reproduction of the guitar Jimi used, the Gibson Custom Flying V even included the psychedelic custom paint job that was a signature of the guitar that Jimi actually played.

In an interesting turn of events in September 2009, the Gibson Guitar Company in cooperation with Experience Hendrix L.L.C. announced plans to issue three different guitar packages inspired by Jimi. The sets were to include Gibson-made Stratocaster copies packaged with the "Voodoo Child" amplifier and "Foxey" Fuzz pedal, along with some reproduction memorabilia and a soft-sided gig bag. What the Gibson/Experience Hendrix collective did not count on was the backlash that they experienced immediately after announcing their plans. Fans were seemingly outraged by Gibson issuing a Strat copy since it was obviously the domain of the Fender Guitar Company. What is certain is that as of September 27, 2009, Gibson had removed information from their press releases on their plans to issue a Stratocaster copy associated with Jimi's legacy.

Another major market for those who emulate Jimi's guitar sound and playing style was the use of the same/similar effects pedals. The story should start with products made by Roger Mayer, Jimi's self-described "effects guru." At the time that Jimi was actively searching for new guitar sounds, he enlisted the early assistance of Mayer who began working on various types of electronic guitar effects pedals for him in 1967. Mayer had already been building guitar effects for the likes of Jimmy Page and Jeff Beck beginning in 1964.

For Jimi, Mayer built an Octavia pedal and a Fuzz box. With Mayer, Jimi explored the outer reaches of guitar sound making capability in the mid-to-late 1960s. Fortunately, Mayer continues to issue effects inspired by his work with Jimi—largely during the creation of *Axis: Bold as Love*. At this time, Mayer offers no fewer than ten effects pedals that either reproduce or were inspired by the effects that he built for Jimi. Including the Octavia and Fuzz, Mayer now markets a host of effects inspired by the guitar god including the Axis Fuzz, Voodoo-Boost, and Stone (fuzz) pedals.

The guitar effects pedal market is crowded and there are numerous others who craft pedals based on those used by Jimi during his life. Dunlop Guitar

Accessories offers the JH-F1 Jimi Hendrix Fuzz Face which is a reproduction of the Dallas Arbiter Fuzz Face that Jimi used with the Band of Gypsys. The Dunlop Company still markets the Original Crybaby Wah Pedal which they continue to make in the style that Jimi helped to popularize alongside Eric Clapton and David Gilmour. They also sell the JH-1B Jimi Hendrix Signature Wah Pedal. The list of guitar effects pedal providers who imitate the sounds that Jimi created live and in the studio is too long to manage—suffice it to say that there are many and they all attempt to give the modern guitarist the ability to recreate that much sought-after sound/tone that Jimi immortalized.

Other guitar-related gear that has received specific attention or alteration based on Jimi's legacy includes strings. The Dean Markley Company offers Jimi Hendrix nickel-plated steel guitar strings. Beyond the standard guitar gear, there now exists a library of books of reproductions of Jimi's music in notated form. Hal Leonard is understandably a front-runner in this race. They have several series of songbooks specific to Jimi's catalogue. One series offers Jimi's music one album at a time in a series called "Learn to Play the Songs from (fill in the album title here)." Additionally, they have "Signature Licks" of the guitar great and a series of technique books that are a "step-by-step breakdown" for reproducing Jimi's songs.

Beyond musical instruments and the gear associated with them and general merchandise such as t-shirts and such, there has recently been a push by Experience Hendrix L.L.C. to reissue some previously released material—but with new or bonus features. As of the summer of 2009, Experience Hendrix L.L.C. teamed with the Sony Legacy imprint to reissue the seminal works of the guitar superstar. This team effort was all focused on the March 2010 release of *Valleys of Neptune*. Also in that month, Sony Legacy reissued six of Jimi's most popular releases in new versions or formats.

Sony Legacy issued Jimi's first three studio albums to coincide with *Valleys of Neptune*. The first of these was their version of *Are You Experienced?*, which was brought out in a new version with added material. In addition to the original eleven songs, which were digitally remastered from the original two-track tapes, the album included six more songs that had been recorded at the same time as the album tracks. These other songs were "Stone Free," "51st Anniversary," "Highway Chile," "Can You See Me?" "Remember," and "Red House." The apparent reason for the inclusion of the additional songs went to the core of how the material on the first album and the singles that surrounded it were released. What one gets with the Sony Legacy reissue are the tracks from both the United States and the United Kingdom releases of the albums—they contained some different songs—plus the B-sides of the first three singles that Jimi released at the same time as the album was being made.

In addition to the deluxe material, the reissue of the album also included a "making of" mini-DVD documentary and lavishly illustrated packaging including a 36-page booklet that contained liner notes, session information for the initial tracking of the songs, and photos. Also during March 2010, Sony Legacy released *Are You Experienced?* and *Electric Ladyland* in deluxe audiophile versions as 180-gram vinyl with original artwork and gatefold covers.

Axis: Bold as Love was also issued in deluxe CD version in March 2010. The original thirteen songs from the album were digitally remastered from the two-track tapes. Added to this was again a lavish package with a 36-page booklet and mini-DVD "making of" documentary. There were no additional songs added to this release during the remastering process. *Electric Ladyland* also got the deluxe edition treatment from Sony Legacy and was also issued in the same month. Here the original sixteen tracks were digitally remastered and packaged in the ornate six-panel package that they call a "digipak." Also in this reissue was another of the mini-DVD "making of" documentaries—this one clocks in at about twelve minutes.

Also part of this set of reissues was *First Rays of the New Rising Sun*. The original album received the deluxe edition treatment by the label and the seventeen tracks were newly remastered. The album also came out in March 2010 and included a "making of" mini-DVD. The last of the current run of deluxe Sony Legacy audio reissues was *Smash Hits*. The seed tracks were digitally remastered and presented in a deluxe package that included the three original photos from the initial release of the album, plus several other photos that have not been previously available.

The most recent part of the reissue catalogue puzzle coming from Experience Hendrix L.L.C. and Sony Legacy was the release of DVD and Blue-Ray versions of Jimi's performance at Woodstock. The material was described as making use of all of the existing footage in reedited form presented uninterrupted in the original live sequence. The fourteen-song expanded Band of Gypsys set was augmented by the following five bonus items: "Road to Woodstock," "Jimi Hendrix: Live at Woodstock: A Second Look," "Jimi Hendrix Press Conference," "Nashville Rooms," and "Recording Woodstock." With this, the merchandizing of Jimi's legacy is current to March 2010. That said, the deal struck between Experience Hendrix L.L.C. and Sony Legacy extends to licensing of all classics, archive, and filmed concerts—so, no doubt there will be more to come.

ISSUES OF JIMI'S ESTATE

When Jimi died on September 18, 1970, he left behind little in material possessions beyond his guitars and his vast catalogue of music recordings. At issue was that fact that he died without a will and with no immediate heir (at one time he had reportedly had a will drawn up, but never signed it), which left the control of his estate in murky territory. Many people took an immediate and vested interest in what would become of Jimi's catalogue—and more significantly where the money that it was generating went.

As Jimi had not assigned a beneficiary prior to his death, his father was his next-of-kin. Recognizing that he was not able to handle Jimi's legacy himself, Al gave much of Jimi's estate to Alan Douglas and attorney Leo Branton. While this was a purposeful move on Al's part, it was one that he ended up regretting. "For many years Al Hendrix received $50,000 annually, as well as some other payments, which was probably far more than he had ever expected to receive in middle and old age."[1] During this period, Michael Jeffery still had a large stake in what happened with Jimi's legacy and he was also part owner of Electric Lady Studios. He ended up buying out Jimi's stake in the studio and gave the money to Al on Jimi's behalf. As stated above, Jeffery's interest in Jimi's legacy abruptly ended on March 5, 1973, with his death in a plane crash.

One can only imagine that Al must have thought that Jimi's star would gradually fade after his death and that eventually he would disappear into the annals of time the way that so many other musicians had and do. Quite oppositely, the value of Jimi's catalogue has steadily risen since his death with at least some credit going to the evolution of sound technology which called for his material to be reissued on CD and also audio engineering advancements which have allowed a great deal of "cleaning" of his original recordings.

Regardless, once Al realized that Jimi's legacy was worth much, much more than what he was getting he filed a lawsuit to regain proper control of the estate. Al quickly realized that he was not going to be able to afford the type of legal counsel that it was going to take to wrestle control of Jimi's estate back from Douglas and Branton. His savior came in the form of Microsoft cofounder Paul Allen who advanced him in excess of $4 million for the purposes of meeting his legal needs.

Shorty after winning the lawsuit with Douglas and Branton, Al set up Experience Hendrix L.L.C. with the expressed purpose of managing the "name, likeness, image and 100% of the music of Jimi Hendrix's legacy." The family-owned and operated business was initially run by Janie Hendrix (Jimi's stepsister), Al (who died in 2002), and Bob Hendrix (Jimi's nephew). At the time of Al's death, Jimi's estate was valued at an estimated $80 million and managing such a vast estate was a daunting task. In 2004, Janie and Bob lost financial control of the estate, which fell into the hands of a board of trustees. However, it is important to note that Janie Hendrix is still the president and CEO of Experience Hendrix L.L.C. The recent licensing deal established with Sony Legacy is just the most recent event in a long series that have had a profound effect on how and in what form Jimi's catalogue continues to be made available to the public.

Regardless of management, Jimi's legacy has remained remarkably vital and largely unblemished. He continues to be revered as a guitar superstar some forty years after his death. There are many tributes to this fact that remain active and ongoing including the Experience Music Project in Seattle, Washington; the Experience Hendrix Tours; and the Red House Tour.

The Experience Music Project was opened in 2000 and maintains an active focus on Jimi's legacy. Since its opening, it has featured memorabilia associated with Jimi's legacy in two important exhibits: *Jimi Hendrix,* which ran from 2003 until 2007 (with some material essentially on permanent display), and *Message to Love: Remembering and Reclaiming Jimi Hendrix,* which ran for much of 2008. Through the work of the Experience Music Project, new and old fans of Jimi's work continue to be able to access some of the most interesting pieces of memorabilia of the guitar hero. The exhibits have included key instruments, clothing, songwriting notebooks, various pieces of correspondence, and a series of movies—all geared toward keeping Jimi's legacy alive and available to the public.

As an ongoing testament to Jimi's legacy, the year 2000 saw the launch of a series of concerts and tours dedicated to Jimi's music. These events were staged in a wide variety of locations, but all had the same purpose: to have noteworthy performers play Jimi's music for the modern audience as a means of keeping his music and legacy alive. The concerts and tours began at the Rock and Roll Hall of Fame in 2000 with the Jimi Hendrix Surround Sound Theater and Exhibit, which included items on loan from Al's own collection of memorabilia from Jimi's youth.

There followed, in 2002, the San Diego Street Scene Concert and the Seattle 60th Birthday Concert. In 2004 there was a series of concerts dubbed the West Coast Tour. In 2006, came the Boston Tribute Concert followed by the St. Paul Tribute Concert. The East Coast Tour commenced in 2007 with a London Tribute Concert that followed. In 2008 came the Nationwide Tribute Concert. More recent events include the 2010 Experience Hendrix Tour. This, like those from the past ten years, includes a series of rock and roll notables performing Jimi's music live and in concert. The 2010 tour features the playing of Joe Satriani, Jonny Lang, Eric Johnson, Kenny Wayne Shepherd, Brad Whitford (of Aerosmith), Doyle Bramhall II, Ernie Isley, Living Colour, Chris Layton (of Double Trouble), and bassist Billy Cox. Additionally, in conjunction with MCA Records from 1999 to 2001, the Red House Tour focused on a multimedia tribute to Jimi's legacy which involved extended nationwide touring with semitrucks outfitted as rolling museums.

Jimi's musical genius was recognized during his abbreviated life through record sales, concert tickets sold, chart positions held, and awards. In 1967, *Melody Maker* magazine named him Pop Musician of the Year. In 1968, *Billboard* magazine dubbed him Artist of the Year. *Rolling Stone* magazine named him Performer of the Year in the same year. Awards and accolades of all sorts have also been posthumously heaped on Jimi, as well. In 1970, *Downbeat* magazine's Reader's Poll named him to their Hall of Fame. Also in 1970, *Guitar Player* magazine named him guitarist of the year (a serious accomplishment in light of the competition in that year).

In 1983, Jimi was given the Lifetime Achievement Award by *Guitar Player* magazine. As a particular highlight, the Jimi Hendrix Experience was inducted into the Rock and Roll Hall of Fame in 1992. Additionally, Jimi's music has received a series of Hall of Fame Grammy Awards beginning in 1999 for *Electric Ladyland*. Another significant milestone was Jimi being named number one in *Rolling Stone* magazine's 2003 "100 Greatest Guitarists of All Time." As an ongoing testament to Jimi's legacy, he continues to appear on the covers of the most significant guitar-oriented magazines to this day. In fact, Jimi is on the cover of the April 2010 edition of *Guitar World, Guitar Techniques*, and *Guitar Player* magazines. Further testament to Jimi's overall importance to the music world is that he has appeared on the cover of *Rolling Stone* magazine four times, so far. With renewed interest in Jimi's catalogue and legacy spurred by the release of *Valleys of Neptune*, there is no question that the music of Jimi Hendrix will continue to be revered long into the future and that his place at the top of the rock pantheon will remain intact.

Tours and Jam Sessions

(When possible, the other acts on the bill with Hendrix are included. If no other acts are listed it may have been a single act show or the other acts are not known.)[1]

Year/Date	Venue/Location	Other Acts
1966		
October 13	Novelty, Evreaux, Paris, France	Supporting Johnny Hallyday
October 14	Cinema Rio, Nancy, France	Supporting Johnny Hallyday
October 15	Salle Des Fêtes, Villerupt, France	Supporting Johnny Hallyday
October 18	*Musicorama* TV show, L'Olympia, Paris, France	Supporting Johnny Hallyday
October 25	Scotch of St. James, London, England	
November 8	Big Apple, Munich, Germany	
November 9	Big Apple, Munich, Germany	
November 10	Big Apple, Munich, Germany	
November 11	Big Apple, Munich, Germany	
November 25	Bag O'Nails, London, England	Press reception
November 26	Ricky Tick, Hounslow, Middlesex, England	Support for the New Animals

Year/Date	Venue/Location	Other Acts
December 10	The Ram Jam Club, Brixton, London	Supporting John Mayall's Bluesbreakers
December 16	Chiselhurst Caves, Bromley, Kent, England	
December 21	Blaises Club, Queen's Gate, London	
December 22	Guild Hall, Southampton, Hampshire, England	
December 26	The Upper Cut, London, England	
December 29	*Top of the Pops*— performed "Hey Joe"	
December 31	Hillside Social Club, Folkestone, Kent, England	
1967		
January 4	Bromely Court Hotel, Kent, England	
January 7	New Century Hall, Manchester, England	
January 8	Mojo Club, Sheffield, England	
January 11	Bag O'Nails, London, England	
January 12	7^1/$_2$ Club, London, England	
January 13	7^1/$_2$ Club, London, England	
January 14	Beachcomber Club, Nottinghamshire, England	
January 15	Kerklevington Country Club, Yorkshire, England	Supported by Rivers Invitation
January 16	7^1/$_2$ Club, London, England	
January 17	*Ready, Steady, Radio*, London, England 7^1/$_2$ Club, London, England	
January 19	Speakeasy, London, England	
January 20	Haverstock Country Hill Club, London, England	
January 21	Refectory, London, England	
January 22	The Astoria, Lancashire, England	
January 24	Marquee, London, England	Supported by the Syn
January 25	Orford Cellar, Norfolk, England	
January 27	Chiselhurst Caves, Bromely, Kent, England	
January 28	The Upper Cut, London, England	

Year/Date	Venue/Location	Other Acts
January 29	Saville Theater, London, England	Supporting The Koobas and The Who
February 1	New Cellar Club, Durham, England	
February 2	The R&B Club, Imperial Hotel, Durham, England	
February 3	Ricky Tick, Middlesex, England	
February 4	The Ram Jam Club, London, England	
February 6	The Flamingo Club, London, England	
February 8	Bromley Club, Bromley, Kent, England	
February 9	Locarno, Bristol, Gloucester-shire, England	
February 10	Plaza Ballroom, Berkshire, England	
February 11	Blue Moon, Gloucestershire, England	
February 12	Sinking Ship, Cheshire, England	
February 14	Gray's Club, The Civic Hall, Essex, England	
February 15	Dorothy Ballroom, Cambridge, England	
February 17	Ricky Tick/Thames Hotel, Berkshire, England	
February 18	Art College, University of York, York, England	
February 19	Blarney Club, London, England	
February 20	The Pavilion, Somerset, England	
February 22	Roundhouse, London, England	The Flies, Sandy and Hilary
February 23	The Pier Pavilion, Sussex, England	
February 24	University of Leicestershire, Leicestershire, England	
February 25	Corn Exchange, Essex, England	Soul Trinity
February 26	St. Mary Cray, Essex, England	
March 1	Orchard Ballroom, Surrey, England	

Year/Date	Venue/Location	Other Acts
March 2	Marquee Club, London, England	
March 4	Omnibus, Paris, France	
March 5	Law Society Graduation Ball, Paris, France	
March 6	The Twenty Club, Lille, France	
March 8	The Speakeasy, London, England	
March 9	Skyline Ballroom, Yorkshire, England	
March 10	Club A Go Go, Northumberland, England	
March 11	International Club, Leeds, London, England	
March 12	Gyro Club, Yorkshire, England	
March 17	Star Club, Hamburg, Germany	
March 18	Star Club, Hamburg, Germany	
March 19	Star Club, Hamburg, Germany	
March 21	The Speakeasy, London, England	
March 23	Guild Hall, Southampton, England	
March 25	Starlight Room, Lincolnshire, England	
March 26	Tabernacle Club, Cheshire, England	
March 28	Assembly Hall, Buckinghamshire, England	
March 30	*Top of the Pops*—performed "Purple Haze"	
March 31	The Astoria, London, England	Package tour in support of Cat Stevens, Engelbert Humperdinck, The Walker Brothers, Californians, Quotations
April 1	Odeon, Ipswich, England	Cat Stevens, Engelbert Humperdinck, The Walker Brothers, Californians, Quotations
April 2	Gaumont, Worcestershire, England	Cat Stevens, Engelbert Humperdinck, The Walker Brothers, Californians, Quotations

Year/Date	Venue/Location	Other Acts
April 5	Odeon, Leeds, England	Cat Stevens, Engelbert Humperdinck, The Walker Brothers, Californians, Quotations
April 6	Odeon, Glasgow, Scotland	Cat Stevens, Engelbert Humperdinck, The Walker Brothers, Californians, Quotations
April 7	A.B.C., Cumberland, England	Cat Stevens, Engelbert Humperdinck, The Walker Brothers, Californians, Quotations
April 8	A.B.C., Chesterfield, England	Cat Stevens, Engelbert Humperdinck, The Walker Brothers, Californians, Quotations
April 9	The Empire, Liverpool, England	Cat Stevens, Engelbert Humperdinck, The Walker Brothers, Californians, Quotations
April 11	Grenada, Bedfordshire, England	Cat Stevens, Engelbert Humperdinck, The Walker Brothers, Californians, Quotations
April 12	Gaumont, Hampshire, England	Cat Stevens, Engelbert Humperdinck, The Walker Brothers, Californians, Quotations
April 13	Odeon, Wolverhampton, England	Cat Stevens, Engelbert Humperdinck, The Walker Brothers, Californians, Quotations
April 14	Odeon, Lancashire, England	Cat Stevens, Engelbert Humperdinck, The Walker Brothers, Californians, Quotations
April 15	Odeon, Blackpool, England	Cat Stevens, Engelbert Humperdinck, The Walker Brothers, Californians, Quotations
April 16	De Monfort Hall, Leicestershire, England	Cat Stevens, Engelbert Humperdinck, The Walker Brothers, Californians, Quotations
April 19	Odeon, Warwickshire, England	Cat Stevens, Engelbert Humperdinck, The Walker Brothers, Californians, Quotations
April 20	A.B.C., Lincolnshire, England	Cat Stevens, Engelbert Humperdinck, The Walker Brothers, Californians, Quotations
April 21	City Hall, Newcastle-upon-Tyne, England	Cat Stevens, Engelbert Humperdinck, The Walker Brothers, Californians, Quotations
April 22	Odeon, Manchester, England	Cat Stevens, Engelbert Humperdinck, The Walker Brothers, Californians, Quotations

Year/Date	Venue/Location	Other Acts
April 23	Gaumont, Staffordshire, England	Cat Stevens, Engelbert Humperdinck, The Walker Brothers, Californians, Quotations
April 25	Colston Hall, Bristol, England	Cat Stevens, Engelbert Humperdinck, The Walker Brothers, Californians, Quotations
April 26	Capital, Cardiff, Glamorgan, Wales	Cat Stevens, Engelbert Humperdinck, The Walker Brothers, Californians, Quotations
April 27	A.B.C., Hampshire, England	Cat Stevens, Engelbert Humperdinck, The Walker Brothers, Californians, Quotations
April 28	Adelphi, Buckinghamshire, England	Cat Stevens, Engelbert Humperdinck, The Walker Brothers, Californians, Quotations
April 29	Winter Gardens, Dorset, England	Cat Stevens, Engelbert Humperdinck, The Walker Brothers, Californians, Quotations
April 30	Granada, London, England	Cat Stevens, Engelbert Humperdinck, The Walker Brothers, Californians, Quotations
May 4	*Top of the Pops*—performed "The Wind Cries Mary "	
May 6	Imperial Ballroom, Lancashire, England	
May 7	Saville, London, England	Supported by Garnett Mimms
May 12	Bluesville '67 Club, London, England	
May 13	Imperial College, London, England	Supported by the band 1984
May 14	Belle Vue, Manchester, London	
May 15	Neue Welt, Berlin, Germany	
May 16	Big Apple, Munich, Germany	
May 19	Konserthallen, Göteborg, Sweden	
May 20	Mariebergsskogen, Karlstad, Sweden	
May 21	Falkoner Centret, Copenhagen, Denmark	
May 22	Kulttuuritalo, Helsinki, Finland	
May 23	Klubb Bongo, Malmö, Sweden	

Year/Date	Venue/Location	Other Acts
May 24	Tivoli Garden, Stockholm, Sweden	
May 25	Star Palace, Kiel, Germany	
May 28	Jaguar Club, Herford, Germany	
May 29	Tulip Bulb Auction-Barbeque '67, Lincolnshire, England	Cream, Pink Floyd, Move, Zoot Money, etc.
May 31	Speakeasy, London, England	Jam session
June 4	Saville Theater, London, England	Supported by The Chiffons, Procol Harum, and Denny Laine's Electric String Band
June 6	Imperial Ballroom, Lancashire, England	
June 18	Monterey International Pop Festival, Monterey, California	
June 20	Fillmore West, San Francisco, California	
June 21	Fillmore West, San Francisco, California	
June 22	Fillmore West, San Francisco, California	
June 23	Fillmore West, San Francisco, California	
June 24	Fillmore West, San Francisco, California	
June 25	The Panhandle, Golden Gate Park, San Francisco, California (during the afternoon) Fillmore West, San Francisco, California (evening show)	
July 1	Earl Warren Showgrounds, Santa Barbara, California	
July 2	Whisky a Go Go, Los Angeles, California	Supporting Sam and Dave
July 3	Scene Club, New York, New York	Jam session
July 4	Scene Club, New York, New York	Supported by the Seeds and Tiny Tim
July 5	Rheingold Festival, Central Park, New York, New York	Supporting the Young Rascals
July 8	Jacksonville Coliseum, Jacksonville, Florida	As support for the Monkees

Year/Date	Venue/Location	Other Acts
July 9	Jackie Gleason Memorial Hall, Miami, Florida	As support for the Monkees
July 11	Charlotte Coliseum, Charlotte, North Carolina	As support for the Monkees
July 12	Greensboro Coliseum, Greensboro, North Carolina	As support for the Monkees
July 14	Forest Hills Stadium, New York, New York	As support for the Monkees
July 15	Forest Hills Stadium, New York, New York	As support for the Monkees
July 16	Forest Hills Stadium, New York, New York	As support for the Monkees
July 18	Gaslight Club, New York, New York	
July 19	Gaslight Club, New York, New York	
July 20	Salvation Club, New York, New York	
July 21	Café Au Go Go, New York, New York	
July 23	Café Au Go Go, New York, New York	
July 26	Gaslight Club, New York, New York	Jam session
July 27	Gaslight Club, New York, New York	Jam session
August 3	Salvation Club, New York, New York	
August 4	Salvation Club, New York, New York	
August 5	Salvation Club, New York, New York	
August 7	Salvation Club, New York, New York	
August 8	Salvation Club, New York, New York	
August 9	Ambassador Theater, Washington, DC	Natty Bumpo
August 10	Ambassador Theater, Washington, DC	Natty Bumpo
August 11	Ambassador Theater, Washington, DC	Natty Bumpo
August 12	Ambassador Theater, Washington, DC	Natty Bumpo

Year/Date	Venue/Location	Other Acts
August 13	*Keep The Faith for Washington Youth Fund*, Washington, DC	
August 15	Fifth Dimension Club, Ann Arbor, Michigan	
August 18	Hollywood Bowl, Hollywood, California	As support for The Mamas and the Papas and Scott McKenzie
August 19	Earl Warren Showgrounds, Santa Barbara, California	Moby Grape, Tim Buckley, Captain Speed
August 22	*The Simon Dee Show*—performed "Lamp"	Burning of the Midnight
August 27	Saville Theater, London, England	Crazy World of Arthur Brown, Tomorrow
	Speakeasy, London, England	Jam session
August 29	Nottingham Blues Festival, Nottingham, England	Supported by Jimmy James and the Vagabonds
September 3	Konserthallen, Göteborg, Sweden	
September 4	Stora Scenen, Tivoli Garden, Stockholm, Sweden	
September 5	Radiohuset, Stockholm, Sweden	
September 6	Västerås Idrottshall, Västerås, Sweden	
September 7	Club Filips, Stockholm, Sweden	Jam session
September 8	Högbo Bruk, Högbo, Sweden	
September 9	Mariebergsskogn, Karlstad, Sweden	
September 10	Akademisha Föreningen, Lund, Sweden	
September 11	Stora Scenen, Tivoli Garden, Stockholm, Sweden	
September 12	Stjärnscenen, Göteborg, Sweden	
September 14	*Top of the Pops*	
September 15	The Manor House Pub, London, England	Jam with Eric Burdon and The Animals
September 25	*Guitar In*, Royal Festival Hall, London, England	Paco Pena, Bert Jansch, Sebastian Jorgensen, and Tim Walker
October 7	The Wellington Club, Dereham, England	
October 8	Saville Theater, London England	Crazy World of Arthur Brown, The Herd, Eire Apparent

Year/Date	Venue/Location	Other Acts
October 9	L'Olympia, Paris, France	
October 12	*Musicorama* TV show, Paris, France	
October 15	Starlight Ballroom, Crawley, Sussex, England	
October 22	Hastings Pier Pavilion, Hastings, Sussex, England	
October 24	Marquee Club, London, England	Supported by The Nice
October 28	California Ballroom, Dunstable, England	
November 8	The Union, Manchester University, England	
November 10	*Hippy Happy Event*, Rotterdam, Holland	
November 11	Sussex University, Brighton, Sussex, England	
November 14	Royal Albert Hall, London, England	The Move, Pink Floyd, Amen Corner, Outer Limits, Eire Apparent, The Nice
November 15	Winter Gardens, Bournemouth, England	The Move, Pink Floyd, Amen Corner, Outer Limits, Eire Apparent, The Nice
November 17	City Hall, Sheffield, Yorkshire, England	The Move, Pink Floyd, Amen Corner, Outer Limits, Eire Apparent, The Nice
November 18	Empire Theater, Liverpool, England	The Move, Pink Floyd, Amen Corner, Outer Limits, Eire Apparent, The Nice
November 19	The Coventry Theater, Coventry, England	The Move, Pink Floyd, Amen Corner, Outer Limits, Eire Apparent, The Nice
November 22	Guild Hall, Portsmouth, England	The Move, Pink Floyd, Amen Corner, Outer Limits, Eire Apparent, The Nice
November 23	Sophia Gardens Pavilion, Cardiff, Wales	The Move, Pink Floyd, Amen Corner, Outer Limits, Eire Apparent, The Nice
November 24	Colston Hall, Bristol, England	The Move, Pink Floyd, Amen Corner, Outer Limits, Eire Apparent, The Nice
November 25	Opera House, Black Pool, England	The Move, Pink Floyd, Amen Corner, Outer Limits, Eire Apparent, The Nice

Year/Date	Venue/Location	Other Acts
November 26	Palace Theater, Manchester, England	The Move, Pink Floyd, Amen Corner, Outer Limits, Eire Apparent, The Nice
November 27	*Festival of Arts*, Belfast, Northern Ireland	The Move, Pink Floyd, Amen Corner, Outer Limits, Eire Apparent, The Nice
December 1	Town Hall, Chatham, Kent, England	The Move, Pink Floyd, Amen Corner, Outer Limits, Eire Apparent, The Nice
December 2	The Dome, Brighton, Sussex, England	The Move, Pink Floyd, Amen Corner, Outer Limits, Eire Apparent, The Nice
December 3	Theater Royal, Nottingham, England	The Move, Pink Floyd, Amen Corner, Outer Limits, Eire Apparent, The Nice
December 4	City Hall, Newcastle-upon-Tyne, England	The Move, Pink Floyd, Amen Corner, Outer Limits, Eire Apparent, The Nice
December 5	Green's Playhouse, Glasgow, Scotland	The Move, Pink Floyd, Amen Corner, Outer Limits, Eire Apparent, The Nice
December 7	Speakeasy, London, England	Jam session
December 12	Speakeasy, London, England	Jam session
December 22	*Christmas on Earth Concert*, London, England	Eric Burdon and the Animals, The Who, Pink Floyd, The Move, Soft Machine, Tomorrow
December 31	Speakeasy, London, England	Jam session
1968		
January 2	Klook's Kleek, London, England	Jam session
January 5	Jernvallen Sports Hall, Sandviken, Sweden	
January 7	Tivolis Koncerthalle, Copenhagen, Denmark	Supported by Page One and Hansson and Karlsson
January 8	Stora Salen, Stockholm, Sweden	
January 22	Speakeasy, London, England	Jam session
January 29	L'Olympia, Paris, France	Eric Burdon and the Animals
February 1	Fillmore West, San Francisco, California	Albert King, John Mayall's Bluesbreakers, Soft Machine
February 2	Winterland, San Francisco, California	John Mayall's Bluesbreakers, Albert King, Soft Machine
February 3	Winterland, San Francisco, California	John Mayall's Bluesbreakers, Albert King, Soft Machine

Year/Date	Venue/Location	Other Acts
February 4	Winterland, San Francisco, California	John Mayall's Bluesbreakers, Albert King, Big Brother and the Holding Company
February 5	Sun Devil's Gym, Arizona State University, Tempe, Arizona	Soft Machine
February 6	V.I.P. Club, Tucson, Arizona	Soft Machine
February 8	Sacramento State College, Sacramento, California	Soft Machine, The Creators
February 9	Anaheim Convention Center, Anaheim, California	Eric Burdon and the Animals, Eire Apparent, Soft Machine
February 10	Shrine Auditorium, Los Angeles, California	Blue Cheer, Electric Flag, Soft Machine
February 11	Robertson Gym, Santa Barbara, California	East Side Kids, Soft Machine
February 12	Center Arena, Seattle, Washington	Soft Machine
February 13	Ackerman Union Grand Ballroom, UCLA, Los Angeles, California	Soft Machine
February 14	Regis College, Denver, Colorado	Soft Machine
February 15	Municipal Auditorium, San Antonio, Texas	Soft Machine, The Moving Sidewalks, Neal Ford and the Fanatics
February 16	State Fair Music Hall, Dallas, Texas	Soft Machine, The Moving Sidewalks, Neal Ford and the Fanatics
February 17	Will Rogers Auditorium, Fort Worth, Texas	Soft Machine, The Moving Sidewalks, Neal Ford and the Fanatics
February 18	Music Hall, Houston, Texas	Soft Machine, The Moving Sidewalks, Neal Ford and the Fanatics
February 20	Scene Club, New York, New York	Jam session
February 21	Electric Factory, Philadelphia, Pennsylvania	Woody's Truck Stop
February 22	Electric Factory, Philadelphia, Pennsylvania	Soft Machine, Woody's Truck Stop
February 23	Masonic Temple, Detroit, Michigan	Soft Machine, MC 5, The Rationals
February 24	Canadian National Exhibition Coliseum, Arena, Toronto, Canada	Soft Machine, The Paupers, Eire Apparent

Year/Date	Venue/Location	Other Acts
February 25	Civic Opera House, Chicago	Soft Machine Illinois
February 27	The Factory, Madison, Wisconsin	Soft Machine, Mark Boyle's Sense Laboratory
February 28	The Scene, Milwaukee, Wisconsin	
February 29	The Scene, Milwaukee, Wisconsin	
March 2	Hunter College, New York, New York	The Troggs
March 3	Veterans Memorial Auditorium, Columbus, Ohio	Soft Machine
March 4	Scene Club, New York, New York	Jam session
March 5	Scene Club, New York, New York	Jam session
March 6	Scene Club, New York, New York	Jam session
March 8	Brown University, Providence, Rhode Island	
March 9	State University of New York at Stony Brook, Long Island, New York	
March 10	International Ballroom, Washington Hilton Hotel, Washington, DC	
March 13	Scene Club, New York, New York	Jam session
March 15	Atwood Hall, Clark University, Worcester, Massachusetts	
March 16	Lewiston Armory, Lewiston, Maine	Terry and the Telstars
March 17	Café Au Go Go, New York, New York	Jam session
March 19	Capital Theater, Ottawa, Ontario	Soft Machine
March 21	Community War Memorial, Rochester, New York	Soft Machine, The Rustics
March 22	Bushnell Memorial Hall, Hartford, Connecticut	
March 23	Memorial Auditorium, Buffalo, New York	Soft Machine
March 24	Masonic Temple, Flint, Michigan	Soft Machine, Fruit of the Looms, Rationals
March 25	Industrial Mutual Association Auditorium, Flint, Michigan	

Year/Date	Venue/Location	Other Acts
March 26	Public Music Hall, Cleveland, Ohio	
March 27	Lion's Delaware County Fairgrounds, Muncie, Indiana	Soft Machine, The Glass Calendar
March 28	Xavier University Fieldhouse, Cincinnati, Ohio	
March 29	Chicago University, Chicago Cheetah Club (after the show) Chicago, Illinios	Jam session
March 30	University of Toledo Fieldhouse, Toledo, Ohio	
March 31	The Arena, Philadelphia, Pennsylvania	Soft Machine
April 2	Paul Sauve Arena, Montreal, Quebec	
April 4	Civic Dome, Virginia Beach, Virginia	
April 5	Symphony Hall, Newark, New Jersey Generation Club, New York, New York (after the show)	Jam session
April 6	Westchester County Center, White Plains, New York	
April 7	Generation Club, New York, New York	Jam session
April 9	Generation Club, New York, New York	Jam session
April 15	Generation Club, New York, New York	Jam session
April 19	Troy Armory, Troy, New York	Soft Machine
May 10	Fillmore East, New York, New York	Sly and the Family Stone
May 18	*The Underground Pop Festival*, Hallandale, Florida	Mother's Invention, John Lee Hooker, Blue Cheer, etc.
May 23	Piper Club, Milan, Italy	
May 24	Brancaccio Theater, Rome, Italy	
May 25	Brancaccio Theater, Rome, Italy	
May 26	Palasport, Bologna, Italy	
May 30	*Beat Monster-Konzert*, Hallenstadion, Zürich, Switzerland	Traffic, Small Faces, John Mayall's Blues Breakers, The Move
May 31	*Beat Monster-Konzert*, Hallenstadion, Zürich, Switzerland	Traffic, Small Faces, John Mayall's Blues Breakers, The Move

Year/Date	Venue/Location	Other Acts
June 8	Fillmore East, New York, New York	Electric Flag
June 15	Scene Club, New York, New York	Jam session
June 22	Scene Club, New York, New York	Jam session
July 6	Woburn Music Festival, Woburn Alley, Bedfordshire, England	Tyrannosaurus Rex, The Family, Geno Washington, etc.
July 18	Sgt. Pepper's Club, Palma, Majorca, Spain	
July 30	Independence Hall, Baton Rouge, Louisiana	Soft Machine, Eire Apparent
July 31	Municipal Auditorium, Shreveport, Louisiana	Soft Machine, Eire Apparent
August 1	City Park Stadium, New Orleans, Louisiana	Soft Machine, Eire Apparent
August 2	Municipal Auditorium, San Antonio, Texas	Soft Machine, Eire Apparent
August 3	Southern Methodist University, Dallas, Texas	Soft Machine, Eire Apparent
August 4	Sam Houston Coliseum, Houston, Texas	Soft Machine, Eire Apparent
August 8	Moody Coliseum, Southern Methodist University, Dallas, Texas	Soft Machine, Eire Apparent
August 10	Auditorium Theater, Chicago, Illinois	Soft Machine, Eire Apparent
August 11	Colonial Ballroom, Davenport, Iowa	Soft Machine, Eire Apparent
August 16	Merriweather Post Pavilion, Columbia, Maryland	Soft Machine, Eire Apparent
August 17	Atlanta Municipal Auditorium, Atlanta, Georgia	Vanilla Fudge, Eire Apparent, Soft Machine
August 18	Curtis Hixon Hall, Tampa, Florida	Eire Apparent, Soft Machine
August 20	The Mosque, Richmond, Virginia	Vanilla Fudge, Eire Apparent, Soft Machine
August 21	Civic Dome, Virginia Beach, Virginia	Vanilla Fudge, Eire Apparent, Soft Machine
August 23	*New York Rock Festival*, New York, New York	Chamber Brothers, Soft Machine, Big Brother and the Holding Company with Janis Joplin
August 24	Bushnell Memorial, Hartford, Connecticut	Vanilla Fudge, Eire Apparent, Soft Machine

Year/Date	Venue/Location	Other Acts
August 25	Carousel Stadium, Framingham, Massachusetts	Vanilla Fudge, Eire Apparent, Soft Machine
August 26	Kennedy Stadium, Bridgeport, Connecticut	Vanilla Fudge, Eire Apparent, Soft Machine
August 30	Lagoon Opera House, Salt Lake City, Utah	Vanilla Fudge, Eire Apparent, Soft Machine
September 1	Red Rocks Park, Denver, Colorado	Vanilla Fudge, Eire Apparent, Soft Machine
September 3	Balboa Stadium, San Diego, California	Vanilla Fudge, Eire Apparent, Soft Machine
September 4	Memorial Coliseum, Phoenix, Arizona	Vanilla Fudge, Eire Apparent, Soft Machine
September 5	Swing Auditorium, San Bernardino, California	Vanilla Fudge, Eire California Apparent, Soft Machine
September 6	Seattle Center Coliseum, Seattle, Washington	Vanilla Fudge, Eire Apparent, Soft Machine
September 7	Pacific Coliseum, Vancouver, British Columbia	Vanilla Fudge, Eire Apparent, Soft Machine
September 8	Spokane Coliseum, Spokane, Washington	Vanilla Fudge, Eire Apparent, Soft Machine
September 9	Memorial Coliseum, Portland, Oregon	Vanilla Fudge, Soft Machine
September 13	Oakland Coliseum, Oakland, California	Vanilla Fudge, Soft Machine
September 14	Hollywood Bowl, Hollywood, California	Big Brother and the Holding Company, The Chamber Brothers
September 15	Memorial Auditorium, Sacramento, California	Vanilla Fudge, Eire Apparent
September 18	Whisky A Go Go, Hollywood, California	
October 5	Honolulu International Center, Honolulu, Hawaii	Times Music Company
October 10	Winterland, San Francisco, California	Buddy Miles Express, Dino Valenti
October 11	Winterland, San Francisco, California	Buddy Miles Express, Dino Valenti (second show)
October 12	Winterland, San Francisco, California	Buddy Miles Express, Dino Valenti (third show)
October 18	Fillmore West, San Francisco, California Whisky A Go Go (after the above show)	Jam session
October 26	Civic Auditorium, Bakersfield, California	
November 1	Municipal Auditorium, Kansas City, Missouri	Cat Mother & the All-Night News Boys

Year/Date	Venue/Location	Other Acts
November 2	Minneapolis Auditorium, Minneapolis, Minnesota	Cat Mother & the All-Night News Boys
November 3	Kiel Auditorium, St. Louis, Missouri	Cat Mother & the All-Night News Boys
November 11	Scene Club, New York, New York	
November 15	Cincinnati Gardens, Cincinnati, Ohio	
November 16	Boston Garden, Boston, Massachusetts	Cat Mother & the All-Night News Boys, The McCoys
November 17	Woolsey Hall, Yale University, New Haven, Connecticut	Cat Mother & the All-Night News Boys, Terry Reid
November 22	Jacksonville Coliseum, Jacksonville, Florida	Cat Mother & the All-Night New Boys
November 23	Curtis Hixon Hall, Tampa, Florida	Cat Mother & the All-Night News Boys
November 24	Miami Beach Convention Hall, Miami Beach, Florida	Cat Mother & the All-Night News Boys
November 27	Rhode Island Auditorium, Providence, Rhode Island Café Au Go Go (jam session after the above show)	
November 28	*An Electric Thanksgiving* at Philharmonic Hall, New York, New York	Fernando Valenti, New York Brass Quintet
November 30	Cobo Hall, Detroit, Michigan	Cat Mother & the All-Night News Boys
December 1	Chicago Coliseum, Chicago, Illinois	Cat Mother & the All-Night News Boys
December 20	Fillmore East, New York, New York	Jam session
1969		
January 8	Lorensberg Cirkus, Göteborg, Sweden	Amen Corner, Burning Red Ivanhoe
January 9	Konserthuset, Stockholm, Sweden	Supported by Jethro Tull
January 10	Falkoner Centret, Copenhagen, Denmark	Supported by Jethro Tull
January 11	Musikhalle, Hamburg, Germany	Eire Apparent
January 12	Rheinehalle, Düsseldorf, Germany	Eire Apparent
January 13	Sporthalle, Köln, Germany	Eire Apparent
January 14	Münsterlandhalle, Münster, Germany	Eire Apparent
January 15	Kongreβsaal, Deutsches Museum, Munich, Germany	Eire Apparent

Year/Date	Venue/Location	Other Acts
January 16	Meistersingerhalle, Nuremburg, Germany	Eire Apparent
January 17	Jahrhunderthalle, Frankfurt, Germany	Eire Apparent
January 19	Liederhalle, Stuttgart, Germany	Eire Apparent
January 21	Wacken, Strasbourg, France	Eire Apparent
January 22	Grosser Saal, Konzerthaus, Vienna, Austria	Eire Apparent
January 23	Sport Palast, Berlin, Germany	Eire Apparent
February 18	Royal Albert Hall, London, England	Mason, Capaldi, Wood & Frog, Soft Machine
February 24	Royal Albert Hall, London, England	Fat Mattress, Van der Graaf Generator, Soft Machine
	Speakeasy Club (after the above show)	Jam session
March 8	Ronnie Scott's, New York, New York	Jam session
March 9	Ronnie Scott's, New York, New York	Jam session
March 10	Speakeasy, New York, New York	Jam session
April 11	Dorton Arena, Raleigh, North Carolina	Fat Mattress
April 12	Spectrum, Philadelphia, Pennsylvania	Fat Mattress
April 18	Ellis Auditorium, Memphis Tennessee	Fat Mattress
April 19	Sam Houston Coliseum, Houston, Texas	Fat Mattress, Chicago Transit Authority
April 20	Memorial Auditorium, Dallas, Texas	Fat Mattress, Cat Mother & the All-Night News Boys
April 26	The Forum, Inglewood, California	Chicago Transit Authority, Cat Mother & the All-Night News Boys
April 27	Oakland Coliseum, Oakland, California	Jefferson Airplane, Fat Mattress
May 2	Cobo Arena, Detroit, Michigan	Fat Mattress, Cat Mother & the All-Night News Boys
May 3	Maple Leaf Gardens, Toronto, Ontario, Canada	Cat Mother & the All-Night News Boys
May 4	War Memorial Auditorium, Syracuse, New York	Cat Mother & the All-Night News Boys
May 7	Memorial Coliseum, Tuscaloosa, Alabama	Fat Mattress, Cat Mother & the All-Night News Boys

Year/Date	Venue/Location	Other Acts
May 9	Charlotte Coliseum, Charlotte, North Carolina	Chicago Transit Authority
May 10	Charleston Civic Center, Charleston, West Virginia	Fat Mattress, Chicago Transit Authority
May 11	Fairgrounds Coliseum, Indianapolis, Indiana	Chicago Transit Authority
May 13	Scene Club, New York, New York	Jam session
May 16	Baltimore Civic Center, Baltimore, Maryland	Buddy Miles Express, Cat Mother & the All-Night News Boys
May 17	Rhode Island Arena, Providence, Rhode Island	Buddy Miles Express, Cat Mother & the All-Night News Boys
May 18	Madison Square Garden, New York, New York	Buddy Miles Express
May 23	Seattle Center Coliseum, Seattle, Washington	Fat Mattress
May 24	Sports Arena, San Diego, California	Fat Mattress
May 25	*San Jose Pop Festival,* Santa Clara County Fairgrounds, San Jose, California	Taj Mahal, Loading Zone, Fat Mattress, etc.
May 30	Waikiki Shell, Honolulu, Oahu, Hawaii	Fat Mattress
May 31	Waikiki Shell, Honolulu, Oahu, Hawaii	Fat Mattress
June 1	Waikiki Shell, Honolulu, Oahu, Hawaii	Fat Mattress
June 20	Newport '69, San Fernando Valley State College, Devonshire Downs, Northridge, California	Albert King, Ike & Tina Turner, Joe Cocker, Taj Mahal, etc.
June 22	*Newport Pop '69,* San Fernando Valley State College, Devonshire Downs, Northridge, California	The Rascals, Booker T & The MG's, The Byrds, etc.
June 29	*Denver Pop Festival,* Mile High Stadium, Denver, Colorado	Three Dog Night, Joe Cocker, etc.
July 7	*The Dick Cavett Show,* New York, New York	
July 10	*The Tonight Show,* NBC Television Studios, New York, New York	
August 10	Tinker Street Cinema, Woodstock, New York	Jam session

Year/Date	Venue/Location	Other Acts
August 18	*Woodstock Music and Art Fair*, Bethel, New York	Johnny Winter, The Band, Ten Years After, etc.
September 5	*Jazz Festival/Benefit*, Harlem, New York, New York	Sam and Dave, Big Maybelle
September 8	*The Dick Cavett Show*, New York, New York	
September 10	Salvation Club, New York, New York	
December 31	Fillmore East Theatre, New York, New York	
1970		
January 1	Fillmore East Theater, New York, New York	Voices of East Harlem
January 28	Winter Festival for Peace, Madison Square Garden, New York, New York	Peter Paul and Mary, Dave Brubeck, Judy Collins, etc.
April 25	The Forum, Inglewood, California	Buddy Miles Express, Ballin' Jack
April 26	Cal Expo, Sacramento, California	Buddy Miles Express, Blue Mountain Eagle
May 1	Milwaukee Auditorium, Milwaukee, Wisconsin	
May 2	Dane County Memorial Coliseum, Madison, Wisconsin	
May 3	St. Paul Civic Center, St. Paul, Minnesota	
May 4	Village Gate (Benefit for Timothy Leary), New York, New York	Johnny Winter, Noel Redding, Jim Morrison
May 8	University of Oklahoma, Norman, Oklahoma	
May 9	Will Rogers Auditorium, Fort Worth, TexasBloodrock	
May 10	HemisFair Arena, San Antonio, Texas	Country Funk
May 16	Temple Stadium, Philadelphia, Pennsylvania	Grateful Dead, Steve Miller Band, Cactus
May 22	Cincinnati, Ohio (Cancelled)	
May 23	Keil Auditorium, St. Louis, Missouri (Cancelled)	
May 24	Veterans Memorial Auditorium, Columbus, Ohio (Cancelled)	
May 30	Berkeley Community Center, Berkeley, CA	Tower of Power

Year/Date	Venue/Location	Other Acts
June 5	Memorial Auditorium, Dallas, Texas	Ballin' Jack
June 6	Sam Houston Coliseum, Houston, Texas	Ballin' Jack
June 7	Assembly Center Arena, Tulsa, Oklahoma	Ballin' Jack
June 9	Mid-South Coliseum, Memphis, Tennessee	
June 10	Roberts Municipal Stadium, Evansville, Indiana	
June 13	Civic Center, Baltimore, Maryland	Ballin' Jack, Cactus
June 19	Civic Arena, Albuquerque, New Mexico	
June 20	Swing Auditorium, San Bernardino, California	
June 21	County Fairgrounds, Ventura, California	Ballin' Jack, Grin
June 23	Mammoth Gardens, Denver, Colorado	Ballin' Jack, Grin
June 27	Boston Garden, Boston, Massachusetts	Cactus, The Illusion,
July 4	*2nd Atlanta International Pop Festival,* Middle Georgia Raceway, Byron, Georgia	Jethro Tull, Mountain, B. B. King, Cactus, etc.
July 5	Miami Jai Alai Fronton, Miami, Florida	
July 17	*New York Pop Festival,* Randall's Island, New York	John Sebastian, Grand Funk Railroad, Steppenwolf, Jethro Tull
July 25	International Sports Arena, San Diego, California	Cat Mother & the All-Night News Boys
July 26	Sick's Stadium, Seattle, Washington	Cactus, Rube Tuben and the Rhondonnas
July 30	*Rainbow Bridge,* Haleakala Center, Maui, Hawaii	
August 1	International Center, Honolulu, Hawaii	
August 30	*Isle of Wight Festival,* Isle of Wight, England	Moody Blues, Jethro Tull, Free, Donovan, etc.
August 31	Tivoli Gardens, Stockholm, Sweden	
September 1	Stora Scenen, Göteborg, Sweden	Cat Mother & the All-Night News Boys
September 2	Vejlby-Risskov Hallen, Århus, Denmark	Blue Sun

Year/Date	Venue/Location	Other Acts
September 3	K. B. Hallen, Copenhagen, Denmark	Blue Sun
September 4	*Super Concert '70*, Deutschlandhalle, Berlin, Germany	Cat Mother & the All-Night News Boys, Ten Years After, Procol Harum, etc.
September 6	*Open Air Love and Peace Festival*, Isle of Fehmarn, Germany	Alexis Korner, Embry Limbus 4, etc.
September 16	Ronnie Scott's, London, England	Jam session

Selected Discography

This discography includes only United Kingdom and United States releases in chronological order. There are many bootlegs that are omitted as they are not part of the sanctioned Hendrix catalogue.

SINGLES

Year/Title (A- and B-sides)	Producer/Label/Label Number
1963	
"Go Go Shoes"/"Go Go Place" *with Lonnie Youngblood*	Youngblood/Fairmount/F-1002
1964	
"Testify I"/"Testify II" *with the Isley Brothers*	?/T-Neck/45-501
1965	
"Move Over and Let Me Dance"/"Have You Ever Been Disappointed?" *with the Isley Brothers*	?/Atlantic/45-2303
1966	
"I Don't Know What You've Got but It's Got Me I"/"I Don't Know What You've Got but It's Got Me II" *with Little Richard and the Upsetters*	Calvin Carter/Vee Jay/JV-698
"Hey Joe"/"Stone Free"	Chandler/Polydor/561329

Year/Title (A- and B-sides)	Producer/Label/Label Number
1967	
"Purple Haze"/"51st Anniversary"	Chandler/Track/604001
"Hey Joe"/"51st Anniversary"	Chandler/Reprise/0572
(United States release)	
"The Wind Cries Mary"/"Highway Chile"	Chandler/Track/604004
"Purple Haze"/"The Wind Cries Mary"	Chandler/Reprise/0597
(United States Release)	
"Burning of the Midnight Lamp"/	Chandler/Track/604007
"The Stars That Play With Laughing	
Sam's Dice"	
"Foxey Lady"/"Hey Joe"	Chandler/Reprise/?
1968	
"Up From the Skies"/"One Rainy Wish"	Hendrix/Reprise/0665
(United States release)	
"All Along the Watchtower"/"Burning of	Hendrix/Reprise/0767
the Midnight Lamp"	
(United States release)	
"All Along the Watchtower"/"Long Hot	Hendrix/Track/604025
Summer Night"	
1969	
"Crosstown Traffic"/"Gypsy Eyes"	Hendrix/Track/604029
(Also released in the United States:	
Reprise 0792)	
"Stone Free"/"If 6 Was 9" (United States	Hendrix/Reprise/0853
release)	
"Fire"/"Burning of the Midnight Lamp"	Hendrix/Track/604033
1970	
"Stepping Stone"/"Izabella"	Hendrix/Reprise/0905
(United States release)	
"Voodoo Child (Slight Return)"/"Hey	
Joe"/"All Along the Watchtower"	
1971	
"Freedom"/"Angel"	Hendrix/Reprise/1000
(United States release/released	
in Japan by Polydor DP 1804)	
"Dolly Dagger"/"Star Spangled Banner"	Hendrix/Reprise/1044
(United States release)	
"Gypsy Eyes"/"Remember"/"Purple	Hendrix/Track/2094 010
Haze"/"Stone Free"	
1972	
"Johnny B. Goode"/"Little Wing"	Hendrix/Polydor/2001 – 277
"Waterfall" (aka "May This Be Love")/	Hendrix/Barclay/61 389
"51st Anniversary"	
(Released in France)	

Year/Title (A- and B-sides)	Producer/Label/Label Number
1973	
"Hear My Train A Comin' "/"Rock Me, Baby"	Hendrix/Reprise/14286
1974	
". . . And a Happy New Year" (Released as a promo)	Hendrix/Reprise Pro/595

This catalogue of singles purposely omits recordings that did not feature Hendrix as the band leader and CD singles, of which there are many.

ALBUMS

The selected album discography below only includes Hendrix's work that was either released during his life or has the most authentication. No attempt was made to create a complete list; instead, the albums listed below are the ones that Hendrix himself released or that bear his direct mark (as opposed to one-offs, unlicensed bootlegs, etc.).

Title	Year/Producer/Label/Label Number
Are You Experienced? (Released in CD format by Polydor/ 825 416-2, in April 1985) Track list for the United Kingdom release: "Foxey Lady" "Manic Depression" "Red House" "Can You See Me?" "Love or Confusion" "I Don't Live Today" "May This Be Love" "Fire" "Third Stone From the Sun" "Remember" "Are You Experienced?"	May 1967/Chandler-Yameta/Track/ 613 001 (612 001)
Are You Experienced? Track list for the United States release: "Purple Haze" "Manic Depression" "Hey Joe" "Love or Confusion" "May This Be Love" "I Don't Live Today"	Sept. 1967/Chandler-Yameta/Reprise/ RS 6261

Title	Year/Producer/Label/Label Number

"The Wind Cries Mary"
"Fire"
"Third Stone From the Sun"
"Foxey Lady"
"Are You Experienced?"

Axis: Bold as Love   Dec. 1967/Chandler/Track/613003
(Released in the United States on
Reprise/RS 6281, in January 1968)
　　"EXP"
　　"Up From the Skies"
　　"Spanish Castle Magic"
　　"Wait Until Tomorrow"
　　"Ain't No Telling"
　　"Little Wing"
　　"If 6 Was 9"
　　"You Got Me Floatin' "
　　"Castles Made of Sand"
　　"She's So Fine"
　　"One Rainy Wish"
　　"Little Miss Lover"
　　"Bold as Love"

Smash Hits   Apr. 1968/Chandler/Track/ 613004
(Released in the United States on
Reprise/MSK 2276, in June 1969)
　　"Purple Haze"
　　"Fire"
　　"The Wind Cries Mary"
　　"Can You See Me?"
　　"Hey Joe"
　　"Stone Free"
　　"Manic Depression"
　　"Foxey Lady"

Electric Ladyland   Oct. 1968/Hendrix/Track/613 008/9
(Released in the United States on
Reprise/2RS 6307, in September
1968)
　　". . . And the Gods Made Love"
　　"Have You Ever Been (to Electric
　　　Ladyland)"
　　"Crosstown Traffic"
　　"Voodoo Chile"
　　"Little Miss Strange"
　　"Long Hot Summer Night"

Title	Year/Producer/Label/Label Number
"Come On (Part 1)"	

"Come On (Part 1)"
"Gypsy Eyes"
"Burning of the Midnight Lamp"
"Rainy Day, Dream Away"
"1983 . . . (A Merman I Should
   Turn to Be)"
"Moon, Turn the Tides . . . gently
   gently away"
"Still Raining, Still Dreaming"
"House Burning Down"
"All Along the Watchtower"
"Voodoo Child (Slight Return)"

Electric Hendrix   1968/?/Track/ 2856 002
(Another "best of" compilation that
was released and immediately
withdrawn)
   "Still Raining, Still Dreaming"
   "House Burning Down"
   "All Along the Watchtower"
   "Voodoo Child (Slight Return)"
   "Little Miss Strange"
   "Long Hot Summer Night"
   "Come On (Part I)"
   "Gypsy Eyes"
   "Burning of the Midnight Lamp"

Band of Gypsys   June 1970/?/Polydor/Track 2406 002
(Released in the United States
by Capitol/STAO-472, in April
1970)
   "Who Knows"
   "Machine Gun"
   "Changes"
   "Power of Soul"
   "Message to Love"
   "We Gotta Live Together"

Woodstock   June 1970/Eric Blackstead/Cotillion/
(Released in the United Kingdom   SD35000
on Atlantic, K60001, also in
June 1970, incomplete song set)
   "Star Spangled Banner"
   "Purple Haze"
   "Instrumental Solo"

Title	Year/Producer/Label/Label Number
Monterey International Pop Festival: Otis Redding/Jimi Hendrix Experience	July 1970/?/Reprise/ MS 2029

Side One-Hendrix
   "Like a Rolling Stone"
   "Rock Me, Baby"
   "Can You See Me?"
   "Wild Thing"

Side Two-Redding
   "Shake"
   "Respect"
   "I've Been Loving You Too Long"
   "(I Can't Get No) Satisfaction"
   "Try a Little Tenderness"

Cry of Love (Released in the United States by Reprise/MS 2034, in March 1971)	Jan. 1971/Hendrix, Kramer, Mitchell/ Track/ 2408 101

   "Freedom"
   "Drifting"
   "Ezy Ryder"
   "Night Bird Flying"
   "My Friend"
   "Straight Ahead"
   "Astro Man"
   "Angel"
   "In From the Storm"
   "Belly Button Window"

Woodstock Two (Released in United Kingdom by Atlantic/K60002, also in April 1971, incomplete song set)	Apr. 1971/Eric Blackstead/Cotillion/ SD 24000

   "Jam Back at the House"
   "Izabella"
   "Getting My Heart Back
      Together Again"

Experience (Live recording from Royal Albert Hall from February 24, 1969)	Aug. 1971/?/Ember/5057

   "The Sunshine of Your Love"
   "Room Full of Mirrors"
   "Bleeding Heart"
   "Smashing of Amps"

Title	Year/Producer/Label/Label Number

Rainbow Bridge
(Released in the United States
by Reprise/MS 2040, in
October 1971)
  "Lover Man"
  "Hey Baby (New Rising Sun)"
  "In From the Storm"
  "Message to Love"
  "Foxey Lady"
  "Hear My Train A Comin' "
  "Voodoo Child (Slight Return)"
  "Fire"
  "Purple Haze"
  "Dolly Dagger"
  "Instrumental"
  "Ezy Ryder"
  "Red House"
  "Jam Back at the House"
  "Land of the New Rising Sun"
	Nov. 1971/Hendrix, Mitchell, Kramer,
	Jansen/Reprise/K44159

Isle of Wight
  "God Save the Queen"
  "Sgt. Pepper's Lonely Hearts
    Club Band"
  "Spanish Castle Magic"
  "All Along the Watchtower"
  "Machine Gun"
  "Lover Man"
  "Freedom"
  "Red House"
  "Dolly Dagger"
  "Midnight Lightning"
  "Foxey Lady"
  "Message to Love"
  "Hey Baby (New Rising Sun)"
  "Ezy Ryder"
  "Hey Joe"
  "Purple Haze"
  "Voodoo Child (Slight Return)"
  "In From the Storm"
	Nov. 1971/?/Polydor/2302 016

Jimi Hendrix at his Best, *Volume 1* (All three of the "At His Best" releases were unauthorized bootlegs—also released in the	1971/?/SagaPan (UK)/SAGA-6313

Title	Year/Producer/Label/Label Number

United States on the Joker
imprint: Joker SM 3271)
  "She Went to Bed With My Guitar"
  "Free Thunder"
  "Cave Man Bells"
  "Strokin' a Lady on Each Hip"
  "Baby Chicken Strut"

Jimi Hendrix at his Best,   1971/?/SegaPan (UK)/SAGA-6314
Volume 2
(On the Joker imprint in the United
States: Joker SM 3272)
  "Down Mean Blues"
  "Feels Good"
  "Fried Cola"
  "Monday Morning Blues"
  "Jimi Is Tender Too"
  "Madagascar"

Jimi Hendrix at his Best,   1971/?/SegaPan (UK)/SAGA-6315
Volume 3
(On the Joker imprint in the United
States: Joker SM 3273)
  "Young Jim"
  "Lift Off"
  "Swift's Wing"
  "Giraffe"
  "Spiked With Heady Dreams"

Jimi Hendrix: In the West   Jan. 1972/Kramer and Jansen/
(Released in the United States on   Polydor/2302 018
Reprise/MS 2049, in February 1972)
  "Lover Man"
  "Johnny B. Good"
  "Blue Suede Shoes"
  "Red House"
  "The Queen"
  "Sgt. Pepper's Lonely Hearts
    Club Band"
  "Little Wing"
  "Voodoo Chile"

More Experience   Mar. 1972/?/Ember/5061
(Live recording from Royal Albert Hall
on February 24, 1969)
  "Little Wing"

Title	Year/Producer/Label/Label Number
"Voodoo Child (Slight Return)" "Fire" "Purple Haze" "Wild Thing"	
War Heroes "Bleeding Heart" "Highway Chile" "Tax Free" "Peter Gunn" "Stepping Stone" "Midnight" "Three Little Birds" "Beginnings" "Izabella"	Oct. 1972/Kramer and Jansen/ Polydor/2302 020
Sound Track From the Film *'Jimi Hendrix'* (Released in the United States on Reprise/2 RS 6481, in July 1973) "Rock Me, Baby" "Wild Thing" "Machine Gun I" "Interviews I" "Johnny B. Goode" "Hey Joe" "Purple Haze" "Like a Rolling Stone" "Interviews II" "The Star Spangled Banner" "Machine Gun II" "Hear My Train A Comin' " "Interviews III" "Red House" "In From the Storm" "Interviews IV"	June 1973/Joe Boyd/Reprise/ K 64017
Jimi Plays Monterey (Released in Germany on Polydor/827 990-1) "Killing Floor" "Foxey Lady" "Like a Rolling Stone" "Rock Me, Baby" "Can You See Me?"	Feb. 1986/?/Reprise/25358-1

Title	Year/Producer/Label/Label Number

"The Wind Cries Mary"
"Purple Haze"
"Wild Thing"

Stages   1992/?/Polydor/511763–2
(Four *Stages* releases were issued—one
live show from 1967 to 1970)
1967–Live at Stockholm's
Radiohuset, September 1967
    "Sgt. Pepper's Lonely Hearts
       Club Band"
    "Fire"
    "The Wind Cries Mary"
    "Foxey Lady"
    "Hey Joe"
    "I Don't Live Today"
    "Burning of the Midnight Lamp"
    "Purple Haze"
1968–Live at the Paris Olympia,
January 29, 1968
    "Killing Floor"
    "Catfish Blues"
    "Foxey Lady"
    "Red House"
    "Drivin' South"
    "Tune Up Song (Spanish Castle
       Magic)"
    "The Wind Cries Mary"
    "Fire"
    "Little Wing"
    "Purple Haze"
1969–Live at the San Diego Sports
Arena, May 24, 1969
    "Fire"
    "Hey Joe"
    "Spanish Castle Magic"
    "Red House"
    "I Don't Live Today"
    "Purple Haze"
    "Voodoo Child (Slight Return)"
1970–Live at the *Atlanta International
Pop Festival*, July 4, 1970
    "Fire"
    "Lover Man"
    "Spanish Castle Magic"

Title	Year/Producer/Label/Label Number

"Foxey Lady"
"Purple Haze"
"Getting My Heart Back Together
    Again"
"Stone Free"
"Star Spangled Banner"
"Straight Ahead"
"Room Full of Mirrors"
"Voodoo Child (Slight Return)"

Jimi Hendrix: Blues   Apr. 1994/?/MCA/MCAD 11060
"Hear My Train A Comin'"
    (Acoustic)
"Born Under a Bad Sign"
"Red House"
"Catfish Blues"
"Voodoo Chile"
"Mannish Boy"
"Once I Had a Woman"
"Bleed Heart"
"Jam 292"
"Red House"
"Getting My Heart Back Together"
    (Electric)

Crash Landing   Feb. 1975/Douglas and Bongiovi/
(Released in the United Kingdom on   Reprise/MS 2204
Polydor/2310 398, in August 1975)
"Message to Love"
"Somewhere Over the Rainbow"
"Crash Landing"
"Come Down Hard on Me"
"Peace in Mississippi"
"With the Power"
"Stone Free Again"
"Captain Coconut"

Midnight Lightning   Nov. 1975/?/Reprise/MS 2229
(Released in the United Kingdom on
Polydor/2310 415, in November 1975)
"Trash Man"
"Midnight Lightning"
"Hear My Train"
"Gypsy Boy (New Rising Sun)"
"Blue Suede Shoes"
"Machine Gun"

Title	Year/Producer/Label/Label Number
"Once I Had a Woman"	
"Beginnings"	
The Essential Jimi Hendrix	July 1978/?/Reprise/2RS 2245
"Are You Experienced?"	
"Third Stone From the Sun"	
"Purple Haze"	
"Little Wing"	
"If 6 Was 9"	
"Bold as Love"	
"Little Miss Lover"	
"Castles Made of Sand"	
"Gypsy Eyes"	
"Burning of the Midnight Lamp"	
"Voodoo Child (Slight Return)"	
"Have You Ever Been (to Electric Ladyland)"	
"Still Raining, Still Dreaming"	
"House Burning Down"	
"All Along the Watchtower"	
"Room Full of Mirrors"	
"Izabella"	
"Freedom"	
"Dolly Dagger"	
"Stepping Stone"	
"Drifting"	
"Ezy Ryder"	
Lifelines: The Jimi Hendrix Story	Nov. 1990/various/Reprise/ 9 26435–2
"Introduction"	
"Testify"	
"Lawdy Miss Clawdy"	
"I'm a Man"	
"Like a Rolling Stone"	
"Red House"	
"Hey Joe"	
"Hoochie Coochie Man"	
"Purple Haze"	
"The Wind Cries Mary"	
"Foxey Lady"	
"Third Stone From the Sun"	
"Rock Me, Baby"	
"Look Over Yonder/Mister Bad Luck"	

Title	Year/Producer/Label/Label Number
"Burning of the Midnight Lamp"	
"Spanish Castle Magic"	
"Bold as Love"	
"One Rainy Wish"	
"Little Wing"	
"Drivin' South"	
"The Things I Used to Do"	
"All Along the Watchtower"	
"Drifter's Escape"	
"Cherokee Mist"	
"Voodoo Child (Slight Return)"	
"1983 . . . (A Merman I Should Turn to Be)"	
"Voodoo Chile"	
"Come On (Part 1)"	
"Manic Depression"	
"Machine Gun"	
"Room Full of Mirrors"	
"Angel"	
"Rainy Day Shuffle"	
"Valleys of Neptune"	
"Send My Love to Linda"	
"South Saturn Delta"	
"Night Bird Flying"	
"Tax Free"	
"Red House"	
"Spanish Castle Magic"	
"Star Spangled Banner"	
"Purple Haze"	
"I Don't Live Today"	
"Voodoo Chile/Sunshine of Your Love"	
Blues	Apr. 1994/Douglas/Polydor/521
"Hear My Train A Comin'" (aka "Getting My Heart Back Together" [acoustic])	037–2
"Born Under a Bad Sign"	
"Red House"	
"Catfish Blues"	
"Voodoo Chile Blues"	
"Mannish Boy"	
"Once I Had a Woman"	
"Bleeding Heart"	
"Jelly 292"	
"Hear My Train A Comin'" (electric)	

Title	Year/Producer/Label/Label Number
Experience Hendrix: The Best of Jimi Hendrix	Sept. 1997/Janie Hendrix and John McDermott/MCA/MCAD-11671

Experience Hendrix: The Best of
Jimi Hendrix
  "Purple Haze"
  "Fire"
  "The Wind Cries Mary"
  "Hey Joe"
  "All Along the Watchtower"
  "Stone Free"
  "Crosstown Traffic"
  "Manic Depression"
  "Little Wing"
  "If 6 Was 9"
  "Foxey Lady"
  "Bold as Love"
  "Castles Made of Sand"
  "Red House"
  "Voodoo Child (Slight Return)"
  "Freedom"
  "Nigh Bird Flying"
  "Angel"
  "Dolly Dagger"
  "The Star Spangled Banner"

First Rays of the New Rising Sun   Apr. 1997/Hendrix, Kramer, Mitchell/
  "Freedom"   MCA/MCAD-11599
  "Izabella"
  "Night Bird Flying"
  "Angel"
  "Room Full of Mirrors"
  "Dolly Dagger"
  "Ezy Ryder"
  "Drifting"
  "Beginnings"
  "Stepping Stone"
  "My Friend"
  "Straight Ahead"
  "Hey Baby (New Rising Sun)"
  "Earth Blues"
  "Astro Man"
  "In From the Storm"
  "Belly Button Window"

South Saturn Delta   Oct. 1997/Chandler, Hendrix, Kramer,
  "Look Over Yonder"   Mitchell, Jansen/MCA/MCAD-
  "Little Wing"   11684
  "Here He Comes (Lover Man)"
  "South Saturn Delta"
  "Power of Soul"

Title	Year/Producer/Label/Label Number
"Message to the Universe (Message to Love)"	
"Tax Free"	
"All Along the Watchtower"	
"The Stars That Play With Laughing Sam's Dice"	
"Midnight"	
"Sweet Angel (Angel)"	
"Bleeding Heart"	
"Pali Gap"	
"Drifter's Escape"	
"Midnight Lightning"	
Jimi Hendrix Experience: Live at Oakland	Feb. 1998/?/Dagger Records/088 23532–2
"Introduction"	
"Fire"	
"Hey Joe"	
"Spanish Castle Magic"	
"Hear My Train A Comin'"	
"Sunshine of Your Love"	
"Red House"	
"Foxey Lady"	
"Star Spangled Banner"	
"Purple Haze"	
"Voodoo Child (Slight Return)"	
The Jimi Hendrix Experience: The BBC Sessions	1998/various/MCA/MCAD 2–11742
"Foxey Lady"	
"Alexis Kroner Introduction"	
"Cay You Please Crawl Out Your Window?"	
"Rhythm and Blues World Service"	
"(I'm Your) Hoochie Coochie Man"	
"Travelling With the Experience"	
"Driving South"	
"Fire"	
"Little Miss Lover"	
"Introducing the Experience"	
"Burning of the Midnight Lamp"	
"Catfish Blues"	
"Stone Free"	
"Love or Confusion"	
"Hey Joe"	
"Hound Dog"	
"Driving South"	

Title	Year/Producer/Label/Label Number
"Hear My Train A Comin'"	
"Purple Haze"	
"Killing Floor"	
"Radio One"	
"Wait Until Tomorrow"	
"Day Tripper"	
"Spanish Castle Magic"	
"Jammin'"	
"I Was Made to Love You"	
"Foxey Lady"	
"A Brand New Sound"	
"Hey Joe"	
"Manic Depression"	
"Driving South"	
"Hear My Train A Comin'"	
"A Happening For Lulu"	
"Voodoo Child (Slight Return)"	
"Lulu Introduction"	
"Sunshine of Your Love"	
Jimi Hendrix: Live at the Fillmore East	1999/Janie Hendrix, Kramer,
"Stone Free"	McDermott/MCA/MCAD2–11931
"Power of Soul"	
"Hear My Train A Comin'"	
"Izabella"	
"Machine Gun"	
"Voodoo Child (Slight Return)"	
"We Gotta Live Together"	
"Auld Lang Syne"	
"Who Knows"	
"Changes"	
"Machine Gun"	
"Stepping Stone"	
"Stop"	
"Earth Blues"	
"Burning Desire"	
"Wild Thing"	
Jimi Hendrix Experience: Live	July 1999/?/Dagger Records/
at Clark University	088 12033–2
"Jimi Hendrix: Preconcert Interview"	
"Fire"	
"Red House"	
"Foxey Lady"	
"Purple Haze"	

Title	Year/Producer/Label/Label Number

"Wild Thing"
"Noel Redding: Postconcert
    Interview"
"Mitch Mitchell: Postconcert
    Interview"
"Jimi Hendrix: Postconcert
    Interview"	

Jimi Hendrix: Live at Woodstock "Introduction" "Message to Love" "Hear My Train A Comin' " "Spanish Castle Magic" "Red House" "Lover Man" "Foxey Lady" "Jam Back at the House" "Izabella" "Fire" "Voodoo Child (Slight Return)" "Star Spangled Banner" "Purple Haze" "Woodstock Improvisation" "Villanova Junction" "Hey Joe"	1999/Janie Hendrix, Kramer, McDermott/MCA/MCAD2–11987

*Jimi Hendrix: Merry Christmas
and Happy New Year*
"Little Drummer Boy/Silent Night/
    Auld Lang Syne"
"Three Little Bears"
"Little Drummer Boy/Silent Night/
    Auld Lang Syne" (extended
    version)
	Nov. 1999/Janie Hendrix, Kramer,
	    McDermott/MCA/115 651–2

Jimi Hendrix: Morning Symphony Ideas "Keep on Groovin' " "Jungle" "Room Full of Mirrors" "Strato Strut" "Scorpio Woman" "Acoustic Demo"	July 2000/?/Dagger/088 12353–2

Title	Year/Producer/Label/Label Number
The Jimi Hendrix Experience	Sept. 2000/Kramer/MCA/088 112
"Purple Haze"	316–2
"Killing Floor"	
"Hey Joe"	
"Foxey Lady"	
"Highway Chile"	
"Hey Joe"	
"Title #3"	
"Third Stone From the Sun"	
"Taking Care of No Business"	
"Here He Comes (Lover Man)"	
"Burning of the Midnight Lamp"	
"If 6 Was 9"	
"Rock Me, Baby"	
"Like a Rolling Stone"	
"Sgt. Pepper's Lonely Hearts Club Band"	
"Burning of the Midnight Lamp"	
"Little Wing"	
"Little Miss Lover"	
"The Wind Cries Mary"	
"Catfish Blues"	
"Bold as Love"	
"Sweet Angel (Angel)"	
"Fire"	
"Somewhere"	
"(Have You Ever Been to) Electric Ladyland"	
"Gypsy Eyes"	
"Room Full of Mirrors"	
"Gloria"	
"It's Too Bad"	
"Star Spangled Banner"	
"Stone Free"	
"Spanish Castle Magic"	
"Hear My Train A Comin' "	
"Room Full of Mirrors"	
"I Don't Live Today"	
"Little Wing"	
"Red House"	
"Purple Haze"	
"Voodoo Child (Slight Return)"	
"Izabella"	
"Message to Love"	
"Earth Blues"	

Title	Year/Producer/Label/Label Number
"Astro Man"	
"Country Blues"	
"Freedom"	
"Johnny B. Goode"	
"Lover Man"	
"Blue Suede Shoes"	
"Cherokee Mist"	
"Come Down Hard on Me"	
"Hey Baby/In From the Storm"	
"Ezy Ryder"	
"Night Bird Flying"	
"All Along the Watchtower"	
"In From the Storm"	
"Slow Blues"	
Morning Symphony Ideas	July 2000/?/Dagger Records/?
"Keep on Groovin'"	
"Jungle"	
"Room Full of Mirrors"	
"Strato Strut"	
"Scorpio Woman (Morning Symphony)"	
"Acoustic Demo"	
Voodoo Child: The Jimi Hendrix Collection	2001/Janie Hendrix, Kramer, McDermott/MCA/088 112 603–2
"Purple Haze"	
"Hey Joe"	
"The Wind Cries Mary"	
"Fire"	
"Highway Chile"	
"Are You Experienced?"	
"Burning of the Midnight Lamp"	
"Little Wing"	
"All Along the Watchtower"	
"Crosstown Traffic"	
"Voodoo Child (Slight Return)"	
"Spanish Castle Magic"	
"Stone Free"	
"Izabella"	
"Stepping Stone"	
"Angel"	
"Dolly Dagger"	
"Hey Baby (New Rising Sun)"	
"Fire"	

Title	Year/Producer/Label/Label Number
"Hey Joe"	
"I Don't Live Today"	
"Hear My Train A Comin' "	
"Foxey Lady"	
"Machine Gun"	
"Johnny B. Goode"	
"Red House"	
"Freedom"	
"Purple Haze"	
"Star Spangled Banner"	
"Wild Thing"	
Jimi Hendrix Experience: Live at Ottawa	Oct. 2001/?/Dagger Records/088 12739–2
"Killing Floor"	
"Tax Free"	
"Fire"	
"Red House"	
"Foxey Lady"	
"Hey Joe"	
"Spanish Castle Magic"	
"Purple Haze"	
"Wild Thing"	
Jimi Hendrix: Baggy's Rehearsal Sessions	June 2002/?/Dagger Records/088 112956–2
"Burning Desire"	
"Hoochie Coochie Man"	
"Message to Love"	
"Ezy Ryder"	
"Power of Soul"	
"Earth Blues"	
"Changes"	
"Lover Man"	
"We Gotta Live Together"	
"Baggy's Jam"	
"Earth Blues"	
"Burning Desire"	
Martin Scorsese Presents the Blues: Jimi Hendrix	Sept. 2003/?/Universal Music Enterprises/602498603642
"Red House"	
"Voodoo Chile"	
"Come On (Let the Good Times Roll)"	
"Georgia Blues"	

Title	Year/Producer/Label/Label Number
"Country Blues"	
"Hear My Train A Comin'"	
"It's Too Bad"	
"My Friend"	
"Blue Window"	
"Midnight Lightning"	
Live at Berkeley (The Second Set)	Sept. 2003/?/Universal Music
"Introduction"	Enterprises/602498607527
"Straight Ahead"	
"Hey Baby (New Rising Sun)"	
"Lover Man"	
"Stone Free"	
"Hey Joe"	
"I Don't Live Today"	
"Machine Gun"	
"Foxey Lady"	
"Star Spangled Banner"	
"Purple Haze"	
"Voodoo Child (Slight Return)"	
Jimi Hendrix Experience: Paris	Apr. 2003/?/Dagger Records/
1967/San Francisco 1968	CAFT-05056–2
"Stone Free"	
"Hey Joe"	
"Fire"	
"Rock Me, Baby"	
"Red House"	
"Purple Haze"	
"Wild Thing"	
"Killing Floor"	
"Red House"	
"Catfish Blues"	
"Dear Mr. Fantasy (Part 1)"	
"Dear Mr. Fantasy (Part 2)"	
"Purple Haze"	
Jimi Hendrix: Hear My Music	Nov. 2004/?/Dagger Records/
"Slow Version"	CAFT-05153–2
"Drone Blues"	
"Ezy Ryder/Star Spangled Banner"	
"Jimi/Jimmy Jam"	
"Jam 292"	
"Trash Man"	
"Message to Love"	

Title	Year/Producer/Label/Label Number
"Gypsy Blood"	
"Valleys of Neptune"	
"Blues Jam at Olympic"	
"Valleys of Neptune" (piano)	

Live at Fehmarn — Dec. 2005/?/Dagger Records/TBA

"Introduction"
"Killing Floor"
"Spanish Castle Magic"
"All Along the Watchtower"
"Hey Joe"
"Hey Baby (New Rising Sun)"
"Message to Love"
"Foxey Lady"
"Red House"
"Ezy Ryder"
"Freedom"
"Room Full of Mirrors"
"Purple Haze"
"Voodoo Child (Slight Return)"

Hendrix: Burning Desire — Dec. 2006/Various/Dagger Records/CAFT-05208–2

"Izabella"
"Ezy Ryder/MLK" (aka "Captain Coconut")
"Cherokee Mist/Astro Man"
"Record Plant 2X" (jam)
"Villanova Junction Blues"
"Burning Desire"
"Stepping Stone/Villanova Junction Blues"
"Slow Time Blues"

Jimi Hendrix Experience: Live at Monterey — Oct. 2007/?/Universal Music Enterprises/B0009843–02

"Introduction by Brian Jones"
"Killing Floor"
"Foxey Lady"
"Like a Rolling Stone"
"Rock Me, Baby"
"Hey Joe"
"Can You See Me?"
"The Wind Cries Mary"
"Purple Haze"
"Wild Thing"

Title	Year/Producer/Label/Label Number
Jimi Hendrix Experience: Live in Paris and Ottawa 1968	Sept. 2008/?/Dagger/02517 79178

    "Killing Floor"
    "Catfish Blues"
    "Foxey Lady"
    "Red House"
    "Drivin' South"
    "The Wind Cries Mary"
    "Fire"
    "Little Wing"
    "Purple Haze"
    "Sgt. Pepper's Lonely Hearts
      Club Band"
    "Fire"
    "Purple Haze"

Title	Year/Producer/Label/Label Number
Jimi Hendrix Experience: Live at Woburn	July 2009/?/Dagger/02527 10325

    "Sgt. Pepper's Lonely Hearts
      Club Band"
    "Fire"
    "Tax Free"
    "Red House"
    "Foxey Lady"
    "Voodoo Child (Slight Return)"
    "Purple Haze"

Title	Year/Producer/Label/Label Number
Jimi Hendrix: Valleys of Neptune	Mar. 2010/Janie Hendrix, Kramer, McDermott/Sony/88698 64056 2

    "Stone Free"
    "Valleys of Neptune"
    "Bleeding Heart"
    "Hear My Train A Comin' "
      (aka "Getting
      My Heart Back Together")
    "Mr. Bad Luck"
    "Sunshine of Your Love"
    "Lover Man"
    "Ships Passing Through the Night"
    "Fire"
    "Red House"
    "Lullaby for the Summer"
    "Crying Blue Rain"

Notes

CHAPTER 1

1. Caesar Glebbeek and Douglas J. Noble, *Jimi Hendrix: The Man, The Music, The Memorabilia* (New York: Thunder's Mouth Press, 1996), 7.

2. Glebbeek and Noble, 7.

3. Glebbeek and Noble, 9.

4. Glebbeek and Noble, 9.

5. There is a level of disagreement in the source work concerning the actual "first" band that Jimi played with. Some consider the first to be the Velvetones and others list the Rocking Kings. The fact is that the Rocking Kings grew out of the Velvetones.

6. Glebbeek and Noble, 10.

7. The Club Del Morocco was on Jefferson Street in Nashville, Tennessee. It was owned by "Uncle" Teddy Acklen and its Blue Room was home to many famous performers in the late 1950s and through the 1960s. In the late 1960s, the club was torn down to make way for an interstate.

8. The term chitlin' circuit refers collectively to the venues in the South and on the East Coast of the United States that allowed black musicians to perform during the period of segregation. The name is derived from "chitterlings" (stewed pig intestines) which is a popular part of the soul food cuisine.

9. Lonnie Youngblood was born Lonnie Thomas in 1941, in Augusta, Georgia. His early influences included saxophonists such as Louis Jordan and King Curtis. He got his start in the late 1950s as a sideman for Pearl Reeves and eventually became a bandleader of his own. Youngblood's career is long and storied and he is known as the "Prince of Harlem."

10. Glebbeek and Noble, 13.

11. The Isley Brothers were born in Cincinnati, Ohio and in 1957 formed a vocal trio that included Ronald, Rudolph, and O'Kelly Isley. After a lackluster start, the Isleys found success with the song "Lonely Teardrops" and secured a recording contract with RCA records. Their first top forty hit came with "Shout" and, after leaving RCA, they had another hit with "Twist and Shout." This began their string of hits. They signed to the Motown subsidiary Tamla and teamed with the Holland-Dozier-Holland creative team. The Isley Brothers went on to years of success that carried them from the rhythm and blues style, to Motown, and ultimately to funk.

12. Rosa Lee Brooks' claim to fame is the recording that she made of Arthur Lee's song "My Diary" with Jimi playing guitar.

13. Curtis Knight was born in Fort Scott, Kansas, in 1929 and died November 29, 1999. He was a famous singer and band leader who had a series of successful singles in the United States and the United Kingdom.

14. Glebbeek and Noble, 16.

15. Linda Keith was an aspiring young model in the mid-1960s with an appetite for the limelight, music, and musicians. In 1965 and 1966, Linda was the girlfriend of Keith Richards, the Rolling Stones' guitarist. In fact, Keith is on record as having written the song "Good Bye, Ruby Tuesday" about the couple's split.

16. Born Bryan James Chandler in 1938, "Chas" Chandler was the bass player, backup singer, and accessional songwriter for the Animals. When the group split in late 1966, Chas went on to manage a host of bands including the Jimi Hendrix Experience, Slade, Nick Drake, and others. He also ran his own studio and launched his own record label called Bam Records. Chandler died of a heart condition in 1996.

CHAPTER 2

1. Michael Jeffery (died March 5, 1973, in a plane crash), who Chandler had known from his work with the Animals. Jeffery was the Animals' business manager and is widely believed to have broken up the band amidst claims that he was embezzling the majority of the band's royalties. Regardless of this Chandler hired Jeffery for the business management of Hendrix once the Experience was formed. Suspicion and speculation continue to swirl around Jeffery even in death as claims have been made that he admitted to killing Hendrix and that he also embezzled money from the Experience.

2. Johnny Hallyday was born Jean-Philippe Smet in 1943. He is a French singer who is widely considered the "French Elvis Presley." He has sold more than 100 million records and has had a long and illustrious recording and touring career. Although wildly famous in France, Hallyday is little known in the United States.

3. Caesar Glebbeek and Douglas J. Noble, *Jimi Hendrix: The Man, The Music, The Memorabilia* (New York: Thunder's Mouth Press, 1996), 21.

4. Chris Potash, *The Jimi Hendrix Companion: Three Decades of Commentary* (New York: Schirmer Books, 1996), 3.

5. The singles described here, the release dates, and the song combinations refer to the original United Kingdom releases. Later singles with different song combinations were released in the United States.

6. Richie Unterberger, *The Rough Guide to Jimi Hendrix* (London: Rough Guides, 2009), 175.

7. Unterberger, 176.

8. *Ready Steady Go* was one of the first popular music television shows to air in the United Kingdom. It aired from 1964 to 1966.

9. *Top of the Pops* was another British popular music program. The show began in 1964 and aired until 2006.

10. Glebbeek and Noble, 26.

11. Philip José Farmer's (1918–2009) science fiction novel *Night of Light* was published in 1957 by Mercury Press. It tells the story of a world whose inhabitants must battle a two-week period of extreme light each five years. The light has transformative powers and its appearance polarizes the battle of good versus evil.

12. John McDermott, preface to *Jimi Hendrix: the Lyrics*, compiled by Janie Hendrix (Milwaukee, Wisconsin: Hal Leonard, 2003), 8.

13. Jimi Hendrix, *New Musical Express* (1/12/67), quoted in Harry Shapiro and Caesar Glebbeek, *Jimi Hendrix: Electric Gypsy* (New York: St. Martin's Griffin, 1995).

14. The Octavia effect pedal was first manufactured in 1967. It electronically created the effect of doubling an octave higher whatever note was being played.

15. David Stubbs, *Jimi Hendrix: The Stories Behind Every Song* (New York: Thunder's Mouth Press, 2003), 24.

16. Cat Stevens was born Steven Demetre Georgiou in 1948. He has enjoyed a long run as a successful singer-songwriter with several multiplatinum albums to his credit. Some of his most notable songs include "Wild World," "Father and Son," and "Peace Train." After several life-changing events, including at least two near-death experiences, Stevens converted to Islam and took the name Yusef Islam. He continues to record and perform, having released his most recent album, *Road-singer,* in 2009.

17. Engelbert Humperdinck was born Arnold George Dorsey in 1936 and rose to fame as a British pop singer. He took his stage name from a famous German opera composer and parlayed his early popularity into a long and storied career with in excess of fifty albums—both live and studio releases. Several of his most well-known songs are "Can't Take My Eyes off of You," "Misty Blue," and "After the Lovin'." Humperdinck's career continues with an album released in 2009.

18. The Walker Brothers were a three-piece American pop group whose heyday came in the late 1960s. The group consisted of Noel Scott Engel (Scott Walker) on bass, John Maus (John Walker) on vocals, and Gary Leeds (Gary Walker) on drums. Together the group released a series of successful albums with hit songs such as "The Sun Ain't Gonna Shine (Anymore)" and "Make It Easy on Yourself."

19. Harry Shapiro and Caesar Glebbeek, *Jimi Hendrix: Electric Gypsy* (New York: St. Martin's Griffin, 1995), 151.

20. Some sources say that the tour promoter, Tito Burns, was not happy with Jimi's antics and others say that he was in on the guitar burning.

21. Glebbeek and Noble, 32.

22. Unterberger, 177.

23. Stubbs, 24.

24. Unterberger, 178.

25. Commonly considered the first "super group," Cream formed in 1966 with Eric Clapton (guitar, vocals), Jack Bruce (bass, vocals), and Ginger Baker (drums). Although the group only lasted for two years, they released four albums and had

multiple hit singles including "Crossroads," "Born Under a Bad Sign," and "Tales of Brave Ulysses." The band has reformed a few times for isolated concert appearances since its original breakup.

26. Pink Floyd formed in 1965 with the union of Syd Barrett (guitar, vocals), Roger Waters (bass, vocals), Richard Wright (keyboards), Nick Mason (drums), and by 1968 David Gilmour (guitar, vocals). Together, the group defined progressive and art rock in the late 1960s and the early 1970s. However, Barrett left the group in 1968 and there ensued a power struggle between Waters and Gilmour. Waters ultimately left for a solo career in 1985. Pink Floyd has enjoyed success for over forty years. Through a series of often dark, but successful albums the group's popularity grew to arena-sized proportions. Gilmour and Mason continue on as Pink Floyd, as Barrett died in 2006 and Wright died in 2008.

27. George Bruno "Zoot" Money is an English-born vocalist, keyboard players, and bandleader who ran a successful working band for long stretches beginning in the early 1960s. In 1961, Money started the Big Roll Band which played in various venues around England. They had success and were popular as they were able to play in a wide range of styles including soul, jazz, R&B, and rock and roll. In 1967, Money changed his band's name to Dantalian's Chariot and continued his successes. He also came to the United States and toured in addition to appearing in several other bands. Of note, a young Andy Summers played guitar for the Big Roll Band and went on to be one-third of the rock group the Police.

28. The Move was formed in Birmingham, England, by Roy Wood (guitar, vocals), Carl Wayne (vocals), Bev Bevan (drums), Chris Kefford (bass), and Trevor Burton (guitar). The group specialized in a mix of rock and psychedelia from 1968 to 1972. By 1972 the group had shrunk to only Wood and Bevan and had added Jeff Lyne on the way to becoming another band, the Electric Light Orchestra.

29. Shapiro and Glebbeek, 167.

30. Heather Taylor is an American model who Roger Daltrey met in 1968. The couple married in 1971.

31. Shapiro and Glebbeek, 525.

32. Unterberger, 178–179.

33. Peter Doggett, *Jimi Hendrix: the Complete Guide to his Music* (London: Omnibus Press, 2004), 12.

34. Stubbs, 31.

35. Unterberger, 180.

36. Unterberger, 181.

37. Doggett, 12.

38. Unterberger, 182.

39. Shapiro and Glebbeek, 525.

40. The wah-wah pedal that Jimi (and Eric Clapton) used was the original Vox "Clyde McCoy" pedal that was first manufactured in 1967. The pedal was named for McCoy who was a big band trumpet player known most for the wah-wah effect he could get from his horn through the use of dampening. The Vox McCoy pedal spawned numerous copies and remains famous as the first such electric effects pedal.

41. Unterberger, 183.

42. Jimi Hendrix, "Third Stone From the Sun," on *Are You Experienced?* Track Records 612 001, 1967.

43. Unterberger, 184.

44. Doggett, 13.

45. Unterberger, 185.

46. The Experience's appearance at Monterey has been written about a great deal. It was at this show that Jimi again lit a guitar on fire on stage. This time it was not to generate publicity, but rather to upstage the Who. Jimi and Pete Townshend (the Who's guitarist) had clashed before the show over who would play first. Jimi ended up playing second and had to do something to contend with Townshend's aerial acrobatics while playing and the Who drummer Keith Moon's destruction of his drum kit at the end of the set.

47. Potash, 38.

48. The Fillmore West was opened by Bill Graham at the corner of Market Street and South Van Ness Avenue. It has been the home of countless famous concerts by artists including Creedence Clearwater Revival, Santana, and the Jimi Hendrix Experience. The Fillmore West location was closed by Graham in 1971.

49. The Whisky A Go Go was opened at 8901 Sunset Boulevard on January 11, 1964. The name is a purposeful misspelling as is attested to by the marquee on the front of the now famous building. Over the past forty-five years the Whisky has played host to many of the most important acts in American popular music in addition to being on the forefront of the evolution of musical style from 1960s psychedelic rock, to 1970s punk, to metal in the 1980s, and grunge in the 1990s. In the 1960s, famous acts who frequented the Whisky included the Doors, Van Morrison, Frank Zappa and the Mothers of Invention, as well as Jimi Hendrix who discovered there the Chicago Transit Authority, which would later be known as the band Chicago. The Whisky a Go Go remains an important West Coast music venue to this day.

50. Glebbeek and Noble, 48.

51. Dick Clark was born Richard Wagstaff Clark in 1929. He rose to fame at an early age as a television and radio personality. He was also a skilled businessman who was successful in the burgeoning American record business in the 1950s and 1960s. He created his own production company in addition to hosting the hugely successful television music program *American Bandstand.*

52. John Paul Hammond was born on November 13, 1943, in New York City. He is a critically acclaimed blues singer, songwriter, and guitarist.

53. The Salvation Club was located at 1 Sheridan Square in New York City. It existed in this location from 1967 to 1970 and was frequented by movie stars and famous rock and roll acts like Jimi Hendrix and the Yardbirds.

54. The Café A Go Go was located in the basement of 152 Bleeker Street in New York's Greenwich Village. It was famous as a home for jazz musicians before being taken over by 1960s musicians including the Grateful Dead, Richie Havens, Van Morrison, Howlin' Wolf, Muddy Waters, Johnny Lee Hooker, John Hammond, Jr., Jefferson Airplane, and others.

55. Natty Bumpo was one of Washington, DC's original psychedelic bands in the late 1960s. In addition to playing with the Experience, Natty Bumpo toured with Creedence Clearwater Revival, Boz Scaggs, Country Joe and the Fish, and others.

56. The Mamas and the Papas formed with two male and two female members, John and Michelle Phillips, Denny Doherty, and Cass Elliot. Due to internal conflict (and affairs) the band lineup changed during the recording of their second album when Michelle Phillips was replaced by Jill Gibson. In addition to releasing

numerous popular songs in the late 1960s, the Mamas and the Papas headlined the first concert that the Jimi Hendrix Experience played in America, the Monterey International Pop Festival of 1967.

57. Moby Grape was formed out of a union between several individuals that were associated with the band Jefferson Airplane in the mid-1960s. In 1966, Jerry Miller (lead guitar), Don Stevenson (drums), Peter Lewis (guitar), Bob Mosley (bass), and Skip Spence (guitar) formed the band whose name comes from the joke "What's big and purple and lives in the ocean?" The band had success in the late sixties releasing several albums before splitting up in 1971. Since then, Moby Grape has reformed with varying membership and continue to put out sporadic albums into the new millennium.

58. Born Timothy Charles Buckley III in 1947, Tim Buckley went on to a successful and critically acclaimed career as a folk singer and songwriter. Buckley's life was tragically short as he was only twenty-eight when he died on June 29, 1975.

59. The Mellotron was one of the earliest sample-playback keyboards. In the body of a wood-grained organ was inserted a series of prerecorded sounds on strips of magnetic tape. When a key was depressed it played the sampled sound underneath. The strips of tape could be created by anyone with a reel-to-reel deck and banks of new sounds could be added with relative ease.

60. Shapiro and Glebbeek, 527.

61. Doggett, 40–41.

Chapter 3

1. Harry Shapiro and Caesar Glebbeek, *Jimi Hendrix: Electric Gypsy* (New York: St. Martin's Griffin, 1995), 527.

2. Johnny Black, *Jimi Hendrix: The Ultimate Experience* (New York: Thunder's Mouth Press, 1999), 113–116.

3. The name Paul Caruso came from an actual friend of Jimi's.

4. Richie Unterberger, *The Rough Guide to Jimi Hendrix* (London: Rough Guides, 2009), 187.

5. The Spanish Castle Club opened in 1959 and lasted until 1964 during which it played host to acts such as Jerry Lee Lewis, Conway Twitty, and Roy Orbison. The site on which the Spanish Castle Club once stood is now a parking lot.

6. Unterberger, 187.

7. Peter Doggett, *Jimi Hendrix: the Complete Guide to His Music* (London: Omnibus Press, 2004), 17.

8. Created by Donald Leslie in the mid-1960s, the Leslie speaker cabinet has long been associated with the sound of psychedelic rock and the Hammond Organ. The technology at work in the speaker was unique in that it had a rotating treble speaker unit that consisted of two actual speakers—one was a dummy counterbalance. The treble speakers actually rotated on an electric motor thus producing the Doppler effect with the sound. The bass speaker was stationary, but its baffling materials rotated on an electric motor. The speaker created the signature Doppler effect along with vibrato, tremolo, and chorus effects. The motors could be run at two different speeds or stopped altogether.

9. In 1953, Eugene Shenk began building handmade audio electronics equipment under the Pultec name. Much of the early Pultec filter technology allowed audio engineers to focus, equalize, and boost specific recorded information, such as Jimi's vocals.

10. Black, 115.

11. Unterberger, 188.

12. As was the case with many of Hendrix's songs, "If 6 Was 9" was cut in several different versions. The original liner notes for the album did not contain a fourth verse, but it does appear in Janie Hendrix's *Jimi Hendrix: the Lyrics* (Milwaukee, WI: Hal Leonard, 2003), 78.

13. Interestingly, the British slang "if 6 was 9" means to be in a state of utter confusion. However, on this song Jimi did not appear to be confused about anything other than the poor reception he got from those who could not relate to the way he looked, acted, or dressed.

14. Unterberger, 188–189.

15. In the movie, two hippie bikers played by Peter Fonda and Dennis Hopper ride their motorcycles across the United States encountering a drug-fueled, countercultural landscape. The movie stands as a popular period piece encapsulating the isolation felt by the "peace and love" generation coming of age in the late 1960s. Interestingly, Jimi would later pen a song called "Ezy Ryder" about the freedom felt by a biker on the highway.

16. Shapiro and Glebbeek, 528.

17. Shapiro and Glebbeek, 528.

18. Doggett, 17.

19. Doggett, 18.

20. Black, 90.

21. Automatic double tracking or artificial double tracking was a recording trick achieved in the analog recording studio in which a voice or instrument was simultaneously recorded on two separate decks to create a dual recording which was then combined into a single track to make the sound achieve "natural" doubling. The technique was first used in 1966 by the Beatles while recording at Abbey Road Studios.

22. Doggett, 18.

23. The lyrics contained in the original LP inside gatefold contained several differences from that found in Janie Hendrix's book containing Jimi's lyrics. Based on the knowledge that Jimi frequently sang songs differently from the album version, this is not surprising. However, the nonsense lyric in the liner notes "would you believe babe, I've been looking for a Suethat feels like you" makes much more sense as "would you believe baby, I've been lookin' for a soul that feels like you for some time?" From Janie Hendrix, *Jimi Hendrix: the Lyrics* (Milwaukee, WI: Hal Leonard, 2003), 87.

24. Doggett, 18.

25. Caesar Glebbeek and Douglas J. Noble, *Jimi Hendrix: The Man, The Music, The Memorabilia* (New York: Thunder's Mouth Press, 1996), 59.

26. Chris Potash, *The Jimi Hendrix Companion: Three Decades of Commentary* (New York: Schirmer Books, 1996), 55.

27. Black, 118.

28. Most popular between 1968 and 1973, the band Ten Years After was Alvin Lee (guitar, vocals), Leo Lyons (bass), Chick Churchill (keyboards), Ric Lee (drums), and Joe Gooch (guitar). The group was an English blues-based rock band that scored several top ten hits with songs such as "I'd Love To Change the World" and "Hear Me Calling."

29. From 1967 to 1969, the Amen Corner released a series of successful United Kingdom chart hits in a rhythm and blues tinged pop style. The group was

composed of Blue Weaver (organ), Andy Fairweather Low (vocals), Neil Jones (guitar), Clive Taylor (bass), Allen Jones and Mike Smith (saxophones), and Dennis Bryon (drums).

30. The Nice formed in 1967 in London, England, and lasted until 1970. The group produced some of the earliest progressive rock songs with Keith Emerson on keyboards, Lee Jackson on bass and vocals, Brian Davison on drums, and David O'List on guitar. After their split, the group's members went on to form other bands including the progressive rock giants Emerson, Lake, and Palmer.

31. The band Eire Apparent ended up teaming up with the Experience as an opening act because they were also managed by Chas Chandler. Active from 1967–1970, the Belfast, Ireland–based group consisted of Mick Cox, Ernie Graham, Davy Lutton, Henry McCullough, and Chris Steward. Together they released one album of rock-tinged psychedelia which was produced by Jimi Hendrix.

32. The Soft Machine took its name from the William S. Burroughs book of the same title. The group formed in Canterbury, England in 1966 with members Robert Wyatt (drums, vocals), Kevin Ayers (bass, guitar, vocals), Daevid Allen (guitar), and Mike Ratledge (organ). Together they played in the proto-progressive rock style and had success helping to pioneer that sound. The band ended up touring with the Experience because they were also managed by Chas Chandler. The Soft Machine existed until 1984, but with a wide-ranging assortment of members that ultimately did not include any of the original four.

33. Albert King was born Albert Nelson in Indianola, Mississippi, in 1923 (he lived until 1992). Known for his blues guitar playing, King's signature instrument was a Gibson Flying V which he played upside down (just as Jimi did). King scored a series of successful singles recording on the Stax Records label and was notorious for his pith-bending abilities, which fit well into the blues style.

34. John Mayall formed the Bluesbreakers in 1963 and the band went on to be a pioneering and influential blues-rock group with wide-reaching influence. The group has included a great range of players since its beginnings and continued to issue recordings as recently as 2009. Over the course of the Bluesbreakers' existence key members (other than Mayall himself) included Eric Clapton (later formed Cream), Jack Bruce (also in Cream), Peter Green (later of Fleetwood Mac), John McVie (also of Fleetwood Mac), Mick Fleetwood (also of Fleetwood Mac), Mick Taylor (later of the Rolling Stones), and many others. The band has issued in excess of fifty-five albums and enjoyed a long and storied history as part of the British blues explosion of the mid-1960s.

35. Black, 131.

36. The Troggs are often described as a novelty band, but in fact had a series of successful singles and were signed in 1964 by Larry Page who also managed the Kinks. The group consisted of Reg Presley (vocals), Chris Britton (lead guitar), Dave Wright (rhythm guitar), Pete Staples (bass), and Ronnie Bond (drums). In addition to "Wild Thing," the Troggs scored hits with "Girl Like You," "I Can't Control Myself," and "Love Is All Around." The Troggs continued to perform and record into the 1990s.

37. Black, 140.

38. Glebbeek and Noble, 65.

39. Black, 142.

40. Unterberger, 190.

41. Dave Mason was born David Thomas Mason, in Worcester, England, in 1946 and achieved fame performing with a variety of United Kingdom—and United States–based bands beginning in the late 1960s. Mason was a driving force in the band Traffic, along with Steve Winwood. He also played with Hendrix, the Rolling Stones, Fleetwood Mac, Michael Jackson, and others. With Traffic, he scored a hit with the song "Feelin' Alright" which has been heavily covered.

42. Unterberger, 192.

43. Shapiro and Glebbeek, 529.

44. Black, 144.

45. Blue Cheer began in San Francisco in 1966 with the early lineup containing Eric Albronda (drums), Dickie Peterson (vocals, bass), Leigh Stephens (guitar), Jerre Peterson (guitar), Vale Hamanaka (keyboard), and Jerry Whiting (vocals, harmonica). Paul Whaley replaced Albronda in one of the many lineup changes that were a trademark of the band. The band took their name from a particularly potent strain of LSD. Soon Albronda moved to a management position with the band and was replaced by Paul Whaley. The group's early style was a blend of blues-based rock and they were credited as early pioneers of the West Coast psychedelic style. After seeing the Experience, Blue Cheer pared down to a power trio with Peterson, Whaley, and Stephens. Over the course of ten albums, several charting singles, and multiple lineup changes, the band continued to record into 2009; along the way they changed style with the times to include metal, punk, and grunge.

46. Black, 149.

47. Formed in 1965, the original lineup of the Small Faces was Steve Marriott, Ronnie Lane, Kenney Jones, and Jimmy Winston. Winston was soon replaced by Ian McLagan and the group went on to success in the late 1960s as one of the pioneers of the English mod sound. The Small Faces scored a series of hits with songs such as "Lazy Sunday," "Tin Soldier," and "All or Nothing" before breaking up in 1969. Out of the ashes of the Small Faces came the popular band the Faces with the addition of Ronnie Wood (guitar, later of the Rolling Stones) and Rod Stewart (vocals).

48. Electric Flag was guitarist Mike Bloomfield's band after he departed the Butterfield Blues Band. Together with Barry Goldberg (keyboards), Buddy Miles (drums), Harvey Brooks (bass), and Nick Gravenites (vocals), the band formed in 1967 and specialized in a hybrid of blues, rock, jazz, and rhythm and blues.

49. Black, 152.

50. Begun under the name Tyrannosaurus Rex in 1967, the band was essentially Marc Bolan (guitar, vocals) and Steve Peregrin Took (drums). Together the pair achieved moderate success and released a series of albums before parting company in 1970. At this point Bolan continued on under the moniker T. Rex. T. Rex was most famous for the song "Get It On."

51. Geno Washington was born William Francis Washington in Indiana. While stationed in England during his military duty, Geno was a club regular singing in the American rhythm and blues style. In 1965, he teamed up with the Ram Jam Band and for three years the group had success through their aggressive touring and popular live performances.

52. Although critically acclaimed and often successful on the charts in the United Kingdom, the Family struggled to get a foothold in the United States. The group

formed in 1966 in Leicester, England, and fostered a blend of psychedelic and progressive rock. Due to a rotating membership that included eleven different artists over a seven-year period, the Family had an oft-changing sound as well. They released seven albums many of which achieved United Kingdom chart position before disbanding in 1973.

53. Vanilla Fudge began in 1967 and stylistically bridged the gap between late 1960s psychedelia and the early incarnations of heavy metal. The original group was Mark Stein (organ), Tim Bogert (bass), Vince Martell (guitar), and Carmine Appice (drums)—all four members also sang. The band has existed in several incarnations since, but their greatest fame was achieved with this lineup on the song "Keep Me Hanging On." The "mob" connection with the band was through their manager Phillip Basile who was allegedly a part of the Luchese crime family.

54. The claim of a mafia connection to Vanilla Fudge is well documented in both Shapiro and Glebbeek (page 166) and Black (page 157).

55. Noel formed Fat Mattress in the late summer of 1968. The group included Neil Landon, Jim Leverton, and Eric Dillon. Together, the group released two albums before breaking up in 1970. Although a short-lived diversion from his work with the Jimi Hendrix Experience, Noel's involvement with Fat Mattress marked the beginning of the end of his time performing as part of any group fronted by Jimi.

56. Shapiro and Glebbeek, 300.

57. Black, 162.

58. Dino Valenti (born Chester Powers, 1947–1994) was a singer and songwriter who was most famous for his song "Get Together." The song was covered by artists such as Jefferson Airplane and the Youngbloods. As part of the San Francisco psychedelic rock era, Valenti helped form Quicksilver Messenger Service. Troubled by a series of drug busts and time in prison, and possessed of a short temper, Valenti's music fame was short lived.

59. Buddy Miles (1947–2008) was born George Allen Miles, Jr. He achieved fame in the music business as a rock and funk drummer—as well as being an accomplished singer. Buddy's early career was spent backing jazz greats such as Duke Ellington, Count Basie, and Dexter Gordon. He went on to work with the Ink Spots, the Delfonics, and Wilson Pickett. Next he formed the group Electric Flag and at this point caught Jimi's attention. The two jammed together and became good friends. Buddy played with Jimi in the Band of Gypsys in 1969 and 1970 before being fired by Jeffery. He went on to continued success in music writing and performing for the stage and screen.

60. James Cotton was born in Tunica, Mississippi, in 1935. Cotton has had a long and successful career as a singer, harmonica player, songwriter, and band leader. Cotton's songs are in the blues/delta blues style and he has performed with a large number of artists from a variety of styles including Janis Joplin, Howlin' Wolf, Muddy Waters, Led Zeppelin, Taj Mahal, B. B. King, the Grateful Dead, and many others.

61. The group Cat Mother & the All-Night News Boys began in 1968 and lasted until 1973. Formed in New York, the group included Bob Smith (keyboards, vocals), Roy Michaels (bass, vocals), William David "Charlie" Chin (guitar, vocals), Larry Parker (violin, guitar), and Michael Equine (drums, guitar). Together the group released a series of four albums and had a string of popular singles including "The Street Giveth and the Street Taketh Away."

62. Linda Eastman (1941–1998) was an American photographer and musician. On March 12, 1969, she married Paul McCartney of the Beatles and subsequently was a member of McCartney's band Wings. Her photographs of music figures of the 1960s are quite popular and have been released as a book called *Linda McCartney's Sixties: Portrait of an Era*. She was diagnosed with breast cancer in 1995 and died in 1998 at age fifty-six.

63. Shapiro and Glebbeek, 530.

64. Shapiro and Glebbeek, 530.

65. Potash, 16.

66. Unterberger, 189.

67. "Crosstown Traffic" was released as a single prior to its appearance on *Electric Ladyland* and was therefore discussed previously.

68. Peter Doggett, *Jimi Hendrix: the Complete Guide to His Music* (London: Omnibus Press, 2004), 22.

69. Shapiro and Glebbeek, 530.

70. Doggett, 22.

71. Hendrix, *The Lyrics*, 90.

72. Al Kooper was born Alan Kuperschmidt in 1944 in New York. Kooper achieved early success with his musical talent and went on to success in several bands and as a session player. In 1965, Kooper teamed with Bob Dylan when Dylan went electric and Kooper provided the keyboard part of Dylan's seminal song "Like a Rolling Stone." Kooper was also instrumental in forming the group Blood, Sweat and Tears—though he was only with the group for a short time. He went on to great success as a session keyboard player and recorded with acts such as the Rolling Stones, B. B. King, the Who, Alice Cooper, Cream, and others—having appeared on over one hundred albums.

73. Earl King was born Earl Silas Johnson in New Orleans, Louisiana, and had a long and successful career as a singer, songwriter, and guitarist (1934–2003). King was a master of the New Orleans blues and R&B styles. In addition to recording and releasing several albums of his own music, King worked with other successful recording artists such as Professor Longhair, Lee Dorsey, and most notably Allen Toussaint and the Meters.

74. Doggett, 23.

75. Lucille Hendrix was buried in a pauper's grave in the same cemetery in which Jimi would be entombed a short twelve years later.

76. Shapiro and Glebbeek, 531.

77. Michael Finnigan, Freddie Smith, and Larry Faucette were members of the Lawrence, Kansas–based band the Serfs in 1968. The group had been advised to go to the Record Plant to record as that was the happening studio at the time. As the story went, the members of the Serfs are at the studio standing in the hall when Jimi proposed that they play together. The Serfs were short-lived as a band, but did release an album called *Early Bird Café* in 1969 on Capitol Records.

78. Richie Unterberger. *The Rough Guide to Jimi Hendrix* (London: Rough Guides, 2009), 191.

79. Shapiro and Glebbeek, 531.

80. Doggett, 24.

81. Unterberger, 192.

82. Doggett, 24.

83. Shapiro and Glebbeek, 531.

84. Because the single of "All Along the Watchtower" was released prior to its appearance on *Electric Ladyland* it was discussed previously.

85. Unterberger, 193.

86. Shapiro and Glebbeek, 302.

87. Glebbeek and Noble, 79.

88. Black, 173.

89. Formed in 1967, Burning Red Ivanhoe was likely Scandinavia's first progressive rock band. Their early music sounded like a jazzy take on the Who which then moved into straight-ahead prog rock. In 1972 the group transformed into Secret Oyster Service and then Secret Oyster, each of which had greater jazz leanings stylistically.

90. Glebbeek and Noble, 79.

91. Led by the singing, flute playing, songwriting, and guitar work of Ian Anderson, Jethro Tull formed in England in 1967. The group has sold in excess of 60 million records in the past forty-plus years and has mastered the rock, folk, and art rock styles.

92. Glebbeek and Noble, 79.

93. Van der Graaf Generator was an English progressive rock band that was run by Peter Hammill and David Jackson. Begun in 1967, their music was darker and heavier than some of the "spaced out" progressive rock bands and was more in the view of King Crimson. After several periods of hiatus and lineup changes, Van der Graaf Generator continues to perform.

94. John McLaughlin was born on January 4, 1942. He is a guitarist of high reputation who has had a long and storied career. In addition to playing with his own bands including Mahvishnu Orchestra, McLaughlin also recorded with the group Lifetime and Miles Davis. His guitar styles range from fusion to classical, Indian to jazz. His current group is called the 4th Dimension and includes McLaughlin (guitar), Gary Husband (drums, keyboards), Mark Mondesir (drums), and Dominique di Piazza (bass).

95. Black, 182.

96. Black, 183.

97. Potash, 19.

98. Black, 187.

99. Born Henry Saint Clair Fredericks, in 1942, Taj Mahal has had a long and storied career in the music business. He is recognized as an international force in American blues guitar, banjo, and harmonica playing and has branched out to work in a wide variety of styles and forms. His music reflects the influences of Africa and the Caribbean and he continues to be an active live performer and recording artist.

100. The San Francisco–based band Loading Zone was an R&B band with a horn line. They formed in 1967 and over the course of three years released two albums. The group included Linda Tillery (vocals), Todd Anderson (woodwinds, keyboards), Steve Dowler (guitar), Paul Faverso (vocals, keyboards), Peter Shapiro (guitar), George Newcom (drums), Bob Kindle (bass), Patrick O'Hara (trombone), and Paul Taormina (trumpet). Although the group's popularity was regional, several members went on to work in larger venues. Patrick O'Hara worked with Boz Scaggs and Paul Faverso worked with Mike Love of the Beach Boys.

101. Black, 194.

102. Tom Doyle, "Stone Free," *Q Magazine* 285 (April 2010): 88.

CHAPTER 4

1. Born Gerardo Velez, Jerry is a popular Puerto Rican percussionist who Jimi met in mid-May 1969 when he saw him playing with the band the McCoys at the Scene. Jimi invited Velez to join him in the studio that night and with this Velez became a member of the group Gypsy Sun and Rainbows which played Woodstock. Velez has deep roots in Latin percussion and plays in a variety of styles. After working with Jimi, Velez went on to be a member of the fusion band Spyro Gyra, has been nominated for seven Grammy Awards, and is currently creating a DVD called *Velez Sez.*

2. Juma Sultan was born in 1942 in Monrovia, California. He worked with Jimi on a series of shows, most significantly appearing with Jimi at Woodstock. He was a part of the band that Jimi called Gypsy Sun and Rainbows and also played live with Jimi on the *Dick Cavett Show.*

3. Johnny Black, *Jimi Hendrix: The Ultimate Experience* (New York: Thunder's Mouth Press, 1999), 196.

4. Tom Doyle, "Stone Free," *Q Magazine* 285 (April 2010): 89.

5. There are several videotaped versions of Jimi's performance at Woodstock. Unfortunately, the film crew hired to record the event took time to change tape in their machine during "Hear My Train A Comin'." However, amateur videographer twenty-two-year old Albert Goodman captured the entire set and has recently made it available.

CHAPTER 5

1. The Hotel Navarro was located at 112 Central Park South with easy access to the types of recording and performing venues that interested Jimi. It was subsequently rebuilt and is now the Ritz-Carlton.

2. The United Block Association was established by Leo Billy Rolle in 1955 with the expressed purpose of serving the many needs of the people of Harlem.

3. Johnny Black, *Jimi Hendrix: The Ultimate Experience* (New York: Thunder's Mouth Press, 1999), 203.

4. Sam and Dave were a soul/R&B duo that formed in 1961 with Samuel Moore singing tenor and Dave Prater singing baritone. The pair went on to fame after they signed with the Stax Records label and began recording with the Stax house band Booker T. and the M.G.'s as well as the Stax horn line the Mar-Keys. The pair quickly became known as "Double Dynamite" on their way to being inducted into the Rock and Roll Hall of Fame. Many of Sam and Dave's songs were chart toppers, but few have remained as popular as "Hold On, I'm Coming" and "Soul Man."

5. Big Maybelle was born Mabel Louise Smith (1924–1972). She gained fame as an American rhythm and blues singer with hits such as "Candy." She released a series of ten popular records during her life and recorded on labels such as King Records, Okeh Records, and Chess Records, among others.

6. Black, 206.

7. Alan Douglas is an American record producer and label boss of Douglas Records. He has famously worked with Miles Davis, Lenny Bruce, the Last Poets, and Jimi Hendrix, among others. While Douglas was helpful to Jimi at the time, his work on Jimi's material after the guitarist's death was quite controversial. On the releases *Crash Landing* and *Midnight Lightning*, Douglas replaced the original drum and bass tracks with newly recorded session players and even overdubbed additional guitar work.

8. The Last Poets are a group of musicians and lyricists/poets who formed in Harlem in 1968 as a part of the civil rights movement. The core membership included Felipe Luciano, Galan Kain, and David Nelson. However after a split the group went on to include Jalal Mansur Nuriddin, Umar Bin Hassan, Abiodun Oyewole, and Nalaja Obabi. The group recorded for Alan Douglas and through him met and worked with Jimi Hendrix. The Last Poets are generally credited as one of the earliest proto-rap groups.

9. Tony Bongiovi is a legendary American music producer and engineer who worked with Jimi when Bongiovi was still establishing his career. The pair worked on several tracks together during the final year of Jimi's life. In the mid-to-late 1970s, Bongiovi went on to great success when he opened the Power Station recording studio. There a wide range of artists recorded for Bongiovi (many of them at the Power Station) including the Ramones, the Talking Heads, Aerosmith, Chic, Gloria Gaynor, Diana Ross, David Bowie, Bruce Springsteen, and many others. Bongiovi remains active and recently pioneered a new breed of car audio. He is the second cousin of John Bon Jovi (who changed the spelling of his last name).

10. The concert was also released in DVD format in 1999 with additional songs and interviews from Jimi, Mitch Mitchell, Noel Redding, Billy Cox, and Buddy Miles, along with Lenny Kravitz, Vernon Reid, Slash, and Eddie Kramer. The DVD is titled *Band of Gypsys: Live at the Fillmore East*.

11. Black, 216.

12. Janie Hendrix, comp., *Jimi Hendrix: the Lyrics* (Milwaukee, WI: Hal Leonard, 2003), 176.

13. Richie Unterberger, *The Rough Guide to Jimi Hendrix* (London: Rough Guides, 2009), 194.

14. Peter Doggett, *Jimi Hendrix: the Complete Guide to His Music* (London: Omnibus Press, 2004), 29.

15. On January 1, 1970, the University of Southern California Trojans played the University of Michigan in the Rose Bowl and won 10–3.

16. Doggett, 30.

17. Black, 221.

CHAPTER 6

1. Due to the lack of consistency in billing, the band that backed Jimi for the tour is referred to here only with the names of the other performers who were on stage.

2. Johnny Black, *Jimi Hendrix: The Ultimate Experience* (New York: Thunder's Mouth Press, 1999), 223.

3. The band Ballin' Jack was formed in Seattle, Washington, by Luther Rabb (bass, vocals) and Ronnie Hannon (drums). The name of the band was a slang term

with many different interpretations. One was that it was the name of a popular dance move in the early 1900s and another was simply to dance or have a good time. Other interpretations reference railroad work and the game bocce ball. Regardless, Rabb and Hammon's band played a mix of rock and jazz-rock fusion with the addition of Glen Thomas (guitar) and Jim Coile and Tim McFarland (horns). The group achieved national success in the United States before breaking up in 1974. Rabb and Hammon went on to work in the band War.

4. The band Blue Mountain Eagle took their name from a Grant County, Oregon, newspaper and formed in the summer of 1969 out of the ashes of the New Buffalo Springfield. The group included David Price (rhythm guitar, vocals), Don Poncher (drums, vocals), Jim Price (horn), Randy Fuller (bass), Bob Jones (lead guitar, vocals), and Joey Newman (second lead guitar). The band released an eponymous album which sold poorly before disbanding in September 1970.

5. Bloodrock was one of the first successful rock and roll bands to come out of Fort Worth, Texas. The group formed in 1969 and included Jim Rutledge (vocals), Rick Cobb (drums), Lee Pickens (guitar), Ed Grundy (bass), Stevie Hill (keyboards), and Nick Taylor (guitar). The band had some success over the course of their six-year run. They released seven albums, several of which cracked the Billboard Top 200.

6. Country Funk was formed in 1968 in Los Angeles by Adam Taylor (lead guitar) and Hal Paris (rhythm guitar, keyboard). The pair recruited a rhythm section of Jeff Lockwood (bass) and Joe Pfeifer (drums) and began making a name for themselves. The band's lineup was unstable and several others entered and exited the band in its first year. Country Funk generated a following on the west and east coasts and released an album on Polydor Records before disbanding.

7. Cactus was formed out of the ashes of Vanilla Fudge. Carmine Appice (drums) and Tim Bogert (bass) recruited Jim McCarty (guitar) and Dusty Day (vocals) and created the group in 1970. For two years Cactus performed live and recorded, generating four albums, before interband tension broke the group up.

8. Black, 229.

9. Although it was not known to Jimi until 1970, Les Paul had actually seen him play at a club in 1965 and had wanted to get together with him to put together a record deal. However the opportunity was missed when Paul was unable to learn Jimi's name at the time.

10. Robert Mackey, "Les Paul, in his own words," *New York Times*, August 13, 2009.

11. The band Grin was the making of guitarist, singer, and songwriter Nils Lofgren. After working with Neil Young for a time, Lofgren formed Grin as a solo project with Bob Gordon (bass) and Bob Berberich (drums). The group began playing together in 1969 and released four albums together by 1974. Along the way, Lofgren added his brother Tom on rhythm guitar. After Grin was released by their label in 1974, Lofgren went on to great success as part of Neil Young's band Crazy Horse and Bruce Springsteen's group the E Street Band.

12. The Illusion was formed in 1965 in Long Island, New York, and lasted until 1972. The group released three albums with their own take on the 1960s psychedelic sound. The band's members were John Vinci (vocals), Richie Ceniglia (lead guitar), Mike Maniscalco (rhythm guitar), Chuck Adler (bass), and Mike Ricciardella (drums).

13. Black, 234.

14. Black, 236.

15. David Weiss, "The Changing Face of New York Studios: Recording, Mixing, and Post Facilities Adapt to Economic Realities," *Mix Professional Audio and Music Production Magazine* 33/10 (October 2009): 32.

16. For a complete list of those who have recorded at Electric Lady Studios along with current news about who is using the studio see http://www.electricladystudios .com/index.html.

17. Black, 238.

18. Black, 241.

19. Blue Sun was a Copenhagen-based jam band that formed in 1969. The original incarnation of the band lasted until 1971 and released two albums (they have reformed several times since). The core players in the Blue Sun band were Bo Jacobsen (drums), Jan Kaspersen (keyboards), Niels Pontoppidan (guitar), Dale Smith (vocals, percussion), and Jesper Zeuthen (saxophone). The group played in an avant-garde jazz-rock style that was marked by long improvisations.

20. Black, 246.

21. Harry Shapiro and Caesar Glebbeek, *Jimi Hendrix: Electric Gypsy* (New York: St. Martin's Griffin, 1995), 470–471.

22. Richie Unterberger, *The Rough Guide to Jimi Hendrix* (London: Rough Guides, 2009), 129.

CHAPTER 7

1. Peter Doggett, *Jimi Hendrix: the Complete Guide to His Music* (London: Omnibus Press, 2004), 34–35.

2. Harry Shapiro and Caesar Glebbeek, *Jimi Hendrix: Electric Gypsy* (New York: St. Martin's Griffin, 1995), 537.

3. Johnny Black, *Jimi Hendrix: The Ultimate Experience* (New York: Thunder's Mouth Press, 1999), 231.

4. Doggett, 35.

5. Black, 233.

6. Richie Unterberger, *The Rough Guide to Jimi Hendrix* (London: Rough Guides, 2009), 196.

7. Peter Doggett, *Jimi Hendrix: the Complete Guide to His Music* (London: Omnibus Press, 2004), 37.

8. Doggett, 47.

CHAPTER 8

1. Unterberger, 135.

2. Harry Shapiro and Caesar Glebbeek, *Jimi Hendrix: Electric Gypsy* (New York: St. Martin's Griffin, 1995), 539.

3. Johnny Black, *Jimi Hendrix: The Ultimate Experience* (New York: Thunder's Mouth Press, 1999), 227.

4. Peter Doggett, *Jimi Hendrix: the Complete Guide to His Music* (London: Omnibus Press, 2004), 94.

5. Doggett, 95.

6. Doggett, 114.

7. Blair Jackson, "'Valleys of Neptune': New Studio Gems from the Hendrix Vaults," *Mix: Professional Audio and Music Production* 34/3 (March 2010): 40.

8. Jackson, 41.

CHAPTER 9

1. Richie Unterberger, *The Rough Guide to Jimi Hendrix* (London: Rough Guides, 2009), 137.

TOURS AND JAM SESSIONS

1. The list of tours reflects a culmination of a variety of sources including Caesar Glebbeek and Douglas J. Noble, *Jimi Hendrix: The Man, The Music, The Memorabilia* (New York: Thunder's Mouth Press, 1996), 195–215, and Johnny Black, *Jimi Hendrix: The Ultimate Experience* (New York: Thunder's Mouth Press, 1999). Also important was the list of tours found at www.jimihendrix.com/encyclopedia.

Bibliography

BOOKS, ARTICLES, AND SONGBOOKS

(n.d. = no printing date)

Aledort, Andy. *Jimi Hendrix: A Step-by-Step Breakdown of His Guitar Styles and Techniques.* Milwaukee, WI: Hal Leonard Corporation, 1996.

Black, Johnny. *Jimi Hendrix: The Ultimate Experience.* New York: Thunder's Mouth Press, 1999.

Blecka, Peter, Jim Fricke, et al. *Crossroads: The Experience Music Collection.* New York: Distributed Art Publishers, 2000.

Cross, Charles. *Room Full of Mirrors: a Biography of Jimi Hendrix.* New York: Hyperion, 2005.

DeCurtis, Anthony. "Beyond the Jimi Hendrix Experience." *New York Times*, February 28, 2010.

Doggett, Peter. *Jimi Hendrix: The Complete Guide to His Music.* London: Omnibus Press, 2004.

Doyle, Tom. "Stone Free." *Q Magazine* 285 (April 2010): 87–91.

Etchingham, Kathy, with Andrew Crofts. *Through Gypsy Eyes.* London: Orion Books, 1998.

Fricke, David. "Jimi's Last Days: Epic Plans, Earthly Troubles and Sweet Music." *Rolling Stone* 1101 (April 2010): 50057.

Glebbeek, Caesar, and Douglas J. Noble. *Jimi Hendrix: The Man, the Music, the Memorabilia.* New York: Thunder's Mouth Press, 1996.

Henderson, David. "Jimi Hendrix Deep Within the Blues and Alive Onstage at Woodstock—25 Years after Death." *African American Review* 29/1 (Summer 1995): 213–216.

Henderson, David. "Jimi Hendrix: Voodoo Child of the Aquarian Age." *Notes* 36/2 (December 1979): 373–374.

Henderson, David. *Scuse Me While I Kiss the Sky: The Life of Jimi Hendrix.* New York: Bantam Books, 1981.

Hendrix, Janie. *Jimi Hendrix: The Lyrics.* Milwaukee, WI: Hal Leonard Corporation, 2003.

Hendrix, Janie, and John McDermott. *Jimi Hendrix: An Illustrated Experience.* New York: Atria Books, 2007.

Hendrix, Jimi. *Experience Hendrix: The Best of Jimi Hendrix.* Milwaukee, WI: Hal Leonard Corporation, n.d.

Hermes, Will. "Hendrix's Deepest Riffs: The New Curators of the Jimi Hendrix Estate Find Gold in the Vaults." *Rolling Stone* 1100 (March 18, 2010): 62.

Jackson, Blair. "'Valleys of Neptune': New Studio Gems From the Hendrix Vaults." *Mix: Professional Audio and Music Production* 34/3 (March 2010): 39–41.

Johnson, Chad. *Jimi Hendrix: A Step-by-Step Breakdown of His Guitar Styles and Techniques.* Volume 2, Milwaukee, WI: Hal Leonard Corporation, 1996.

Keena-Levin, Richard. "Jimi Hendrix." *Popular Music* 10/1 (January 1991): 89–91.

Lawrence, Sharon. *Jimi Hendrix: The Intimate Story of a Betrayed Music Legend.* New York: HarperCollins Publishers, 2006.

Lawrence, Sharon. *Jimi Hendrix: The Man, the Magic, the Truth.* New York: HarperCollins Publishers, 2005.

Lentz, Harris. "Buddy Miles, Obituaries." *Classic Images* 395 (May 2008): 53.

Mackey, Robert. "Les Paul, in His Own Words," *New York Times,* August 13, 2009.

McDermott, John, with Eddie Kramer. *Hendrix: Setting the Record Straight.* Edited by Mark Lewisohn. New York: Grand Central Publishing, 1992.

McDermott, John, with Eddie Kramer. *Ultimate Hendrix: An Illustrated Encyclopedia of Live Concerts and Sessions.* Milwaukee, WI: Hal Leonard Corporation, 2008.

Morse, Tim. *Classic Rock Stories: The Stories Behind the Greatest Songs of All Time.* New York: St. Martin's Griffin, 1998.

Perone, James. *Woodstock: An Encyclopedia of the Music and Art Fair.* Westport, CT: Greenwood Press, 2005.

Potash, Chris. *The Jimi Hendrix Companion: Three Decades of Commentary.* New York: Schirmer Books, 1996.

Redding, Noel, and Carol Appleby. *Are You Experienced?: The Inside Story of the Jimi Hendrix Experience.* New York: Da Capo Press, 1996.

Robinson, John. "Cry Freedom!" *Uncut Magazine* 153 (February 2010): 44–57.

Roby, Steven. *Black Gold: The Lost Archives of Jimi Hendrix.* New York: Billboard Books, 2002.

Rooksby, Rikky. *Inside Classic Rock Tracks: Songwriting and Recording Secrets of 100 Great Songs, from 1960 to the Present Day.* San Francisco, CA: Backbeat Books, 2001.

Shapiro, Harry, and Caesar Glebbeek. *Jimi Hendrix: Electric Gypsy.* New York: St. Martin's Griffin Press, 1995.

Snow, Mat. "Ten More Years of Hendrix: Jimi's Estate Talks Archive Releases." *Mojo: The Music Magazine* 196 (March 2010): 17.

Stubbs, David. *Jimi Hendrix: The Story Behind Every Song.* New York: Thunder's Mouth Press, 2003.

Unterberger, Richie. *The Rough Guide to Jimi Hendrix.* London: Rough Guides, 2009.

Weiss, David. "The Changing Face of New York Studios: Recording, Mixing and Post Facilities Adapt to Economic Realities." *Mix Professional Audio and Music Production Magazine* 33/10 (October 2009): 32–37.

Whiteley, Sheila. "Progressive Rock and Psychedelic Coding in the Work of Jimi Hendrix." *Popular Music* vol. 9/1 (January 1990): 37–60.

Zak, Albin J. "Bob Dylan and Jimi Hendrix: Juxtaposition and Transformation 'All Along the Watchtower'." *Journal of the American Musicological Society* 57/3 (Autumn 2004): 599–644.

WEB SITES

http://www.jimihendrix.com/us/home
http://www.legacyrecordings.com/artists/the-isley-brothers/bio
http://www.electricladystudios.com/index.html

Index

About the Author

DAVID V. MOSKOWITZ is an associate professor of music at the University of South Dakota. He is the author of *Caribbean Popular Music: an Encyclopedia of Reggae, Mento, Ska, Rock Steady, and Dancehall, Bob Marley: A Biography,* and *The Words and Music of Bob Marley.*